ROUTLEDGE LIBRARY EDITIONS: T. S. ELIOT

Volume 5

T.S. ELIOT AND THE ROMANTIC CRITICAL TRADITION

T.S. ELIOT AND THE ROMANTIC CRITICAL TRADITION

EDWARD LOBB

LONDON AND NEW YORK

First published in 1981 by Routledge & Kegan Paul Ltd

This edition first published in 2016
by Routledge
2 Park Square, Milton Park, Abingdon, Oxon OX14 4RN

and by Routledge
711 Third Avenue, New York, NY 10017

Routledge is an imprint of the Taylor & Francis Group, an informa business

© 1981 Edward Lobb

All rights reserved. No part of this book may be reprinted or reproduced or utilised in any form or by any electronic, mechanical, or other means, now known or hereafter invented, including photocopying and recording, or in any information storage or retrieval system, without permission in writing from the publishers.

Trademark notice: Product or corporate names may be trademarks or registered trademarks, and are used only for identification and explanation without intent to infringe.

British Library Cataloguing in Publication Data
A catalogue record for this book is available from the British Library

ISBN: 978-1-138-18484-8 (Set)
ISBN: 978-1-315-64488-2 (Set) (ebk)
ISBN: 978-1-138-12100-3 (Volume 5) (hbk)
ISBN: 978-1-138-12103-4 (Volume 5) (pbk)
ISBN: 978-1-315-65132-3 (Volume 5) (ebk)

Publisher's Note
The publisher has gone to great lengths to ensure the quality of this reprint but points out that some imperfections in the original copies may be apparent.

Disclaimer
The publisher has made every effort to trace copyright holders and would welcome correspondence from those they have been unable to trace.

T.S. Eliot
and the Romantic Critical Tradition

Edward Lobb

Routledge & Kegan Paul
London, Boston and Henley

First published in 1981
by Routledge & Kegan Paul Ltd
39 Store Street, London WC1E 7DD,
9 Park Street, Boston, Mass. 02108, USA, and
Broadway House, Newtown Road,
Henley-on-Thames, Oxon RG9 1EN

Set in Baskerville by
Computacomp (UK) Ltd
Fort William, Scotland
and printed in the United States of America by
Vail-Ballou Press, Inc.,
Binghampton, New York

Copyright Edward Lobb 1981

No part of this book may be reproduced in
any form without permission from the
publisher, except for the quotation of brief
passages in criticism

British Library Cataloguing in Publication Data

Lobb, Edward
T. S. Eliot and the Romantic critical tradition
1. Eliot, Thomas Stearns – Criticism and interpretation
I. Title
820'.9   PS3509.L43Z/   80-41283
ISBN 0 7100 0636 5

For three sisters
G.K., N.L. and H.S.

Tanto son belle e di tanta vertute

Contents

	Preface	ix
	Acknowledgments	xi
	Note on Abbreviations	xiii
	Introduction	1
1	History and Poetry	11
2	Romantic Criticism and the Golden Age	60
3	Eliot as Rhetorician	93
	Conclusion	135
	Appendix A Eliot, Pound and Modernist Criticism	150
	Appendix B Eliot and Philosophical Aesthetics	158
	Notes	162
	Index	189

Preface

Since revising the manuscript of this book in 1978, I have read a number of works which bear, directly or indirectly, on some of the topics I have discussed. Several of the essays in David Newton-de Molina's collection *The Literary Criticism of T. S. Eliot* (London: Athlone, 1977) deal specifically with issues raised in the following chapters. For reasons of space I have avoided repeating arguments or referring to any material not relevant to my immediate subject, but the reader should be aware that these essays are complementary to my own treatment of Eliot. Thus William Righter's 'The Philosophical Critic' is a necessary supplement to my discussion of Eliot's use of philosophical terms in Chapter 1 and Appendix B; C. K. Stead's 'Eliot, Arnold and the English Poetic Tradition' completes the picture of Eliot's relation to Arnold in Chapter 2; and Roger Sharrock's essay 'Eliot's "Tone" ' should be read with my Chapter 3, 'Eliot as Rhetorician'. As the issue of Eliot's classicism falls into perspective, more attention has been given to his place in Romantic and post-Romantic tradition. A. Walton Litz's essay ' "That strange abstraction, 'Nature' " : T. S. Eliot's Victorian Inheritance' in *Nature and the Victorian Imagination* (ed. U. C. Knoepflmacher and G. B. Tennyson, Berkeley: University of California Press, 1977) is one example of good new work in this area – which, again, falls outside the limits of this study. In other instances, I have been scrupulous in acknowledging earlier work, perhaps to the point of obscuring what I believe to be genuinely new in my discussion of Eliot as a critic.

I am indebted to many people for their help. R. G. Harrison, formerly of the University of Toronto Schools, and Brian

Preface

Hennessey, C.S.B., of St Michael's College in the University of Toronto, introduced me to Eliot's shorter poems and *The Waste Land* respectively: to these men I owe my first enthusiasm for Eliot and my realization that teaching is an art. A. Walton Litz, another superb teacher, supervised my dissertation at Princeton and has provided me with invaluable help, advice, and moral support for the better part of a decade; my debt to him can be acknowledged but not repaid. Dame Helen Gardner shared, during an afternoon's conversation, both her memories of Eliot and some of the fruits of her long study of his work. Lyndall Gordon guided me through the early Eliot manuscripts in the Berg Collection of the New York Public Library. I am, finally, deeply grateful to Valerie Eliot for her kindness in allowing me to study her husband's unpublished manuscripts, for her interest in my project, and for her suggestions, corrections and encouragement.

A number of organizations have also assisted me. Doctoral fellowships from the Canada Council enabled me to complete my graduate education. The American Philosophical Society and the American Council of Learned Societies provided grants to cover expenses during summer research at King's College, Cambridge, in 1975, and the staff of the library at King's made working there a pleasure. The Canadian Federation for the Humanities provided criticism which enabled me to improve the manuscript substantively.

I am also indebted to my colleagues Dillon Johnston, Elizabeth Phillips, and Lee Potter, who read my first draft and made helpful suggestions; and to my student assistant, Ira Lackey, who checked the quotations and footnotes for accuracy. Most of all, I wish to thank my parents and the friends who helped me through difficult times – Madeleine Darte, John Meanwell, Gerald McKoy, Mary Jane Boland, John Tucker – and Ron Boyd, without whose help and support the book could not have been finished. In conclusion, I want to express my thanks to Stephen Brook and Angela Quinn of Routledge & Kegan Paul for their imperturbable helpfulness.

R.E.L.
Toronto
26 September 1979

Acknowledgments

Excerpts from *Selected Essays* by T. S. Eliot are reprinted by permission of Faber & Faber Ltd; excerpts from *Selected Essays* and *Essays on Elizabethan Drama* by T. S. Eliot are reprinted by permission of Harcourt Brace Jovanovich, Inc. (copyright 1932, 1936, 1950 by Harcourt Brace Jovanovich, Inc.; copyright 1960 by T. S. Eliot; copyright 1971, 1978 by Esme Valerie Eliot). Excerpts from *The Sacred Wood* by T. S. Eliot are reprinted by permission of Methuen & Company Ltd. Excerpts from *For Lancelot Andrewes* by T. S. Eliot are reprinted by permission of Faber & Faber Ltd. Excerpts from *The Use of Poetry and the Use of Criticism* by T. S. Eliot are reprinted by permission of Faber & Faber Ltd and Harvard University Press. Excerpts from *On Poetry and Poets* by T. S. Eliot, copyright © 1943, 1945, 1951, 1954, 1956, 1957 by T. S. Eliot, are reprinted by permission of Faber & Faber Ltd and Farrar, Straus & Giroux, Inc. Excerpts from *To Criticize the Critic* by T. S. Eliot, copyright © 1965 by Valerie Eliot, are reprinted by permission of Faber & Faber Ltd and Farrar, Straus & Giroux, Inc.

Selections from T. S. Eliot's uncollected writings are reprinted by permission of Mrs Valerie Eliot and Faber & Faber Ltd from sources as indicated in Donald Gallup, *T. S. Eliot: A Bibliography* (revised and extended edn, New York: Harcourt Brace, 1969). Extracts from T. S. Eliot's unpublished writings are reprinted by permission of Mrs Valerie Eliot and Faber & Faber Ltd from the manuscript of the Clark Lectures at King's College, Cambridge, © Mrs Valerie Eliot 1980. Excerpts from the poetry of T. S. Eliot are reprinted from his volume *Collected Poems 1909–1962* by permission of Faber & Faber Ltd and Harcourt Brace Jovanovich,

Acknowledgments

Inc. (copyright 1936 by Harcourt Brace Jovanovich, Inc.; copyright © 1943, 1963, 1964 by T. S. Eliot).

Excerpts from 'The Eye' by Richard Wilbur are reprinted from his volume *The Mind-Reader: New Poems* by permission of Harcourt Brace Jovanovich, Inc. and Faber & Faber Ltd (© 1975 by Richard Wilbur).

Note on Abbreviations

Wherever possible, notes refer the reader to *Selected Essays* rather than the volumes in which the essays first appeared. The following abbreviations are used throughout the book:

SW	*The Sacred Wood: Essays on Poetry and Criticism*, 2nd ed. (London: Methuen, 1928).
HJD	*Homage to John Dryden: Three Essays on Poetry of the Seventeenth Century* (London: Hogarth Press, 1924).
FLA	*For Lancelot Andrewes: Essays on Style and Order* (London: Faber, 1970).
UPUC	*The Use of Poetry and the Use of Criticism: Studies in the Relation of Criticism to Poetry in England*, 2nd ed. (London: Faber, 1964).
EAM	*Essays Ancient and Modern* (London: Faber, 1936).
SE	*Selected Essays*, 3rd ed. (London: Faber, 1951).
CPP	*The Complete Poems and Plays, 1909–1950* (New York: Harcourt, Brace, 1952).
OPAP	*On Poetry and Poets* (London: Faber, 1957).
TCTC	*To Criticize the Critic and Other Writings* (London: Faber, 1965).

Full references to uncollected essays are given in the notes.

Introduction

> En Amérique, professeur;
> En Angleterre, journaliste;
> C'est à grands pas et en sueur
> Que vous suivrez à peine ma piste.
> 'Mélange Adultère de Tout'
>
> All critical judgments excite criticism.
> T. S. Eliot, in a review[1]

In 1951, R. P. Blackmur wrote an essay for the *Kenyon Review* on T. S. Eliot's literary criticism. It was called 'In the Hope of Straightening Things Out', and it remains, decades later, among the best short treatments of Eliot as a critic.[2] The title of the essay, a phrase from Eliot's 'Dante' (1929), might stand as the motto of all serious criticism; but it often seems, particularly with Eliot, that we are as far from straightening things out as we have ever been. Eliot as a literary critic is unmistakably *there* – a formidable presence – but he is also remarkably elusive. We do not know him as we know I. A. Richards or Northrop Frye, both of whom have explained themselves at length. Eliot's relative reticence and his elliptical statements are, however, only part of the problem: a fog of academic commentary – called up, no doubt, by some protective goddess – has surrounded the criticism, and much discussion has unwittingly avoided the real issues altogether.

The confusion has existed almost from the beginning of Eliot's career as a literary critic. If, as some claim, Eliot stated all of his

Introduction

major critical ideas in *The Sacred Wood* (1920), it can fairly be said that the reviews of that book established the questions with which subsequent discussion has dealt. That discussion has generated much more heat than light, but after sixty years it is possible to see which problems have been disposed of and which remain to be solved.

It was not clear in 1920, for example, that Eliot's criticism was 'a by-product of my private poetry-workshop', nor that he was 'implicitly defending the sort of poetry that I and my friends wrote'.[3] A large part of Eliot's intention was to review the literary past in the light of present needs, as Dryden, Keats, and Arnold had done before him. Eliot had said in 1919 that 'the important critic is the person who is absorbed in the present problems of art', and it was perhaps inevitable that modernist criticism be as misunderstood as modernist poetry.[4] The reviewer, encountering one of Eliot's generalizations, too seldom saw it in relation to the present state of literature; he took it at face value, and often felt obliged to disagree.

A second problem was Eliot's style. The Preface to the second edition of *The Sacred Wood* (1928) acknowledged a 'stiffness and an assumption of pontifical solemnity which may be tiresome to many readers'. (*SW* vii) In 1961, reviewing his criticism as a whole, Eliot found 'errors of tone: the occasional note of arrogance, of vehemence, of cocksureness or rudeness, the braggadocio of the mild-mannered man safely entrenched behind his typewriter'.[5] The tone served, presumably, to protect statements which Eliot felt to be true but which were not easily demonstrable; it also served, less conveniently, to stimulate opposition. On a different level, there was the matter of Eliot's whimsy. As Eliot the banker took delight in looking as much like a City businessman as possible, so Eliot the critic delighted in assuming various critical masks. He was by turns solemnly obvious ('from the point of view of literature, the drama is only one among several poetic forms'), fastidious ('it is a question of some nicety to determine how much must be read of any particular poet'), or owlish and avuncular.[6] As a result, it did not occur to the reviewers that the sneers at Meredith in *The Sacred Wood*, for example, were not to be taken too seriously. Sweetness and light and high seriousness were still the

Introduction

touchstones of 'bellettristic' criticism; sarcasm and levity – aspects of what Bernard Bergonzi has called 'the supercilious urbanity of Eliot's manner' – were bound to be misunderstood.[7]

Finally, there were Eliot's inconsistencies. The critic, Eliot declares, 'must simply elucidate: the reader will form the correct judgment for himself'.[8] But *The Sacred Wood* is, as the *Times* critic noted, full of value judgments and opinion.[9] Eliot asserts that Swinburne 'is certainly right in putting Webster above Tourneur, Tourneur above Ford, and Ford above Shirley', and he mentions as matter of fact the 'degeneration [of blank verse] from Shakespeare to Milton'.[10] These are tenable opinions, but they are not simply elucidation, nor are they supported by argumentation or evidence. One could easily compile, as his opponents have done from time to time, a little anthology of similar contradictions between Eliot's expressed principles and his own practice.

These three 'problems' have largely taken care of themselves. We now take for granted, for example, that Eliot's criticism was, in part, written in defence of modernism; we likewise recognize the mixture of argument and rhetorical persuasion in the essays. Even the inconsistencies seem less important with the passage of time: complete consistency is a minor virtue, and we expect it of none but the dullest writers and critics. Furthermore, as M. C. Bradbrook has noted, the essays have the *essential* unity of any extended body of work – however various the statements, they are recognizably the products of a single mind and voice.[11]

One problem, however, remains obstinately unsolved. Eliot's view of literary history, and of the 'dissociation of sensibility' which functions as its Great Divide, is central to our understanding of his literary criticism. But on these, of all subjects, Eliot's reticence seems to have been almost compulsive. A few paragraphs of elusive argument in 'The Metaphysical Poets' (1921) and fugitive comments in essays here and there were all one had to go on; the dissociation seemed to lie behind many of Eliot's pronouncements, but its exact relation to them remained mysterious. The sketchiness of the material prompted various attempts at reconstruction of the whole: the texts were gone over with rabbinical thoroughness by scholars and critics who could not agree on the meaning of these oracular fragments. Like the

Introduction

blind wise men around the elephant, commentators came to various conclusions about the nature of the beast depending on the part of it they happened to touch.

The alternative was to ignore the elephant altogether, and we have had, as a result, commentators who speak as if Eliot's criticism involved no historical sense at all. This approach has the practical advantage of simplicity, and serves to locate Eliot in the modernist reaction against one kind of historical criticism, which is more comfortable with ideas than with literature – the kind of criticism which discusses Renaissance cosmology rather than the poem which employs it. It is true that Eliot rarely discusses the background of ideas behind a work, and he has been seen as an early 'new' critic. But his critique of Romanticism and his generalizations about various periods of literature clearly imply a specifically *literary* history, which focuses less on ideas than on the way in which those ideas are given literary form.

In 'Andrew Marvell' (1921), for example, Eliot compares Marvell's 'The Nymph and the Fawn' with Morris's 'Nymph's Song to Hylas', and argues that Marvell's poem is superior to Morris's. We seem to be in the realm of pure criticism and removed from historical considerations altogether, but Eliot argues throughout the essay in covertly historical terms. The comparison of Marvell and Morris is really a juxtaposition of ages, and the whole history of poetry is involved in Eliot's attempt to define a tradition of 'wit'; thirty-seven poets from classical to modern times are mentioned by name in the essay. When Eliot asserts that the 'alliance of levity and seriousness' which characterizes wit is a quality which 'expands in English literature just at the moment before the English mind altered', we look for elaboration and detail, but we look in vain.[12] Until recently, then, discussion of Eliot's criticism was hampered in one way or another by the historical problem: Eliot's ideas about literary history could neither be satisfactorily explained nor ignored. They seemed, like the metre in Eliot's description of free verse, 'to advance menacingly as we [dozed], and withdraw as we [roused]'.[13]

This situation has been changed radically by the recovery of Eliot's unpublished Clark Lectures, delivered in 1926. These lectures are discussed at length in Chapter 1, 'History and Poetry',

Introduction

and they provide a much fuller picture of Eliot's developing view of literary history than we have had. There is, for example, a gap between the praise of Donne in 'The Metaphysical Poets' (1921) and the strictures set forth in 'Lancelot Andrewes' (1926) and later essays which nothing in Eliot's published criticism quite fills. One possible explanation – the 'expansion or development of interests' which Eliot refers to in the 1928 Preface to *The Sacred Wood* – is usually taken as a covert reference to Eliot's conversion, which in turn is seen as evidence of his growing conservatism. But, as Lyndall Gordon has shown, Eliot's interest in religious and metaphysical questions was essentially defined during his career at Harvard: a dramatic particular change, such as his conversion, occurred against the background of long-standing concerns.[14]

Similarly, the revaluation of Donne represents both consistency and change in Eliot's thinking about literature. In setting the lectures against the background of Eliot's published criticism, I have tried to chronicle the development of Eliot's critique of Donne as closely as possible. In other ways, however, the lectures fit naturally into the context of Eliot's published criticism of the 1920s and 1930s, and provide a natural *entrée* to more general questions. I have consequently used the historiography of the lectures and the principles set forth in *Selected Essays* as glosses on each other when it seemed appropriate to do so. Eliot himself objected to critics who ignored the chronology of his writings; all quotations from Eliot are therefore dated in the text or in footnotes.

The lectures contain some ambiguities, as Eliot realized, but it seems pointless to raise objections – to interrupt – before the whole argument is set forth. I have tried to explain or amplify Eliot's more obscure points, and to fill in *lacunae* when they occur; parts of Chapter 1 may, as a result, sound more like advocacy of Eliot's ideas than simple exposition of them.

But the clarification of Eliot's ideas is only the first stage in our understanding of them. Eliot's version of literary history constitutes a kind of historical myth[15] which centres on the idea of a crisis in language (the dissociation of sensibility) and the diminished power of poetry in the ages following: it is the story of Eden applied to the secular history of literature. This literary myth was first put forward by the Romantics, and Eliot's use of it – in his own way and for his own purposes, *mutatis mutandis* – suggests that there is a considerable Romantic heritage in Eliot's literary criticism.

The extent to which modernism as a whole was a revision or extension of Romanticism is still a matter of debate; the answers to the questions raised in that debate depend in large part upon how those protean '-isms' are defined. Eliot's dislike of Romanticism, and his sarcasms at the expense of the Romantic poets, are a matter of record. On the other hand, Eliot himself said that a poet in a Romantic age could be classical only in tendency,[16] and recent scholarship has revealed parts of Eliot's own relationship to Romantic tradition. Three important books have focused on the central, seemingly antithetical, figures of Yeats and Eliot, and found in each a continuation and modification of Romantic doctrine. Frank Kermode, in *Romantic Image* (1957), has dealt with the origins of the Symbolist concern with non-discursive images; C. K. Stead, in *The New Poetic: Yeats to Eliot* (1964), has discussed the modern poets' desire to reunite the roles of seer and public spokesman. More recently, George Bornstein has traced *Transformations of Romanticism in Yeats, Eliot, and Stevens*.[17] He has much of interest to say about Eliot's resistance to, and reconciliation with, Romanticism. All three critics (and one could list others) deal with Eliot's divided loyalties and the tension between his public classicism and his deep, often inarticulate, Romanticism.

The subject is nevertheless far from exhausted. Eliot's view of literary history is, as I shall argue in Chapter 2, basically Romantic in its nostalgia for a lost golden age: it reveals, in particular, a debt to three Romantic poet-critics (Keats, Wordsworth, and Arnold) which has never been properly analysed. Eliot's use of the Middle Ages as an argumentative 'image' likewise owes much to the Romantics and their Victorian successors. To note these affinities is not to diminish Eliot's originality in any way; as the author of 'Tradition and the Individual Talent' knew, it is only in the acceptance and use of a living tradition that any real originality is possible.

The historical myth about language which Eliot adopts and

adapts in the Clark Lectures is important primarily to our understanding of his criticism of poetry, but it implies a theory of prose style as well. If the language we inherit is, for whatever reason, corrupt, it cannot be used for pure argument; rhetorical strategies become more important, particularly in the absence of shared beliefs. As John Holloway has shown in *The Victorian Sage*, argument undergoes fundamental and permanent changes during the nineteenth century. In the hands of writers as diverse as Coleridge and Arnold, Carlyle and Newman, the art of persuasion develops in new directions, largely because the ideas of these writers are not susceptible of reasoned argument in the usual sense of the term – a fact to which Eliot himself referred in several essays.

The study of Eliot's own style emerges naturally, then, from consideration of his view of language and the history of rhetoric. It is not surprising that Eliot shows his Romantic heritage in the style and strategy of his essays, in his very conception of how argument works. The rhetorical element in the prose has long been recognized, as I said earlier, and there is external evidence to show that Eliot was, as one would expect, fully aware of what he was doing. Despite these facts, no one has yet made a thorough rhetorical analysis of Eliot's literary criticism. Such an analysis need not be destructive: the aim should not be to prove that Eliot's essays are 'merely' rhetorical, but rather to analyse the art of Eliot's prose and to trace another of his links to the Romantic tradition.

Eliot's style can, without exaggeration, be compared to Johnson's or Ruskin's in rhetorical complexity. I cannot, obviously, claim to have analysed that style completely, but Chapter 3, 'Eliot as Rhetorician', is sufficiently detailed, I believe, to show the consistency between Eliot's myth of language and his practice of criticism. I have avoided traditional rhetorical terms, partly for simplicity's sake, but mostly because Eliot's usage does not fit the classical categories. Many of the examples I use are taken from Eliot's uncollected essays, which show his critical rhetoric at its most exuberant: I have tried to balance these with more moderate examples from the collected work. The number of examples in Chapter 3 may seem excessive, but it is necessary, I believe, to show that real *patterns* of usage exist. The examples are, moreover, often delightful in themselves. Eliot's wit, his control of tone, the ways in which his argument ranges between pedantry and *sprezzatura* – all of these mark him as a master stylist. He is among our most serious critics, but he is almost never solemn.

It is appropriate, at this point, to indicate what this study does *not* do. It does not, for example, offer a general study of Eliot's criticism; it takes for granted a knowledge of the texts and of Eliot's opinions on a number of subjects. Similarly, I have not attempted to relate Eliot's criticism to his poetic and dramatic work. The unity of these chapters lies in their common concern with Eliot's place in the Romantic tradition of historiography and rhetorical persuasion, and the preservation of that unity involves certain limits of inquiry. In Eliot's criticism, as in Arnold's, there is a steady widening of perspective: as early as 1928, Eliot announced that he was concerned with 'the relation of poetry to the spiritual and social life of its time and of other times'.[18] That same year, the polemical Preface to *For Lancelot Andrewes* made it clear that Eliot's literary position was tied up in his own mind with political and religious loyalties, that neo-classicism, royalism, and anglo-catholicism were somehow intimately related – were, perhaps, *sub specie aeternitatis*, aspects of a single whole. In fact, as more and more work on Eliot's thought appears, the parts of that thought seem more complex and the unity of the whole more impressive. Several studies have touched on this unity: Lyndall Gordon's book, for example, reveals much about the relation of Eliot's preoccupation with metaphysical issues to things as disparate as his dissertation, his early satiric poems, his first marriage and conversion.

We know that the lines which separate various kinds of critical activity are not always clearly drawn; Eliot himself obliterated most of them in *After Strange Gods* (1934), a farrago of literary, social, and religious criticism. Nevertheless, the lines of division are fairly clearly marked in the rest of Eliot's critical work, and, apart from a few remarks towards the end of Chapter 1 on the unity of Eliot's thought, I have avoided the temptation to write a grand synthesis of Eliot's work in literary, political, and religious criticism. Several recent studies have given us materials towards such a synthesis,

Introduction

but it is beyond the scope of this study.[19]

It is during the first twenty years of Eliot's career as a critic that his view of literary history develops, changes, and assumes a nearly final form. I have therefore concentrated on the years 1916–36 in Chapter 1. The year 1936 is not, however, a cut-off point. I have dealt with Eliot's return, in 1947, to the idea of 'dissociation of sensibility', and with some other matters which are clarified by reference to the later criticism. My discussion of Eliot's rhetoric in Chapter 3 likewise focuses on, but is not restricted to, Eliot's criticism before 1936 – the work which is probably his best and certainly his most interesting rhetorically. It is true, as George Bornstein says, that 'the later lectures gain in detachment what they lose in daring',[20] but it is Eliot's earlier criticism which continues to stimulate us, and which we re-read with the sense of new discovery. Eliot's best essays were always the product of his search for whatever was alive and useful in the past, and for a means of integrating the 'really new' work of art and the tradition.[21] With the publication of 'Burnt Norton' in 1936, Eliot consolidated a mature and flexible style, and, as M. C. Bradbrook has written,

> When he stabilized his own style as a poet, some informing power departed from his critical writing. If for example the essay on *In Memoriam* be compared with that on Massinger, or the introduction to the volume of Kipling's verse with the essay on Dryden, it will be seen that Mr. Eliot has withdrawn from his subjects: he is no longer so closely engaged – this may allow a wider scale of social reference, but it weakens the characteristic virtue of his critical writing, which may be termed its involution. The portion of his criticism which records the growth of a poet's mind is also the portion which is germinal for his readers.[22]

I am well aware that in trying to define the tradition of thought about language to which Eliot belongs I risk the charge of having neglected Herder's essay on language, or Rousseau's, or the ideas of Emerson and a dozen others. And there is no wholly adequate defence against such a charge: when one is dealing with a poet-

Introduction

critic who is a polymath as well, no influence can be definitively discounted. I can plead only that I have followed what seem to me the most *direct* lines of descent. Thus, although I discuss Schiller and Gourmont briefly, my analysis of Romantic historiography centres on the English tradition.

This study deals, as I have said, with a fairly limited subject – a Romantic myth of literary history and its effects on the process of argument in Eliot's criticism. But this limited subject is of immense importance not only to our understanding and revaluation of Eliot as a literary critic, but also to our culture as a whole. For the lectures are more than one man's view of the tradition: they are a suggestive account of the malaise of modern and post-modern literature, a prescient analysis of tendencies which would lead, finally, to the literature of silence. The lectures, nominally about a particular strain of poetry, are also about the crisis in our culture; and if such a subject seems absurdly large, we should keep in mind that Eliot was at the centre of that culture in its modernist phase. He had the kind of perspective that only the makers have, and the half-century since the lectures were given has shown us, in criticism as well as literature, the extremes of that tendency towards solipsism which Eliot saw as characteristic of post-Renaissance literature. In the 'Conclusion', I attempt to relate Eliot's ideas to the present state of literary criticism.

Kermode, Stead, and Bornstein have enlarged our understanding of Eliot's place in modernist aesthetics and of the Romantic heritage in his criticism. This study attempts to carry our understanding of Eliot still further – in the hope of straightening things out.

1
History and Poetry

History has many cunning passages, contrived corridors
And issues, deceives with whispering ambitions,
Guides us by vanities.
'Gerontion' (1920)

... he not unnaturally laid down in abstract theory what is in reality a personal point of view.
'Ben Jonson' (1919)

T. S. Eliot's stature as the great poet-critic of our century is generally acknowledged, but there remains much disagreement as to the meaning of his critical work as a whole. During the 1920s and 1930s, his essays on individual writers precipitated, in the words of Hugh Kenner, 'that view of the literature of the past which the twentieth century recognizes as peculiarly its own'.[1] Certain of Eliot's enthusiasms – for the metaphysical poets and the lesser Elizabethan dramatists, for example – have been fixed in the curriculum wherever English literature is taught; certain of his aversions, notably *Hamlet*, have survived his criticism and will continue to do so. The reasons for Eliot's praise or censure of particular works are usually expressed clearly: it is only his generalizations about historical periods which are vague in outline. Eliot remains, as did Coleridge for a century, a critic whose broad formulations are unmistakably important but not always quite clear.

The phrase 'dissociation of sensibility' is emblematic of the whole problem. For many, it is exasperatingly vague and essentially devoid of meaning; for others it summarizes a real sense of the diminished power of poetry after the Renaissance. The phrase occurs in Eliot's 1921 essay 'The Metaphysical Poets'. The title is misleading, for the essay, which was a review of Grierson's historic anthology,[2] attempts to isolate a quality apparent in all the best verse of the Renaissance. Even Jonson and Chapman, not usually thought of as metaphysicals,

> were notably erudite, and were notably men who incorporated their erudition into their sensibility: their mode of feeling was directly and freshly altered by their reading and thought. In Chapman especially there is a direct sensuous apprehension of thought, or a recreation of thought into feeling, which is exactly what we find in Donne.... (SE 286)

Eliot's earliest formulations of the idea of unified sensibility suggested a union between intellect and *sense*-perception – 'feeling' in the physiological sense. The point is made quite clearly in several essays written in 1919 and 1920:

> It is probable that men ripen best through experiences which are at once sensuous and intellectual; certainly many men will admit that their keenest ideas have come to them with the quality of a sense-perception; and that their keenest sensuous experience has been 'as if the body thought'.[3]

> And, indeed, with the end of Chapman, Middleton, Webster, Tourneur, Donne we end a period when the intellect was immediately at the tips of the senses. Sensation became word and word was sensation. The next period is the period of Milton (though still with a Marvell in it)....[4]

> In common with the greatest – Marlowe, Webster, Tourneur, and Shakespeare – [Donne and Chapman] had a quality of sensuous thought, or of thinking through the senses, or of the senses thinking, of which the exact formula remains to be defined.[5]

But, as this last passage suggests, Eliot had not quite decided how to describe the phenomenon; by 1921 he was speaking not only of a 'direct sensuous apprehension of thought' but also of 'sensibility', a word which, like 'feeling', can denote physical sensation or qualities of mind, as when we speak of the artist's sensibility. It is apparent from Eliot's usage in 'The Metaphysical Poets' that he is talking about something more than mere physical perception: 'The poets of the seventeenth century, the successors of the dramatists of the sixteenth, possessed a mechanism of sensibility which could devour any kind of experience.'[6] To the dwellers in this happy age – the most sensitive of them, at any rate – there was no such thing as a thought which was not felt (experienced emotionally) or a feeling which was devoid of intellectual significance. But this Eden, like the other, endured a fall: 'In the seventeenth century a dissociation of sensibility set in, from which we have never recovered. ...'[7]

The same idea occurs in Eliot's later critical writings, and is present in his poetry from its beginnings. In the early 'Whispers of Immortality' (*CPP* 32–3), for example, sensation is a means of perception for Webster and Donne.

>Donne, I suppose, was such another
>Who found no substitute for sense,
>To seize and clutch and penetrate;
>Expert beyond experience,
>
>He knew the anguish of the marrow
>The ague of the skeleton;
>No contact possible to flesh
>Allayed the fever of the bone.

Modern carnality, on the other hand, exemplified by the pneumatic Grishkin, is devoid of any intellectual meaning and is therefore *merely* carnal.[8] The same theme appears, with ironic qualifications, in *The Waste Land*. Eliot does not suppose that some further dimension of perception, uniting intellect and senses, informed the Middle Ages and the Renaissance. Rather, the set of beliefs which prevailed then was so universal and, in its broad outlines, so unquestioned that it affected even the most elementary forms of perception.

An argument which is both sweeping and vague is easy to criticize, and the half-century since 'The Metaphysical Poets' has seen Eliot's capsule history frequently attacked. Frank Kermode, the most trenchant of Eliot's critics in this matter, points out that the 'dissociative' force of scepticism has been constantly at work in all of Europe's great ages, and that the rise of science, most spectacular in the seventeenth century, challenged the theocentric unity of European thought from the thirteenth century onwards. 'It would be quite as reasonable', Kermode concludes, 'to locate the great dissociation in the sixteenth or the thirteenth century as in the seventeenth; nor would it be difficult to construct arguments for other periods.'[9]

Kermode is, in a way, quite right, but the logic of his criticism works ultimately against any definition of historical or literary periods. 'Romanticism' and 'the Renaissance' resist demarcation either as movements or as periods of time: their supposed distinguishing features can be discerned elsewhere, and we might say, in Kermode's terms, that it would be quite as reasonable to locate the beginning of the Renaissance in the twelfth century as in the fourteenth – such arguments have frequently been made. Nevertheless, we continue to believe in these periods, aware that any definition which takes on more than the *minutiae* of cultural history will not be watertight.[10] We look for the general features of the age, and seek to describe the different types of experience represented by metaphysical, Augustan and Romantic verse. The appeal of Eliot's theory is that is suggests, darkly, some reason for the phenomenon it describes; its great shortcoming is that the reason is never, in his published writings, set forth in detail.

There is some evidence that Eliot's reticence was deliberate. F. H. Bradley called criticism the finding of bad reasons for what we believe upon instinct, and Eliot seems to have been shy of exposing the background of his theory – his 'bad reasons' – to matter-of-fact criticism such as Kermode's. In 'The Metaphysical Poets' he refers to 'this brief exposition of a theory – too brief, perhaps, to carry conviction' (*SE* 288); and when the essay was reprinted in *Homage to John Dryden* three years later, Eliot's fears were apparent in the Preface:

> I hope that these three papers may in spite of and partly because of their defects preserve in cryptogram certain notions which, if expressed directly, would be destined to immediate obloquy, followed by perpetual oblivion.[11]

A detailed argument would have been mocked, but in their present elliptical form the essays might serve as a suggestive means of approach to seventeenth-century literature.

Two years later, however, Eliot explained his ideas at considerable length. In 1925 he was invited to give the Clark Lectures at Trinity College, Cambridge; early in 1926 he delivered eight lectures on the metaphysical tradition from Dante to Laforgue and Corbière. He came to his task at the height of his early fame. *The Waste Land* was scarcely three years old, and *Poems 1909-1925* had just appeared. *The Sacred Wood* and *Homage to John Dryden* had fixed Eliot's reputation as the most interesting young critic in England or America, and those who came to hear the lectures no doubt expected to be disturbed and entertained. They cannot have been disappointed. The lectures have all of the virtues and most of the faults of Eliot's early criticism. They generalize freely and frequently leave a dogmatic statement suspended in mid-air to puzzle and stimulate the auditor; what Bernard Bergonzi has called 'the cool outsider's gaze and the poised intellectual gaiety' are much in evidence.[12] One gets the impression that Eliot is striving to express a point of view which is inexpressible or indemonstrable, and I believe that he did not publish the eight lectures for this reason. As a whole, they nevertheless provide us with a far more detailed picture of Eliot's 'tradition' than his published work, collected and uncollected, affords, and they suggest certain sources for his view of the great change in European sensibility in the seventeenth century. They also provide us with a view of Donne which differs sharply from that in 'The Metaphysical Poets'.[13]

It is apparent, both from the scope of the Clark Lectures and the range of quotation in 'The Metaphysical Poets', that the word 'metaphysical' is used in a particular sense by Eliot, and that it is an evaluative term rather than a descriptive one. Dryden's original use of 'metaphysical' as a literary term focused on the intellectual and speculative aspects of some seventeenth-century poets, which to Dryden smacked of remoteness from nature: the suggestion of scholastic dryness in the word was pejorative, and was taken up by Johnson in the famous 'Life of Cowley'. To use the word as narrowly as Johnson did was, as Eliot notes, more of a libel on metaphysics than a clarification of the authors he discussed (CL I: 7). Eliot, as a student of philosophy, uses the term with more of its original sense. Metaphysics is the science of being and knowing, and 'metaphysical poetry', in Eliot's critical vocabulary, is that poetry in which the word, the image, perfectly embodies the experience it is meant to encompass; the knowing, the communication of sense, is entirely subsumed in feeling or emotion.

> It is a function of poetry both to fix and make more conscious and precise emotions and feelings in which most people participate in their own experience, and to draw within the orbit of feeling and sense what had existed only in thought. It creates a unity of feeling out of various parts ... the union of things hitherto unconnected in experience. (CL I: 10)

This passage from the first of the lectures is interesting in several ways. Eliot implies here a distinction between 'feeling and sense': as in the 1921 essay, both physical sensation and sensibility are included in his definition of metaphysicality. Further, in constructing this definition, Eliot employs both the traditional literary concept of the metaphysical and his own earlier attempt at a modern definition of the term. Johnson found that in metaphysical verse 'the most heterogeneous ideas are yoked by violence together';[14] Eliot, more moderately, sees 'the union of things hitherto unconnected in experience' and finds it justified, when it works, by the resulting unity of feeling.[15] The language of the passage and the emphasis on unity recall a passage from 'The Metaphysical Poets':

History and Poetry

When a poet's mind is perfectly equipped for its work, it is constantly amalgamating disparate experience; the ordinary man's experience is chaotic, irregular, fragmentary. The latter falls in love, or reads Spinoza, and these two experiences have nothing to do with each other, or with the noise of the typewriter or the smell of cooking; in the mind of the poet these experiences are always forming new wholes. (SE 287)

The great example of the perfect union of feeling and thought is the work of Dante, which Eliot uses throughout his career as a touchstone of poetic perfection. Donne, too, is credited in Eliot's early essays with a 'mechanism of sensibility' which could take in any kind of experience; but by 1926 Eliot had had troubling second thoughts about the Dean of St Paul's. The metaphysical image depends for its success upon the unity of conceptual truth and truth of feeling; the idea is incarnated in the image and validated by the emotional effect of that image. In Donne, however, conceptual truth and truth of feeling seem to diverge, and in accounting for this change Eliot begins an apparent digression on the difference between theological writing in the thirteenth and seventeenth centuries.

In the thirteenth century theologians held certain beliefs in common, and the Church, not preoccupied with polemic or self-defence, allowed great liberty in philosophical discussion; philosophy was disinterested inquiry within the *sensus communis* of Europe. In the seventeenth century, however, an age of controversy forced Catholic and Protestant theology alike in the direction of polemic: the intent was no longer the pursuit of truth, but the necessity of persuasion.

> Theology which is bent to political controversy, theology at bay, extinguishes the light of pure ideas, the Greek disinterestedness of mind, which the middle ages had revived; but it does not extinguish religious sentiment. ... Religion and theology, abandoning the pursuit of metaphysical truth, develop in the XVII century in the direction of psychology. ... (CL II: 12)

'Psychology' as it is used here does not simply mean rhetorical persuasion. In 1925, reviewing Mario Praz's *Secentismo e Marinismo in Inghilterra* for *TLS*, Eliot spoke of the difference between the religion of the seventeenth century and that of the thirteenth as being 'the difference between psychology and metaphysics'.[16] In the Clark Lectures a year later, he uses similar terms in discussing 'the difference between what I call *ontologism* and *psychologism* – which is perhaps a ... [variant] of the old difference between realism and nominalism'.[17]

The words which Eliot uses in approaching the larger issues necessitate a brief discussion of philosophical terminology. Eliot explicitly denied the influence of philosophy upon his criticism. He claimed to have, like F. H. Bradley, no capacity for abstruse thought, and asserted that only three philosophers had influenced him, and then by their prose styles rather than their points of view.[18] In general, we can take Eliot's word that, despite the dissertation on Bradley, his mind was not philosophical in bent. But a significant part of Eliot's criticism rests upon a view of history, and this view is expressed in philosophical terms which require some elaboration. We must understand something of the difference between ontologism and psychologism, or realism and nominalism, to follow the argument.[19]

The latter pair of terms suggests something of the nature of Eliot's analogy. 'Realism' and 'nominalism' are the names given to opposed views on one of the perennial problems of philosophy – the correspondence between universal or general concepts in the mind and in extramental reality. Extreme realism holds that the correspondence is exact, that a word denotes an actually existent object or concept in the external world. The difficulty with such a view is that there are concepts ('white', for example) which have no external existence without a specific object. The contrary extreme, usually called nominalism, maintains that only individuals exist, and that universal concepts are mere mental constructions. This view, too, encounters difficulties: for if our categories are simply fictional conveniences, then scientific knowledge, which depends upon classification and is, practically speaking, a *fact*, becomes philosophically impossible.

The issue is, obviously, far more complex than this summary suggests. There are positions between the extremes, and

History and Poetry

differences between Thomist and Scotist forms of realism.[20] The importance of the question in the Middle Ages was theological by implication. Its general philosophical significance is indicated by Frederick Copleston:

> If the fact that subsistent objects are individual and concepts general means that universal concepts have no foundation in extramental reality, if the universality of concepts means that they are mere ideas, then a rift between thought and objects is created and our knowledge, so far as it is expressed in universal concepts and judgments, is of doubtful validity at the very least.[21]

This view, and the nominalism of William of Ockham, are part of the *via moderna* of medieval philosophy, which, despite condemnations by the Parisian Faculty of Arts, eventually prevails over the *via antiqua* of Thomas and Duns Scotus. It makes little apparent sense to talk of a transition from realism to nominalism in the Renaissance, as Eliot seems to be doing, since both attitudes are present in the Middle Ages; but to make such an objection is to mistake analogy for history. Eliot is talking about two ways of looking at the world, and goes on to use Descartes as an example of the modern world's point of view. A revolution occurred

> when he clearly stated that what we know is not the world of objects, but our own ideas of these objects. The revolution was immense. Instead of ideas as meanings, as references to an outside world, you have suddenly a new world coming into existence, inside your own mind and therefore by the usual implication inside your own head. Mankind suddenly retires inside its several skulls.... (CL II: 15)

When perception becomes primarily an individual matter, when it occurs to large numbers of people that what *they* perceive is not necessarily what anyone else experiences, any act of true communication – including poetry – becomes virtually impossible. The importance of the distinction between ontology and psychology in Eliot's mind is, then, related to faith in the adequacy of language to encompass and convey experience. The medieval poet knew that words had exact and inviolable meanings, and he used them with a confidence in their solidity which gives to his poetry an indefinable air of authority. This authority, the poet's mastery of what is not so much his world as *the* world, makes Dante supreme among poets even for those who share none of his beliefs, for his ideas and emotions are conveyed exactly. Kermode's objection – that the dissociative and presumably nominalist force of intellect is always at work in a society – is supported by the history of philosophic dispute. But poets are not philosophers: they take their sense of the world not from treatises, but, most often, from current ideas, which are seldom those of the philosophical vanguard. Regardless of what the nominalists were doing in the universities, the spirit of the Middle Ages was incorrigibly realist.

Ontology is defined as the science of the essence of things. The word refers, in Eliot's critical vocabulary, to the realists' belief in the ability of words to embody objective reality. One *locus classicus* of the realist conception of language is Adam's naming of the animals in Book VIII of *Paradise Lost*:

> ... each bird and beast behold
> Approaching two and two, these cowering low
> With blandishment, each bird stooped on his wing.
> I named them, as they passed, and understood
> Their nature, with such knowledge God endued
> My sudden apprehension. ... (ll. 349–54)

The naming, the knowledge of the animals' nature, and the divine assurance that this is accurate knowledge are all more or less simultaneous: naming and knowing are virtually the same act, since language naturally expresses essence. A few lines later, God reiterates the point; he finds Adam

> ... knowing not of beasts alone,
> Which thou hast rightly named, but of thy self,
> Expressing well the spirit within thee free. (ll. 438–40)

But this is language in the unfallen world of paradise: the rhetoricians Belial and Satan can use language for other ends, and it is significant that Satan's appeal to Eve is to see things for *herself*. In the post-lapsarian world, words divide us: Book IX ends with the first human quarrel, after 'point of view' has entered Eden.[22]

By the seventeenth century, then, there is less confidence in the adequacy of words to deal with the reality of the world. The difference between Dante and Donne is, one might say, the difference between the statement 'This is right and that is wrong' and the formulation 'I believe that this is right and that is wrong'. The second is no less firmly believed in than the first, but the very form of the statement admits the possibility of another point of view and focuses upon the way in which an object or idea impinges upon one's self. Donne is self-consciously aware of his mental processes; in Eliot's view, those private processes rather than the shared external world are already becoming the subject matter of poetry. Donne has retired into his skull.

To the commonsensical, the whole issue is likely to seem absurd: words are man's creation, and surely we know what they mean. But history as well as philosophy suggests that we do not. During the Reformation and Counter-Reformation, Catholic and Protestant exegesis of the Bible produced, as Eliot suggests, a bewildering variety of interpretations of any one text; reason, acting upon words, revealed their essential mysteriousness. Destructive verbal criticism (the Biblical criticism of Hobbes, for example) became a possibility when words were first conceived of as *constructions* rather than as *references*. Words do not, then, explain the world: at best they tell us about the way in which *A* perceives the world. Words are internal, connotative, subjective. Science, which deals with the certainties of mass and extension, gains new prestige in the seventeenth century as a rational basis for agreement about the nature of the world; if you and I cannot agree on the Real Presence in the sacrament – if we wonder what 'real' and 'presence' *mean* in such a context – we can at least agree on Boyle's Law. The Cartesian outlook, as it appears in the *Discours sur la méthode*, tends to disparage non-rational forms of knowledge. Basil Willey long ago remarked on the consequences:

And as both religion and poetry (whatever may be our conception of them) spring from quite other modes of knowing, the Cartesian spirit, in so far as it prevailed, was really hostile to both. Descartes himself is perhaps only the most conspicuous representative of a way of thought which was irresistibly gaining ground as the century proceeded, and we must not, therefore, ascribe to him all the consequences of that thought. But the fact remains that by the beginning of the eighteenth century religion had sunk to deism, while poetry had been reduced to catering for 'delight' – to providing embellishments which might be agreeable to the fancy, but which were recognized by the judgment as having no relation to 'reality'. As Dryden wrote in his *Apology for Heroic Poetry and Poetic Licence*, we were to be 'pleased with the image, without being cozened by the fiction.' The Cartesian spirit made for the sharper distinction of the spheres of prose and poetry.... The cleavage then began to appear, which has become so troublesomely familiar to us since, between 'values' and 'facts'; between what you *felt* as a human being or as a poet, and what you *thought* as a man of sense, judgment, and enlightenment.... Prose was for conveying what was felt to be true, and was addressed to the judgment; poetry was for conveying pleasure, and was addressed to the fancy.

These developments could not fail to result in a lowering of the status of poetry, as an activity which by its very nature foreswore the only means by which, it was now felt, truth could be reached.[23]

As Willey suggests, this crisis of confidence, if we can call it that, is not the work of Descartes himself. Ockhamism is its first symptom, a symbol of the crisis to come, and Descartes is merely a convenient representative of the rationalist tendencies of his age.[24] As such, he had become a symbolic villain of sorts long before Eliot; Willey cites Jean-Baptiste Rousseau's remark on Descartes's baleful influence:

J'ai souvent oui dire à Despréaux que la philosophie de Descartes avait coupé la gorge à la poésie, et il est certain que ce

qu'elle emprunte des mathématiques dessèche l'esprit et
l'accoutume à une justesse matérielle qui n'a aucun rapport
avec la justesse metaphysique, si cela se peut dire, des poètes et
des orateurs.²⁵

It is interesting to note that for Rousseau, too, the metaphysical is
more inclusive than the rational. The 'reason' of the Middle Ages
– the basis of metaphysics – is not pure Cartesian reason but *recta
ratio*, right reason, which includes common sense and cannot go
against the truth of normal bodily experience. It would not occur
to a medieval thinker to doubt his own existence, as Descartes
does: it is perfectly obvious that he exists, and he would refute
Descartes's doubt as Johnson refuted Berkeley, by kicking a stone.
It is this bodily thinking, this union of feeling and thought, which
characterizes the true metaphysical poet as Eliot sees him.

Returning to the lectures, we find Eliot asserting that by the
time of Donne, every aspect of thought has been influenced by the
separation of the various elements that comprise sensibility. In the
thirteenth century, Richard of St Victor could write even of
mysticism in an external, reasonable manner, refraining from
autobiography.²⁶ To the Spanish mystics of the seventeenth
century, on the other hand, the experience is intensely personal,
to be communicated, if at all, in lyric poetry (St John of the Cross)
or autobiographical narrative (St Theresa of Avila) (CL III: 10–12).
It is 'psychological', individualist, written from a point of view.²⁷
The experiences described are suprarational, and rational
discourse is inadequate to them.

Some of the reasons for Eliot's failure to publish the lectures are,
I hope, clearer by this point. In striving to express his sense of
historical crisis, Eliot performed an act of great critical courage.
As he realized, his view of history is not really arguable because,
like the poetry it attempts to describe, it issues from a perception
wider than that of reason alone: it is a poet's *felt* history, a myth in
the non-reductive sense of the word.²⁸ But as a myth, Eliot's
history is liable to attack on the narrow grounds of its failure to
establish cause and effect, or even to describe the effects with any
great precision: hence the fears that Eliot expressed in the Preface
to *Homage to John Dryden* that his ideas, if expressed directly, would

experience 'immediate obloquy, followed by perpetual oblivion'. (HJD 9).

But the ideas had been there in one form or another from the beginning of Eliot's career as a critic. In 1920 he had asked his readers to

> Compare a medieval theologian or mystic ... with any 'liberal' sermon since Schleiermacher, and you will observe that words have changed their meanings. What they have lost is definite, and what they have gained is indefinite.[29]

The same ideas are developed in the Clark Lectures; Eliot is simply more specific and detailed about what happened.

> Between 1580 and 1680 the Word – verb, substantive, and adjective – undergoes a very great change, a change which may be apprehended by studying the language of Donne in contrast with the language of Marlowe, and [then] studying the language of Donne in contrast with the language of Dryden. (CL VII: 13)

The capitalized 'Word' calls to mind the *logos* of St John's gospel, and the analogical significance of the allusion is clear. Just as Christ is the incarnation of an ethical system and a concept of God – things otherwise abstract and impalpable – so the poetic image *in its highest form* is a kind of knowledge which 'clothes the abstract, for a moment, with all the painful delight of flesh'. (CL I: 14)

The enemy of such unified perception is any view of the mind which places more emphasis upon the perceiver than upon the perceived. Ockham (by implication: he is not named in the lectures) and Descartes are representative villains, but Eliot provides a fuller demonology in some offhand remarks in his second lecture. Locke, he suggests, would be the principal figure in any history of ideas which attempted to trace the course of the dissociation, presumably – Eliot does not elaborate – because his new psychology transferred the locus of reality from the external world to the perceiving mind.[30] The prophet of 'point of view', of perception on an individual rather than a communal basis, is Luther, a century before Descartes, and the culminating figure in the pandemonium is Jean-Jacques Rousseau. (CL II:9) As I have said, none of these men is a *cause* of the change; each is, however, a signpost on the road to Babel, an example of the concept 'This is true *for me*'. But truth for oneself precludes communication, as Eliot noted in a *Criterion* article a few months after the lectures.

> And this is a capital difference: a different way of facing the 'moral' problem: Mr. [Ramon] Fernandez as a psychologist, Mr. [Herbert] Read as a metaphysician. Mr. Read is interested in St. Thomas [and] ... metaphysical and logical truth; Mr. Fernandez is interested in Newman ... [and] *personality* ... for Mr. Read, I imagine, there is ... no 'nature' of truth, there is only truth and error.[31]

Once again, the philosophical vocabulary is apparent. One can see, by this point, that although the terms on each side are not interchangeable, there are two basic clusters which stand for different types of literature and different ways of looking at the world. They might be arranged, in descending order of abstraction, thus:

realist	nominalist
ontological	psychological
objects	ideas of objects
impersonal	personal

And to the list one could add any number of further pairs – denotation and connotation, for example, or description and emotional reaction to the scene described.

These oppositions adumbrate the more conventional terms 'classic' and 'romantic' which Eliot had employed in earlier essays. 'The Function of Criticism' (1923) focuses on the difference between external and internal reference as the essential distinction between the classic and the romantic:

> There is accordingly something outside of the artist to which he ... must surrender and sacrifice himself in order to earn and to obtain his unique position. ... The second-rate artist, of

course, cannot afford to surrender himself to any common action; for his chief task is the assertion of all the trifling differences which are his distinction. ... (*SE* 24)

'Tradition and the Individual Talent' (1919) makes a similar assertion about the proper role of the poet, who

> has, not a 'personality' to express, but a particular medium, which is only a medium and not a personality, in which impressions and experiences combine in peculiar and unexpected ways. Impressions and experiences which are important for the man may take no place in the poetry, and those which become important in the poetry may play quite a negligible part in the man, the personality. (*SE* 19–20)

In Eliot's essays on particular works the same criterion is used; 'Hamlet and His Problems' (1919) criticizes the play for its failure to provide an external justification for the hero's anxieties which would render them comprehensible to the audience. Shakespeare, too, occasionally retired into his skull.

These particular criticisms, however, are not Eliot's concern in the Clark Lectures. Here he is occupied simply in stating that the change occurred: we must think with Locke or feel with Rousseau, for thought and emotion, outside of an intellectual system which reconciles them, produce contradictory understandings. This dispersed understanding, too, is apparent in the work of Descartes, where

> the various elements are, so to speak, released from each other, so that you need only to press one aspect of his philosophy or another to produce the extremes of materialism or idealism, rationalism or blind faith.[32]

The stage is set for the Age of Reason and for Romanticism, as thought and feeling predominate in turn. But in certain poets – and Donne here becomes the crucial example – the separation is evident much earlier.

These explanations and elaborations of Eliot's often elliptical argument may seem to have brought us quite a distance from Donne's poetry; but, as Eliot himself said, in order to understand poetry it is necessary first to examine things which at first glance appear to have little to do with poetry. (*UPUC* 76) The basic problem for Donne, in Eliot's view, is that he has no philosophy by which to order his experience. Widely read, he has ideas from all ages, schools and sects at his command, and is apt to fly from one to another in his poetry; but if he cannot believe all of these ideas (as clearly he cannot) he must be using some for their emotional effect and others for the conceptual truth they contain. Some of Donne's ideas are 'entertained' rather than believed, and this fact suggests a lack of sincerity on Donne's part. But, Eliot notes, the way in which Donne *feels* the thought is quite sincere: the thought becomes an object of aesthetic delight, and its truth or falsehood becomes irrelevant to its function in the poem – a state of affairs which could hardly have existed before the seventeenth century.[33]

If an intellectually false concept can be used to convey a supposed truth of feeling, the beliefs of the age obviously no longer have a strong emotional attraction for the poet; Donne is often unable or disinclined to find an idea which he believes *and* which will have the desired emotional effect. As the false idea produces the 'true' feeling Donne desires, so the feeling is then embodied in an image – and thus is built up the surface of ideas, emotions, and images which provide the characteristic dazzle, movement, and interest of a Donne poem. Like Leacock's hero, the poem gets on its horse and rides off in all directions: the intellectual tendency of Donne's poetry is catabolic, and reflects the chaos of his age. (CL, II: 10) Such unity as there is in the poems is provided by what we must call Donne's personality. We are interested not in the objects of this man's thought, but in the way his mind itself moves, and this emphasis upon the perceiver and the individuality of his perception is part of what Eliot means by psychologism.

When Donne remains faithful to the vagaries of his own mind, he is one of the moderns, and we sympathize with his fluid emotional reactions to ideas. (CL IV: 10) But emotion is difficult to keep up, even if it is constantly changing, and Donne's attention is often diverted from his subject by ideas. In the 'Fifth Elegy', for example, we have the emotion of parting:

> Here take my Picture; though I bid farewell,
> Thine, in my heart, where my soule dwels, shall dwell.
> Tis like me now, but I dead, 'twill be more
> When wee are shadows both, than 'twas before.
> When weather-beaten I come backe; my hand,
> Perhaps with rude oars torne, or sunbeams tanned,
> My face and brest of haircloth, and my head
> With cares rash sodaine stormes, being o'erspread,
> My body a sack of bones, broken within,
> And powders blew staines scatter'd on my skin.

By the end of this passage Donne has been distracted by the idea of his changed self into the description of mere possibilities ('Perhaps'). As Eliot notes, 'The image of the powder-blue-stained skin is admirable, but what remains of the idea of parting? Even the notion of the meaning of the picture is overlaid; even the image of the sailor himself breaks into its component details.' The original emotion, which in a conventional lyric poet would provide the keynote for the whole, is interrupted by what Eliot, citing Mario Praz, calls 'an anticlimax of ratiocination'. Passion 'fades into the play of suggested ideas; and Donne is the great ruler of that borderland of fading and change'.[34]

The anticlimax of ratiocination is, however, often preferable to Donne's steady focus upon an emotion. For if thought and emotion yield separate truths, they are free of each other's moderating influence and tend towards self-indulgence. The 'entertained' idea is thought indulging itself, thought as an object of aesthetic delight; the indulgence of emotion yields worse things yet. Eliot takes lines from Donne's 'First Anniversary' as an example:

> Shee, shee is dead; she's dead, when thou know'st this,
> Thou know'st how lame a cripple this world is ...
> Shee, shee is dead; she's dead: when thou know'st this,
> Thou know'st how ugly a monster this world is ...

Shee, shee is dead, she's dead: when thou know'st this,
Thou know'st how wan a Ghost this our world is ...
She, shee is dead; she's dead: when thou know'st this,
Thou know'st how dry a Cinder this world is. ...

This technique of quotation is rather unfair, for the lines are taken from several pages of a long poem (ll. 237-8, 325-6, 369-79, 427-8), and have quite a different effect when read *en bloc*. Eliot's point is simply that there is in the 'First Anniversary' something excessive. The idea of Elizabeth Drury's death does not seem to have sufficient emotional impact in itself; the emotion must be worked up, then reinforced by the repetition of a morbid refrain. It is as if – this analogy is mine, not Eliot's – a jaded libertine, unable to respond to the sight of a beautiful woman, were obliged to resort to pornography instead. 'This deliberate overstimulation, *exploitation* of the *nerves* ... has in it, to me, something unscrupulous.' Donne is a 'voluptuary of thought.' (CL V : 20, V : 21)

The separation of feeling and thought is apparent also in Donne's use of the conceit, which can be contrasted with Dante's use of simile. In Dante, the simile always has a rational necessity; it is there to make an emotion or an idea more intelligible to the reader. Eliot uses the example of Dante's entry into the first heaven (*Paradiso*, II, 11. 34–6):

>Per entro sé l'etterna margarita
>ne ricevette, com'acqua recepe
>raggio di luce permanendo unita.
>
>('Within itself the eternal pearl received us,
>as water doth receive a ray of light,
>though still itself uncleft.')

Despite the beauty of the language in which it is conveyed, the simile itself has only one function, which is to clarify the experience. The conceit, on the other hand, is excessive almost by definition. It is a simile carried as far as possible, and occasionally further; its aim is not to make something intelligible, but to

display ingenuity. (CL IV:3, IV:2, VI:19–20) We do not think
'Now I understand', for the idea seldom requires so complicated
an image to render it comprehensible. We think, as we are meant
to, 'How wonderful that he can carry this on so long!' The conceit
directs us to the poet rather than to the point: it is 'psychological'.

Eliot is here on what may seem very questionable ground. If
length and ingenuity of comparison are hallmarks of the conceit,
we surely have a wealth of examples before Donne: patristic
commentary on the Scriptures, for example, abounds with point-
by-point analysis of Old Testament incidents which are seen as
emblems of theological truths or as prefigurations of the life of
Christ. To many people, such comparisons are as ingenious and
fantastic as any conceit, perhaps more so. But in a society with a
complete and coherent theocentric view of life, these parallels are
not ingeniously and tortuously worked out. They come as
naturally as leaves to a tree, since feeling (one's reaction to the Old
Testament story in question) is, in Eliot's terms, simply another
way of thinking: image and idea, story and meaning, are two ways
of stating the same thing – as myth, for the Greeks, was as valid a
way of talking about human nature as philosophical discourse.
Fourfold interpretation of the Bible, or the four levels of
interpretation outlined in Dante's 'Letter to Can Grande', are the
logical outgrowths of an age of intellectual and emotional unity.
In Donne, on the other hand, it often seems that the image has
created the idea. Eliot cites a celebrated image from Donne's
'Valediction Forbidding Mourning' –

> Our two soules therefore, which are one,
>   Though I must goe, endure not yet
> A breach, but an expansion,
>   Like gold to airy thinnesse beat

– and criticizes the simile for its over-ingenuity. It does not clarify
the situation or an idea, for there really is no idea until the image
suggests the possible ductility of the soul. Even the image of the
compasses, which is a successful *tour de force*, leaves one feeling that
the image is more important than the idea. (CL IV:16, IV:17)

It is important to understand that Eliot is not talking about the fact that Donne's poetry reflects the break-up of the Renaissance world-view. The often-cited lines (11. 205–8) from the 'First Anniversary' –

> And new Philosophy cals all in doubt,
> The Element of fire is quite put out;
> The Sun is lost, and th'earth, and no mans wit
> Can well direct him, where to looke for it[35]

– do not appear in the lectures, because Eliot is concerned rather with the way in which the break-up affects the relationships among thought, feeling, and language.

Even so, the indictment of Donne seems too severe. One's first reaction is to ask whether the case has not been overstated, and of course it has. Any ordering of intellectual history is a simplification, and we have seen that what Eliot seeks is not a complete history, nor the establishment of cause and effect, but illustrations of stages in the relationship of belief to expression. He acknowledges, at one point, the impossibility of tracing changes in the use of language authoritatively: the transformation is too gradual for analysis; there are infinite degrees of distinction between the Dantesque simile and the Donne conceit; we cannot fix a date before which there are no conceits of Donne's type; and there are, in any age of poetry, problematic cases. (CL IV:14, IV:3, IV:6, VIII:20) These are sensible qualifications, but, especially in lectures given at weekly intervals, it is the large bold outlines of criticism which matter. If the case is overstated, it is at least clearly stated, and it is, ironically, because of the shortcomings of the lecture as a form of criticism that we are able to clarify ideas which remain shadowy in Eliot's published criticism.

The change in Eliot's thinking about Donne between 1921 and 1926 is obvious, and is reflected in his published essays.[36] In 'Lancelot Andrewes', written in 1926 for the *TLS* and reprinted in *For Lancelot Andrewes*, we find the following:

> About Donne there hangs the shadow of the impure motive; and impure motives lend their aid to a facile success. He is a

little of the religious spellbinder, the Reverend Billy Sunday of his time, the flesh-creeper, the sorcerer of emotional orgy. We emphasize this aspect to the point of the grotesque. Donne had a trained mind; but without belittling the intensity or the profundity of his experience, we can suggest that this experience was not perfectly controlled, and that he lacked spiritual discipline. (SE 345)

The essay goes on to compare Donne, 'a "personality"', with Andrewes, whose emotion is 'wholly evoked by the object of contemplation', in whom 'intellect and sensibility were in harmony'. (SE 351, 345) By 1931, the criticism of Donne is expressed in terms even more reminiscent of the Clark Lectures:

In Donne, there is a manifest fissure between thought and sensibility, a chasm which in his poetry he bridged in his own way, which was not the way of medieval poetry. His learning is just information suffused with emotion, or combined with emotion not essentially relevant to it. In the poetry of Dante, and even of Guido Cavalcanti, there is always the assumption of an ideal unity in experience, the faith in an ultimate rationalization and harmonization of experience, the subsumption of the lower under the higher, an ordering of the world more or less Aristotelian. But perhaps one reason why Donne has appealed so powerfully to the recent time is that there is in his poetry hardly any attempt at organization; rather a puzzled and humorous shuffling of the pieces. ...[37]

Although Donne 'was not a believer, in the sense in which it was a category of medieval thought that there was a unity in existence, *a relation of real to ideal*, which was not beyond the mind of man to trace in its outlines', we must not think of him as a modern sceptic.[38]

The question that naturally arises in the Clark Lectures is whether, if Donne is guilty of such lapses from the objective Dantesque ideal, he can be considered a 'metaphysical' poet at all. Rather surprisingly, Eliot suggests that he can. The job of the poet, as Eliot defined it in his first lecture, is 'to draw within the orbit of feeling and sense what had existed only in thought' (CL I: 10), and Donne's conceits, when they succeed, do just that. They overemphasize the idea (which Donne may not believe), they stress the image and its peculiar personal effect rather than its intelligibility, and Donne's attention soon strays to something else in any case; but if he is a poet of chaos, as Eliot claims, he at least makes 'an exact statement of intellectual disorder'. (CL V: 17, VI: 14) 'There is no *structure* of thought, but every thought is felt, every image has a peculiar feel to it.' (CL V: 10, cf. VIII: 14) The image may be a mundane one ingeniously treated (such as the compasses), or actually nonexistent (the round earth's imagined corners), but of the reality of Donne's reactions, and his honesty in treating them, there can be no doubt. He is not of the company of Dante, but this fact is perhaps more the fault of his age than of Donne himself.

Since Eliot is not writing a history of metaphysical poetry but rather what might be called 'Notes Towards the Definition of Metaphysical Poetry', he does not deal with George Herbert, Vaughan, or Traherne in the lectures; for his purposes Crashaw's poetry alone is the ideal contrast to Donne's. Eliot suggests that if we are to understand Crashaw we must realize that he was, although intelligent and learned, primarily a man of feeling, a devotional rather than an intellectual writer. (CL VI: 2) The forms which his emotion takes are influenced by his reading, especially his reading of Donne and the poets of the Italian *seicento*. Many of the influences can be traced, and many are noted in L. C. Martin's edition of Crashaw, which appeared in 1927.[39] But any formal resemblance to Donne or to Marino, the greatest Italian writer of *concetti*, is overshadowed by Crashaw's emotional affinities with St Theresa of Avila.

It is dangerous to assert a resemblance between temperaments, which is always difficult to demonstrate convincingly, and Eliot's argument is occasionally vague. In its essentials, it runs thus: in Dante and his contemporaries, there is an awareness of the difference between human and divine love. One may lead to the other, but they are different in kind.[40] In Italian poetry of the *seicento*, on the other hand, and in St Theresa, there is a tendency to speak of divine love in terms of human love, and this tendency is developed by Crashaw. Eliot quite uncharacteristically suggests that the celibacy of Theresa and of Crashaw contributed to the transference. I have already mentioned that for Eliot the intensely personal mysticism of the seventeenth century, and of St Theresa in particular, is part of 'psychologism': it emphasizes a personal relationship with God rather than knowledge of Godhead itself, and tends to be highly emotional as well as arational or suprarational. And herein lies the danger. In the rational mind, one idea can confront another, and the outcome is subject to internal – and external – criticism. But when an idea enters the mind through the sensibility, the sum of one's emotional tendencies and susceptibilities, it does not have a rationally apprehensible form; it is therefore subject to no critical principle external to itself, and, lacking the counterbalance of reason or of an emotionally unified age, tends towards self-indulgence. As Donne indulges thought in his use of 'entertained' ideas, so Crashaw indulges his devotional urges. 'Donne might be called a voluptuary of thought; Crashaw could be called a voluptuary of religious emotion.'[41]

Eliot's argument is assisted, of course, by the fact that there is nothing in Donne – nothing, one might say, in all poetry – to equal Crashaw at his extraordinary, bathetic best, and Eliot makes use of the contrast between the two poets to emphasize the dissociation that has taken place. Again, the emblematic quality of Eliot's history is apparent: Donne as Thought and Crashaw as Feeling serve his purpose well, but the more problematic metaphysicals (Herbert and Vaughan, for example) are not discussed. One's sense of the age is rather with Eliot's in the case of Crashaw. Earlier in the lectures, Eliot notes that the origins of the conceit in Italy are analogous to those of baroque art, (CL IV: 21) and some acquaintance with baroque art and architecture helps to clarify Eliot's point. The same exuberance, the same assertion of freedom from the trammels of reason, are apparent in Longhena's church of Santa Maria della Salute, for example, or in Bernini's theatrical *Ecstasy of St Theresa*, as in the work of Crashaw.[42] In the Middle Ages, no such excess would have been possible.[43] 'Sensibility', a word which admits of no very precise definition, is communicated readily by the experience of works of art which incorporate a given sensibility.

It seems likely, however, that we assert freedom only when we feel that it is threatened, and the exuberance of the baroque suggests that thought and feeling are already seen as adversaries. In Crashaw, thought is not the other side of feeling, as in Dante, nor that which arouses feeling, as in Donne; it exists only as a stimulus, lest feeling begin to abate. And feeling does tend to flag, so Crashaw piles 'emotion ... on emotion, as a man drinks when he is afraid of becoming sober'. (CL VI: 8–9) The eight stanzas of 'The Tear', for example, give us various fancies about its subject. In the sixth, Crashaw apostrophizes the tear:

> Fair drop, why quak'st thou so?
> 'Cause thou streight must lay thy head
>   In the dust? O no,
> The dust shall never be thy bed;
> A pillow for thee will I bring,
> Stuft with down of Angels wing.

The passage is an easy one to mock, and Eliot does note the grotesqueness of the image; but he admits that the stanza has an odd sort of beauty as well.⁴⁴ There is intelligence involved not only in Crashaw's making of such an image, but in our appreciation of it. Eliot suggests that our pleasure in Crashaw's effects derives from the destruction of the usual connections between things and the creation of something original and arbitrary in their place. (CL VI: 12) The process is analogous, I would suggest, to that of surrealist painting, in which the literally inconceivable – a flaming tuba, a castle on a rock in mid-air – is used to produce a new sense of what constitutes the 'real'. Like Crashaw, though for different reasons, the surrealists deny the sufficiency of reason and choose to work in the realm of the mind, where the fantastic can be commonplace.

Crashaw is the ultimate reach of the baroque in poetry, going beyond his Italian models, but Eliot includes him among the metaphysicals. He is not merely a writer of conceits because, despite the substitution of human love for divine, Crashaw does bring into the realm of feeling a certain kind of thought – not, presumably, reason, but the thought in his ingenious images. (CL VI: 22) He accomplishes new things with rhythm, and his work as a whole is the quintessence of the religious feeling of 'that strange period of sensual religious intensity'. (CL VI: 19)

The different emphases of Donne and Crashaw are emblematic of the directions of poetry after them: like the philosophy of Descartes, which contains contradictory elements taken up by later philosophers, the English metaphysicals show the catabolic tendencies of the age. The eighteenth century, Eliot will later argue, develops thought and feeling in isolation from each other, but he needs an example of the transition to that period, and he chooses Cowley. The demonstration is necessarily a sketchy one, and depends ultimately upon Eliot's belief that

> It is a postulate implicit in all metaphysical poetry that nothing is ineffable... If you cease to be able to express feelings you cease to be able to have them, and sensibility is replaced by sentiment, in the end by the vague expression of the vague, and poetry degenerates into a diversity of noises. (CL VII: 16–17)

This idea, as Eliot admits in the last of the lectures, places extraordinary responsibility upon the artist for the development and maintenance of the human mind. (CL VIII: 12) If he fails to achieve exact expression, he assists in the decline of sensibility, of clear meaning, ultimately of civilization itself. If, on the other hand, a given view of the world can no longer generate an emotionally compelling poetic vision, that world-view is probably inadequate for poetic purposes and moribund.

Hence the interest of Cowley. As the generally acknowledged 'transitional' poet between Donne and Dryden, he displays characteristics of both; we see in the intellectual order of his work much of the emerging eighteenth-century world-view, and in his language much of the school of Donne. As a metaphysical poet, however, he is unsatisfactory. Eliot cites three stanzas from Cowley's 'Mistress' in support of his point:

> Now by my love, the greatest oath that is,
>   None loves you half so well as I:
>   I do not ask your love for this;
> But for heaven's sake believe me, or I dye.
>   No servant e'er but did deserve
> His master should believe that he does serve;
> And I'll ask no more wages, though I starve.
>
> 'Tis no luxurious diet this, and sure
>   I shall not by't too lusty prove;
>   Yet shall it willingly endure,
> If't can but keep together life and love.
>   Being your pris'ner and your slave,
> I do not feasts and banquets look to have,
> A little bread and water's all I crave.
>
> On a sigh of pity I a year can live,
>   One tear will keep me twenty at least,
>   Fifty a gentle look will give;
> An hundred years on one kind word I'll feast:
>   A thousand more will added be,
> If you an inclination have for me;
> And all beyond is vast eternity.

All of the elements of Donne's poetry are here: the situation, the forceful opening lines, and the images are all characteristic. There are more or less obvious echoes, too, of Donne's 'Good-Morrow' and Marvell's 'Coy Mistress'. What is missing, Eliot finds, is the *movement* of a Donne poem; Cowley's imitation is exact but lifeless. Such a judgment is not really susceptible of proof, but it is apparent that a dimension of some kind has been lost in Cowley's poetry. 'In Donne there is an emotional requirement of the conceit; in Marino, in Crashaw, there is an emotion *in* the conceit; with Cowley there is an effort to reconstitute that curious amalgam of thought and feeling through the conceit.' (CL VII: 5)

The thought, then, does not have an emotional equivalent or completion. Cowley no doubt believes his ideas, as Donne could not have believed all of his, but they do not stir him, and his emotions, courtly and religious, are not a form of knowledge. His love of Hobbes and his love of God necessarily exist in different parts of his mind: his theology and his science are both diminished in order to keep them separate. (CL VII:3) Eliot feels that eighteenth-century belief is inferior to that of earlier epochs, and is particular in pointing out that he does not mean the *objects* of belief, but the believing itself.[45] The 'rift between thought and objects' mentioned by Copleston has presumably had its effects.

It should be apparent by now that Eliot regards the Renaissance in England, especially in its later phases, as a very mixed affair: if it is true that things fall apart, we must not regard the fact as a purely modern development. As early as 1924, Eliot had said that in the Renaissance

> there was a general philosophy of life, if it may be called such, based on Seneca and other influences which we find in Shakespeare as in the others. It is a philosophy which, as Mr. Santayana observed in an essay which passed almost unheeded, may be summarized in the statement that Duncan is in his grave. Even the philosophical basis, the general attitude toward life of the Elizabethans, is one of anarchism, of dissolution, of decay. It is in fact exactly parallel and indeed one and the same thing with their artistic greediness, their desire for every sort of effect together, their unwillingness to accept any limitation and abide by it.[46]

In the Renaissance essays written after the Clark Lectures, this idea of the decay of intellectual order recurs almost as a leitmotif. The dissolution is particularly apparent in drama; in 'A Dialogue on Dramatic Poetry' (1928), 'B' says that 'the age of Shakespeare moved in a steady current, with back-eddies certainly, towards anarchy and chaos'.[47] 'B' may not be Eliot himself – though one is inclined to think that the remark has his approval – but essentially the same point is made again in 'Seneca in Elizabethan Translation' (1927), where Eliot speaks in his own voice: medieval drama, which reaches its highest point in *Everyman*, is more classical than the 'sanguinary' Elizabethan drama, and Eliot feels that 'the change is due to some fundamental release of restraint'.

History and Poetry

(*SE* 83) The Grand Guignol of Jacobean tragedy is just around the corner.

The same degeneration is visible in seventeenth-century poetry. In the Clark Lectures Donne, Crashaw, and Cowley are the examples, but in 'The Silurist', a 1927 review article, Eliot compares the emotion of Herbert's verse, which is 'clear, definite, mature and sustained' with that of Vaughan, which is 'vague, adolescent, fitful and retrogressive'.[48] Certain of Eliot's mysterious generalizations are clearer in the light of the lectures as well. The English civil war, which Eliot feels has been carried on into our own day, is a symbolic watershed, the point at which the new division of mind against senses assumes a political form.[49] In *The Use of Poetry* (1933), Eliot asserts that 'the history of every branch of intellectual activity provides the same record of the diminution of England from the time of Queen Anne'. (*UPUC* 62) This 'diminution' is clearly, in Eliot's mind, the legacy of Cowley's age, which dwarfs both feeling and thought by keeping them separate. 'The inspissation of poetic style throughout Europe after the Renaissance' is the inevitable result of the dissociation.[50]

With the divorce accomplished, Eliot's argument appears to be heading, albeit by a new route, towards an old generalization — that the eighteenth century 'thought' and the nineteenth century 'felt'. But neither thought nor feeling can be completely dispensed with by a particular period. The danger is rather that men will develop 'a petty intellect uncriticized by feeling, and an exuberant feeling uncriticized by thought'. (CL VIII: 12) Eliot had made the same point in earlier essays: 'the eighteenth century was in part cynical and in part sentimental, but it never arrived at complete amalgamation of the two feelings'.[51] Eliot finds that the rise of sentiment (as opposed to whole sensibility) is already apparent in the poetry of Pope, and overt in the work of Gray and Collins; excluded from satire, it gains strength in Thomson and Young and emerges full-blown in Wordsworth and Coleridge. (CL VII: 18) The history at this point in the lectures is very sketchy. Eliot skips from England in the seventeenth century to France in the nineteenth, and his published essays on eighteenth- and nineteenth-century literature are few and contribute little to our knowledge of Eliot's historiography.

Nothing, presumably, will convince a partisan of eighteenth-century literature that Eliot is right in thinking that the Augustans began to develop a petty intellect uncriticized by feeling and an exuberant feeling uncriticized by thought. I find it interesting, however, that at least one eighteenth-century writer – Sterne – was aware of the phenomenon. In *A Sentimental Journey*, Yorick is converted to an enthusiasm for liberty by a starling calling 'I can't get out' from its cage. He apostrophizes the 'thrice sweet and gracious goddess' of Liberty and allows his imagination full scope in conjuring up the miseries of prisoners; but he does not free the bird, and eventually gives it away. Sterne, mocking the cult of sentiment, is aware that feeling often fails to find its completion in considered action.

It is more difficult to explain Eliot's lack of sympathy for the Romantics, whose professed aim was to restore the place of feeling in poetry. Restore it they did; but they could not reunite it with thought. 'The sort of reassociation that was effected, in English verse, was inorganic', Eliot says in the lectures, and he does not elaborate. (CL VI:15) I believe he means that the attempt was contrary to the spirit of the age, that it could not emerge naturally from the thought of the period (primarily rationalist and materialist) and the feeling of the same period, which was generally idealist and transcendental. In a review written for *The Athenaeum* in 1919, Eliot asserts that 'the Romantic Generation in England attained no unity of temper in any sympathy of society and art, and no unity of expression in any individual.'[52] Two years later, in 'The Metaphysical Poets', he acknowledges that 'in one or two passages of Shelley's *Triumph of Life*, in the second *Hyperion*, there are traces of a struggle towards unification of sensibility, but Keats and Shelley died....' (*SE* 288)

As a result of their divorce, feeling and thought enter each other's realms rather awkwardly; they corrupt rather than complete. Philosophy, which ought to be disinterested within its premises, takes on an emotional colouring in the work of Fichte, Schopenhauer, Hegel, James and Bradley, each of whom, Eliot suggests, passionately *wants* something to be true without being able to demonstrate it satisfactorily. Poetry, on the other hand, which should incarnate rather than analyse experience, becomes 'philosophical', 'corrupted by thought', in the work of Wordsworth and Shelley, Tennyson and Browning. (CL VIII: 13)

Here again, Eliot is harking back to points he had already made. In 'The Metaphysical Poets' he said that 'Tennyson and Browning ruminated' – talked about their thoughts rather than conveying them purely in image and incident. (*SE* 288) As for prose, Eliot stated in a 1923 article for *Vanity Fair* that

> In English prose [after Carlyle], no matter how antithetical to the prose of Carlyle it may be, there is usually some exaggeration, some peculiar emotional limitation, as it were a slightly feverish temperature, and of no writer is this more true than Walter Pater. ...[53]

This emotional tone, most obvious in Carlyle, is discernible in the writings of Ruskin, Arnold, and Newman, and the influence of Pater is detectable in Wilde, Yeats, and Bradley.[54] In the Clark Lectures, these ideas are reiterated: the element of emotional temperature in English prose is now said to begin with Newman and to include Francis Thompson and Lionel Johnson. (CL II: 25, VI: 2) The reason for including the poets of the 1890s is clear enough; Eliot explains, in 'Arnold and Pater' (1930), the 'sensationalism' which derives from Pater. Ruskin, Newman, Arnold, and Bradley are less obvious, but the common feature is again 'psychologism' – the conduct of an argument with primary reference not to truth or to the external world, but to its effect upon the reader.

At first glance, these remarks may seem to be merely a smear upon a number of writers whom Eliot happens not to like. It is significant, however, that John Holloway, in *The Victorian Sage*, has made essentially the same point. Many Victorian prose writers quite consciously wrote to persuade rather than to 'prove': in Carlyle, as in the others, 'the nerve of proof – in the readily understood and familiar sense of straightforward argument – simply cannot be traced'.[55] Aware that his ideas are not demonstrable, but feeling that they are vitally important, the sage attempts to communicate his sense of things, the *feel* of a particular point of view. Holloway supports his argument with analyses of literary style in Carlyle, Disraeli, George Eliot, Newman, Arnold, and Hardy – the proof, in so far as proof is possible, of an assertion made by Eliot thirty years earlier.[56]

Did the metaphysical disappear during the seventeenth century, then, not with a bang but a whimper? Not quite. It reappears in France during the nineteenth century in a way which Eliot has patent difficulty in defining. The central figure, not surprisingly, is Jules Laforgue, and the theme is the perennial one of the conflict of thought and feeling.[57] Eliot cites one of Laforgue's 'Dimanches' –

> Bref, j'allais me donner d'un 'Je Vous Aime'
> Quand je m'avisai non sans peine
> Que d'abord je ne me possedai pas moi-même

– and goes on to say that

> That *je m'avisai* is always interrupting, just as the disparity between the meaning of human lives and what they should mean is always driving his Hamlet back onto himself. But he is one who 'ne croit à son Moi qu'à des moments perdus,' in disaccord, and later in the same poem ... he repeats the theme of Baudelaire and Emerson 'je ne suis qu'un faux accord' or 'Seigneur, donnez-moi la force et le courage De contempler mon corps et mon coeur sans dégoût.' (CL VIII: 4)

Donne's poetry depends upon the juxtaposition of thought and the feeling which thought arouses; Laforgue's depends, according to Eliot, upon the contrast and confusion of these elements. Laforgue's philosophical reading, primarily in Schopenhauer and Hartman, was itself based on the conflict of will (nature, which is essentially irrational) and idea, and he is always aware of the two sides of his being. 'He is at once the sentimentalist day-dreaming over the *jeune fille* at the piano with her geraniums, and the behaviourist inspecting her reflexes.' (CL VIII:6) He experiences both the desire for a system which will give his actions some significance in the order of the universe, and the knowledge that no system is adequate to his scepticism. The moral passion, the desire to make sense of things, confronts the non-moral, unintellectual void.

It is surely not enough, however, for one's mind and feelings to be in conflict: the modern metaphysical must be fully aware of this conflict and able to turn it to artistic gain. The irony implied by this awareness is something we recognize in Stendhal, Flaubert – particularly the Flaubert of *L'Education Sentimentale* – and Baudelaire as well as Laforgue.[58] It does not characterize Lord Tennyson, who had the conflict without the irony, and it is perhaps for this reason that Eliot could not admit Tennyson to the ranks of the greatest poets, those who were 'metaphysical' in one sense of the word or another.[59] Irony, a classical quality, suggests the ability to see oneself from without. It is a quality which the English Romantics, with the great exception of Byron, are devoid of.

Eliot concludes his survey of literary history with a few suggestive remarks on Tristan Corbière, and concludes the lectures with some remarks on the consequences of his theory of metaphysical poetry, which 'implies a theory of the history of belief'.[60] One's first inclination is to ask how seriously this version of literary history is to be taken. I have already indicated that as a cut-and-dried affair, with each poet representing a distinct stage in the disintegration of the intellect, it is not at all convincing. The characteristics of Donne and Crashaw are exaggerated, and all the writers Eliot discusses are placed in certain relationships with each other for the sake of the larger argument about the relationship of belief and language.

But as symbolic history, as a means of imposing order upon genuine, perceived differences in the mental outlooks of various ages, Eliot's history is legitimate. In reviewing *Ulysses*, Eliot noted that Joyce's use of myth was 'a way of controlling, of ordering, of giving a shape and significance to the immense panorama of futility and anarchy which is contemporary history',[61] and he was himself aware that 'History has many cunning passages, contrived corridors/And issues, deceives with whispering ambitions,/ Guides us by vanities.'[62] The sense of loss which clearly characterizes so much of English literature from the Romantics on almost inevitably suggests historical myth as explanation.[63]

Writers as diverse as Carlyle, Ruskin, and Henry Adams have been drawn to the Middle Ages, and I shall show in the next chapter Eliot's relationship to this tradition: what I wish to insist on here is the importance of the ideas behind the emblematic examples Eliot uses. To say, with the Renaissance specialist, 'Donne and Crashaw are rather more complicated than that' is not to dispose of Eliot's argument. We naturally wish to understand the mysterious accord among society, the artist, and the means of expression which results in the Gothic cathedrals, the sculpture of classical Greece, the poetry of Dante. The questions Eliot raises about the relationship of language and belief to reality – if not his way of handling them – are of literally vital interest.[64]

The source of the term 'dissociation of sensibility' has been the subject of much bootless controversy. F. H. Bradley and Remy de Gourmont are often mentioned as sources, and both are indeed possible.[65] We might expect that Gourmont had some influence on Eliot's developing view of history: the acknowledged critical debt and the frequent references in Eliot's occasional articles seem to indicate a certain amount of common ground.[66] But the debt is easily overestimated since, as Glenn Burne notes, Eliot's 'ultimate ideas differ considerably from those of the Frenchman'.[67] Eliot first read Gourmont at Pound's urging, but was never in agreement with more than a few of Gourmont's often contradictory ideas.[68] By 1928 he had worked through the influence and was preoccupied with other problems. (See *SW* viii)

Gourmont's essay on the dissociation of ideas is concerned only with the separation of ideas which are conventionally associated by mere habit (sex and procreation, for example).[69] The starting-point of Eliot's use of the term is Gourmont's essay on 'La Sensibilité de Jules Laforgue':

> Mais à force de vivre, on acquiert la faculté de dissocier son intelligence de sa sensibilité: cela arrive, tôt ou tard, par l'acquisition d'une faculté nouvelle, indispensable quoique dangereuse, le scepticisme.[70]

Eliot's striking development of Gourmont's idea is to transfer to literary history the process which Gourmont sees in the psychological growth of the individual.[71] Even in his early articles, Eliot had discussed the growth of the English language as though he were tracing the development of an individual's mind: thus he speaks of the 'maturity' of a language and, in the later *Use of Poetry*, of 'the maturing of the English mind' between Sidney and the latter part of Jonson's lifetime.[72]

But the maturation of language and thought is accompanied by the scepticism which lies behind the concept of words as mere labels, with no necessary or inevitable connection to reality. The dissociation begins, and one of its first fruits, ironically enough, is criticism in the modern sense: 'The important moment for the appearance of criticism seems to be the time when poetry ceases to be the expression of the mind of a whole people.' (*UPUC* 22) The advent of criticism, which is mere rational discourse, represents the failure of the 'felt thought' of poetry as complete communication. *The Use of Poetry*, in which Eliot makes the statement cited above, can be read as an obscure book-length gloss upon the ideas set forth in the Clark Lectures. These later lectures, delivered at Harvard in 1932–3, set out to examine 'the process of readjustment between poetry and the world in and for which it is produced' (*UPUC* 27); but they do not succeed, despite frequent brilliance, because of Eliot's diffidence about stating his theory plainly. At the beginning of 'The Modern Mind', for example, Eliot cites with approval Maritain's remark that 'Work such as Picasso's shows a fearful progress in self-consciousness on the part of painting.' (*UPUC* 121) In its context, the remark is suggestive but not particularly illuminating. In the light of the Clark Lectures, on the other hand, it is apparent that the self-consciousness referred to is, as Eliot sees it, the painter's awareness of the individuality of his vision, the Cartesian awareness 'that what we know is not the world of objects, but our ideas of these objects'.[73]

The role of self-consciousness in separating us from the world suggests that the proper alternative is a kind of naïveté of vision; this in turn suggest the influence of Friedrich von Schiller, whose best-known essay, 'On Naïve and Sentimental Poetry', deals with many of the issues Eliot discusses. Schiller does not suggest a cause for the phenomenon, but remarks on the separation of the modern poet from nature. We react strongly to nature

> because nature, in our time, is no longer in man, and ... we no longer encounter it in its primitive truth, except out of humanity, in the inanimate world. It is not because we are more *conformable* to *nature* – quite the contrary; it is because in our social relations, in our mode of existence, in our manners, we are in *opposition with nature*.[74]

When we encounter the exact descriptions of the Greeks, on the other hand, we are struck by the fact that 'so few traces are met among them of that sentimental interest that we moderns ever take in the scenes of nature and in natural characters'.[75] Schiller admits to initial displeasure with Shakespeare's works, in which he could not find the poet's heart or personality, and he includes Shakespeare and Homer among the 'simple' or 'naïve' poets.

There is, obviously, nothing pejorative in Schiller's use of the word 'naïve', despite his desire to justify modern, 'sentimental' poetry. He implies no lack of craft; he means only that the naïve poet and his audience are in some way closer to nature than their modern counterparts. They are a part of nature, and there is consequently no need for an emotional addition to the scene as it stands.

> As long as man dwells in a state of pure nature (I mean pure and not coarse nature), all his being acts at once like a simple sensuous unity, like a harmonious whole. The senses and reason, the receptive faculty and the spontaneously active faculty, have not been as yet separated in their respective functions: *a fortiori* they are not yet in contradiction with each other. Then the feelings of man are not the formless play of chance; nor are his thoughts an empty play of the imagination, without any value. His feelings proceed from the law of necessity; his *thoughts* from *reality*. But when man enters the state of civilization, and art has fashioned him, this *sensuous* harmony which was in him disappears, and henceforth he can only manifest himself as a *moral unity*, that is, as aspiring to unity.[76]

History and Poetry

There is some vagueness in Schiller's account, as there is in Eliot's; one wonders, for example, how the society of Shakespeare's day, hardly 'pure nature', allowed the poet to develop as a harmonious whole. The similarities between Schiller's argument and Eliot's are striking. There is not only the primitive unity of thought and feeling, and the rift between nature and ourselves (aspects of the Eden metaphor which I shall not belabour), but also the use of the word 'moral' to describe the longed-for unity of one's actions with some system which renders them meaningful – the same sense in which Eliot uses the word in his discussion of Laforgue.

Schiller's 'sentimentality', Gourmont's 'scepticism', and Eliot's 'dissociation' emerge in different ways from consideration of the same crisis. Eliot's account is the fullest and therefore the most controversial, but the basic argument is as old as Romanticism itself, and is one aspect of Eliot's relation to the Romantic tradition.[77] Eliot's ideas do not constitute a break with the past; the author of 'Tradition and the Individual Talent' built, as we might expect, upon the accumulated wisdom of the English and European critical traditions. But – and again this is in keeping with the ideas set forth in 'Tradition' – Eliot's theory does extend the old argument: its greatest novelty is the suggestion that the change in the nature of our perception of the world has parallels in philosophic thought and in our conception of poetic language.

It would be difficult to overestimate the importance of these unpublished lectures to our view of Eliot as a literary critic. The relatively detailed history of sensibility which they provide gives us a means of defining what 'Romanticism', a notoriously protean term, represents in Eliot's mind. The usual facile distinction between classic restraint and romantic freedom, or the classical emphasis on thought and the romantic emphasis on feeling, obviously does not apply here. All poetry, in Eliot's view, deals with feeling as the visceral equivalent of thought, with thought absorbed through the nerve endings. The real distinction between the romantic and classic sensibilities is the difference between subject and object as focus of attention, between the direct evocation of 'feeling' and the portrayal of that which will cause the desired feeling in the reader, or render it comprehensible in the poet or a dramatic character.

This concern for the objective (though not disinterested) portrayal is one of the unifying threads in Eliot's criticism. It appears most obviously in the idea of the 'objective correlative', the external source of and justification for the feelings of a dramatic character:

> The artistic 'inevitability' lies in this complete adequacy of the external to the emotion; and this is precisely what is deficient in *Hamlet*. Hamlet (the man) is dominated by an emotion which is inexpressible, because it is in *excess* of the facts as they appear. ... Hamlet's bafflement at the absence of objective equivalent to his feelings is a prolongation of the bafflement of his creator in the face of his artistic problem.[78]

Whether this is a justifiable censure of *Hamlet* is a vexing question, but there is no doubt that it is a clear statement of Eliot's requirements of a work of art. There is to be no *angst*, no objectless anxiety, no emotion without a clear source. 'Dans ce genre' – Stendhal was talking about prose, but Eliot would make the requirement a general one – 'on n'émeut que par la clarté.'[79]

Hence, in 'Andrew Marvell', Eliot's attack upon poetry which depends for its effect upon 'the mistiness of the feeling and the vagueness of its object'.[80] 'The Nymph's Song to Hylas' in William Morris's *Life and Death of Jason* is compared to Marvell's 'The Nymph and the Fawn'. 'The emotion of Morris is not more refined or more spiritual; it is merely more vague: if anyone doubts whether the more refined or spiritual emotion can be precise, he should study the treatment of the varieties of discarnate emotion in the *Paradiso*.'[81] After further quotation from Marvell's poem, Eliot concludes that

> These verses have the suggestiveness of true poetry; and the verses of Morris, which are nothing if not an attempt to suggest, really suggest nothing; and we are inclined to infer that the suggestiveness is the aura around a bright clear centre, that you cannot have the aura alone.[82]

The 'bright clear centre' is the external situation; the 'aura', the emotion desired.

Thus far, I am sure, the connections are obvious. It may not be as apparent that Eliot's standards imply a theory of style. If the 'bright clear centre' is indeed there, but is described in a highly mannered style, our attention is likely to be diverted from the scene to the style or from the sense to the 'music' of the verse. Ideally, of course, these elements are inseparable:

> Shakespeare, or Dante, will bear innumerable readings, but at each reading all the elements of appreciation can be present. There is no interruption between the surface that these poets present to you and the core. While therefore, I cannot pretend to have penetrated to any 'secret' of these poets, I feel that such appreciation of their work as I am capable of points in the right direction; whereas I cannot feel that my appreciation of Milton leads anywhere outside of the mazes of sound.[83]

This passage is analogous to Eliot's censure of Donne's conceits, which divert attention from the matter they are supposed to convey.

In 'Tradition and the Individual Talent' Eliot had said audaciously that 'Poetry is not a turning loose of emotion, but an escape from emotion; it is not the expression of personality, but an escape from personality',[84] and in the light of our discussion so far, the importance of 'impersonality' should be apparent. What are we to do, then, with Eliot's praise of Renaissance dramatists for the very thing they are meant to avoid? Even the most cursory reading of the Elizabethan essays will show that Eliot tries, in each instance, to isolate the personal element in a dramatist's work. Middleton has 'a quiet and undisturbed vision of things as they are', Ford 'a whole pattern formed by the sequence of plays' and 'a distinct personal rhythm'; Marston has 'a positive, powerful and unique personality', Jonson 'created his own world' and we can recognize 'the Webster pattern'.[85] Eliot goes so far as to make the requirement a general one:

> A man might, hypothetically, compose any number of fine passages or even of whole poems which would each give satisfaction, and yet not be a great poet, unless we felt them to be united by one significant, consistent, and developing personality.[86]

We must, it seems, accuse Eliot of inconsistency at the very least.

But the inconsistency is only apparent. We cannot hope to escape from our personalities: we necessarily see the world from a point of view and write from our own, at least partly private, sense of the world. The artist therefore need not eliminate what is distinctive and personal in his view of things, but he must be careful to prevent its seeming *merely* personal, an addition to the facts. Ideally, personality is transmuted into a world, and the writer's view emerges naturally from the world of the work.

> Dostoevsky had the gift, a sign of genius in itself, for utilizing his weaknesses; so that epilepsy and hysteria cease to be the defects of an individual and become – as a fundamental weakness can, given the ability to face it and study it – the entrance to a genuine and personal universe.[87]

Such transmutation is a difficult and delicate process; there are bound to be more failures than successes. The usual result of such a failure, in Eliot's eyes, is to draw attention to the artist's personality – usually, if he is a bad artist, to a rather immature personality. Tourneur, for example, is said to have an 'intense and unique and horrible vision of life', and this sounds very much like the sort of praise Eliot has used in discussing Marston and Middleton.[88] The vision is, however, a little too intense:

> We may think as we read Swift, 'how loathsome human beings are'; in reading Tourneur we can only think 'how terrible to loathe human beings so much as that.' For you cannot make humanity horrible merely by presenting human beings as consistent and monotonous maniacs of gluttony and lust.[89]

Attention is diverted, in such a case, from the world to its maker.

Massinger, a similar failure, has a fault described by Eliot as 'precisely a defect of personality'.[90]

Romantic art, in Eliot's view, frequently fails to get beyond the personality, and we are aware of a speaker rather than a situation. Classic art, by making us see through the author's eyes, renders the eyes themselves invisible to us.[91] It focuses our attention upon the dramatic situation, the 'objective correlative' which renders the emotion comprehensible. Thus 'the world of a great poetic dramatist is a world in which the creator is everywhere present, and everywhere hidden.'[92] Like Stephen Dedalus's artist-god, he is 'behind or beyond or above his handiwork, invisible, refined out of existence, indifferent, paring his fingernails'.[93]

The Clark Lectures open all areas of Eliot studies for new work, and there is not space, in a study such as this, to indicate more than the outlines of possible future discussion. In our understanding of Eliot's literary criticism, the lectures will be of use not only in defining some terms more precisely, as we have defined 'Romanticism' above, but also in settling the question of whether Eliot is a 'systematic' critic or not. No entirely systematic critic is anything but dull; the predictability of his responses deprives them of any interest. Nevertheless, there have been commentators over the years who have contended that Eliot's criticism is based – *obscurum per obscurius* – on the aesthetics of Aristotle, Kant, or R. G. Collingwood. In opposition to these points of view, there has arisen the counter-assertion that Eliot has no real critical principles at all. According to this school, which tends to minimize the abilities of poets as thinkers, we can count on Eliot for a poet's *aperçus* of other poets, but ought not to expect any general structure of critical thought.[94]

But these extremes are not, of course, the only possibilities. While Eliot does not have a 'system' in the sense in which Lukács or Frye may be said to have one, he does have definite ideas about the relationship of language to belief. The historical myth generated by these ideas is not, however, a means of evaluation. Poets after Donne find it more difficult to unite thought and feeling, but the task is not an impossible one; a gifted and highly conscious poetic mind can wring poetry even out of the conflict, as Baudelaire, Laforgue, and Eliot himself have managed to do.

History and Poetry

When Eliot declared, in the 1928 'Preface' to *The Sacred Wood*, his interest in the relationship of poetry to the spiritual and social life of its time, he was not, as some of his own critics have supposed, attempting to make the moral factor an element in critical judgment. (*SW* x) He was, rather, recognizing the inevitable effect of belief and *Weltanschauung* upon the weight and meaning of the word in poetry, upon the significance of the poetic act itself: and in the best of Eliot's essays there is a constant concern with the authority of the poetic line, its ability to convey both a credible external world and 'a network of tentacular roots reaching down to the deepest terrors and desires'.[95]

The view of the mind set forth in the lectures has interesting parallels with various situations in Eliot's poetry. One thinks, for example, of the recurrent motif of the mind isolated from the world and human contact:

> *Dayadhvam*: I have heard the key
> Turn in the door once and turn once only
> We think of the key, each in his prison
> Thinking of the key, each confirms a prison. ... (*CPP* 49)

Eliot's note on these lines includes a passage from F. H. Bradley's *Appearance and Reality* which makes the meaning explicit:

> My external sensations are no less private to myself than are my thoughts or my feelings. In either case my experience falls within my own circle, a circle closed on the outside; and, with all its elements alike, every sphere is opaque to the others which surround it. ... In brief, regarded as an existence which appears in a soul, the whole world for each is peculiar and private to that soul. (*CPP* 54)

The great themes of *Four Quartets* – love, poetry, and eternity – all involve transcendence of the limitations of self and individual perception; the meditations on poetry deal with the impermanence and inevitable imprecision of our attempts to communicate. The first epigraph to 'Burnt Norton' is a line from Heraclitus which summarizes the whole problem: 'Although there is but one Centre, most men live in centres of their own.'[96]

Knowledge of our isolation fosters the kind of irony we see in Prufrock, Gerontion, the male speaker in 'Portrait of a Lady', and Tiresias. 'Real irony', Eliot notes in the Clark Lectures, 'is an expression of suffering' (CL VIII:9), and this peculiar form of suffering – the awareness of a disjunction between our thoughts and the experience they try to encompass – is one of Eliot's obsessive poetic concerns. Its significance is clarified by the theory of language set forth in the lectures.

In the chronology of Eliot's writing, the lectures occupy an intriguing place. They not only clarify certain critical concepts and poetic themes, but confirm that the years 1923 through 1925 were pivotal in Eliot's intellectual development generally. Lyndall Gordon has shown how Eliot was concerned, from his college days, with the problem of verifying experience of any kind, and discusses the dissertation on Bradley, which shows Eliot 'torn between the truth of his visions and his rational distrust of them'.[97] There is a sense, then, in which the Clark Lectures, like *The Waste Land*, are autobiographical. All of Eliot's various concerns can be seen, in fact, as aspects of the central epistemological problem of subject and object; it is therefore not surprising that his literary, political, and religious ideas were worked out at the same time.[98]

I have already mentioned the analogical relationship between the word in language, as conceived by the realists, and the *logos* of St John, Christ. Both entities incarnate the abstract, and Eliot even capitalizes 'Word' once in discussing language.[99] If Eliot had come to believe that some form of realism was essential for the existence of poetry, it would be natural for him to be drawn to the faith which makes realism a logical possibility. The sacraments, as defined by Catholic theology, are the ultimate example of the power of the word in its relationship to the world: liturgical words effect, ultimately, changes of essence – most obviously, the transformation of bread and wine into Christ's body and blood. Since the transformation is not physical, it is, to the sceptic, absurd; but the same sceptic may react with sympathy and understanding to poetic metaphor. Strictly considered, a metaphor is either a lie (my love is not a rose, for she is neither quite so red nor is she made of petals) or an assertion of the reality of the non-material concept which connects the physical referents (my love is as *delicate* and *beautiful* as a rose). To treat the equation literally is to reduce it to nonsense, but to take it at its intended level is to accept, in some sense, the reality of the unseen.

For Eliot, I would suggest, religion was not only a means of affirming the reality of concepts, but was also, in a very limited sense, a kind of poetry. In both activities, the end is the perception of truth; in both, we must accept the reality of the non-physical; and in both the best means of perception is through concrete detail – the poetic image, parables, incidents in the life of Christ.[100] To accept the validity of poetic statement is not, of course, to accept the religious outlook, but the activities are in some respects parallel.[101]

This concern with the concrete is reflected in Eliot's politics as well. Just as in poetry the vague and connotative can exist only as the corona around a bright clear centre of images; just as, in religion, the divine is brought to earth in bodily form or through concrete symbolic ritual, so in politics the ideal towards which one strives can be encompassed only by beginning with what is. Eliot noted in an address to the Conservative Club that

> A political party may find that it has had a history, before it is fully aware of or agreed upon its own permanent tenets; it may have arrived at its actual formation through a succession of metamorphoses and adaptations, during which some issues have been superannuated and new issues have arisen. What its fundamental tenets are, will probably be found only by careful examination of its behaviour throughout its history and by examination of what its more thoughtful and philosophic minds have said on its behalf. ...[102]

This Burkean preference for the organic, the concrete, the physically present (as opposed to the mechanical or the abstract) is the unifying idea in Eliot's literary, political, and religious thought. It lies behind the famous declaration, in the Preface to *For Lancelot Andrewes*, for classicism, royalism, and anglo-catholicism. (*FLA* 7)

But the final and greatest importance of the Clark Lectures does not have to do with the clarification of problems in Eliot's work at all. The work of any poet-critic worthy of the name is not simply an accumulation of ideas which illuminate his poetry or his belief; if his criticism is to be valid as anything more than personal commentary, it must in some way account for the literature of its age. Thus Eliot's 'Ulysses, Order and Myth'[103] tells us something not only about Eliot's poetic and poetic practice, but also about modernism as a whole in its relation to the past. Similarly, Eliot's history of sensibility is not only an intriguing way of looking at the English tradition, but, even in its details, a perceptive view of the malaise of much modern literature. One thinks, for example, of the anguished Cartesians of Samuel Beckett who carry on their meditations, denying bodily experience as their limbs become paralysed and the sand rises to their necks and beyond. Beckett is surely a 'metaphysical' in the same sense that Laforgue is: the passion for order and meaning which his characters display is at odds with their experience and the void which they attempt, at all costs, to ignore. The resulting irony is of a particularly bitter kind. Ratiocination in what has been called 'post-modern' literature is comic in itself; the absurdity of trying to perceive or create order in a world which does not conform to our mental categories is the source of such comedy as we are still capable of.

In fiction, the technical emphasis has been, since Henry James, on limited point of view. The sophisticated use of this technique, originally a liberating force in the artist's exploration of the mind, has become in the last half-century a millstone around the novelist's neck: no statement about the external world is now admissible, save in the mouth of a character, and the world has virtually disappeared in the mass of misprisions by which the novelist conveys the inevitability of our private worlds and ideas of order.[104] Virginia Woolf, whose treatment of individual perception shows her awareness of the problem, longed for the older writers' confidence in their knowledge of the world:

> Only believe, we find ourselves saying, and all the rest will come of itself... you will not only make people a hundred years later feel the same thing, but you will make them feel it as literature.

History and Poetry

For certainty of that kind is the condition which makes it possible to write. To believe that your impressions hold good for others is to be released from the cramp and confinement of personality.[105]

For Woolf, as for Eliot, literature is ideally 'an escape from personality'.[106]

In modern poetry – in one strain of it, at least – the individual imagination has been extolled at the expense of the world which is its subject. Wallace Stevens's line 'Your world is you. I am my world', with its placing of 'your world' and 'my world' at opposite ends of the line and its emphatic full stop between 'you' and 'I', could well stand as the epitaph of poetry as an act of communication.[107] Between those who have nothing in common, no conversation is possible.

These ideas are not new, and I do not introduce them here to attack the achievements of James or Woolf or Stevens. But serious literature in our time is read by few people: it has, generally, ceased to deal with the world which most people – realists – recognize as their common possession, and Eliot's theory of language and belief is a suggestive account of why.

The Clark Lectures were the first version of what was to become a book on metaphysical poetry. In a prefatory page to the lectures, Eliot indicates the ambitious scope of his project. *The School of Donne* was to be longer and more detailed than the lectures, and would include analyses of other poets. This long book would itself be part of a trilogy with the grand and ominous title *The Disintegration of the Intellect*: the other two volumes would deal with *Elizabethan Drama* and with *The Sons of Ben* – 'the development of humanism, its relation to Anglican thought, and the emergence of Hobbes and Hyde. The three together will constitute a criticism of the English Renaissance.'[108] In 1924, Eliot had written the preface to a projected book on 'Four Elizabethan Dramatists' – Webster, Tourneur, Middleton, and Chapman. Although he wrote essays on Middleton (1927) and Tourneur (1930), and shorter pieces on Webster and Chapman, the book never materialized. The Preface to *For Lancelot Andrewes* (1928) mentions three 'small volumes which I have in preparation: *The School of Donne*, *The Outline of Royalism*,

56

and *The Principles of Modern Heresy*', but this is probably only a whimsical extension of the declaration for classicism, royalism, and anglo-catholicism, not a serious project.[109] By the late 1920s, Eliot seems to have realized that he would not have, at least for some time, the leisure in which to undertake a sustained critical work.

There remained, moreover, the problem of 'proof' and the question of whether his ideas could be clarified without incurring 'immediate obloquy, followed by perpetual oblivion'. (*HJD* 9)

> Beyond the obvious alterations – the conversational style and the constant repetitions to be removed – the whole argument is to be reformed; assertions must be proved; much detail of fact and authority must be added. The divers parts must be made more coherent; I am aware that in the present form my fundamental ideas remain quite obscure.[110]

If completed, the series would have given us a picture of Eliot's views in great detail; but, apart from a few ideas which reappear in later lectures and essays, the material in the lectures was not developed.

And it could hardly, by its very nature, *be* developed. To account adequately for the change in the European mind, Eliot would have had to write a complete intellectual history of Europe from the Middle Ages through modern times. Instead, he seems to have agreed with Valéry that 'a little metaphysics, a little mysticism, and much mythology will for a long time yet be all we have to take the place of positive knowledge in this kind of question'.[111] Like Coleridge, whose 'sad ghost' is invoked on the last page of *The Use of Poetry*, Eliot was destined not to complete his great synthesis. We can, in a sense, hardly regret the fact, for the amount of time and energy required to complete the critical trilogy would almost certainly have prevented the writing of Eliot's major poems from 'Fragment of a Prologue' (1926) through *Four Quartets*.

When Eliot returned, years later, to his early historiography, he had changed his mind about a good many things. What attracted most attention in his second Milton paper (1947) was Eliot's conclusion that Milton was no longer a pernicious influence upon modern poetry, that poets might 'approach the study of his work without danger, and with profit to their poetry and to the English language'.[112] Eliot's view of the seventeenth century, however, remained substantially the same:

> I believe that the general affirmation represented by the phrase 'dissociation of sensibility' (one of the two or three phrases of my coinage – like 'objective correlative' – which have had a success in the world astonishing to their author) retains some validity; but I now incline to agree with Dr. Tillyard that to lay the burden on the shoulders of Milton and Dryden was a mistake. If such a dissociation did take place, I suspect that the causes are too complex and too profound to justify our accounting for the change in terms of literary criticism. All we can say is, that something like this did happen; that it had something to do with the Civil War; that it would even be unwise to say it was caused by the Civil War, but that it is a consequence of the same causes which brought about the Civil War; that we must seek the causes in Europe, not in England alone; and for what these causes were, we may dig and dig until we get to a depth at which words and concepts fail us.[113]

The idea itself is not retracted: it is simply referred to a larger arena of discourse, and ultimately to the realm of mystery. Eliot re-states, in effect, his declaration of interest in 'the relation of poetry to the spiritual and social life of its time and of other times'.[114]

The view of literary history which Eliot developed in the 1920s remained with him, then, throughout the rest of his critical career. His opinion of Donne changed radically between 1921 and 1926; his opinion of Milton clearly moderated between 1936 and 1947; and Eliot himself records some of his other changes of heart in 'To Criticize the Critic'. But the large pattern, the central myth, remained essentially the same.

'To Criticize the Critic' – Eliot's last essay, written in 1961 – was, appropriately, retrospective of his whole career as a critic. It is a curious essay, a mixture of whimsy and seriousness in which Eliot appears at times to make little of his criticism. He confesses that he is now unable to defend his most famous phrases 'with any forensic plausibility', and suggests that they will prove to be of historic interest only. He admits that 'these concepts, these generalizations, had their origin in my sensibility', and that his theorizing as a whole has been 'epiphenomenal of my tastes'. (*TCTC* 19, 20) But these are *a posteriori* considerations, and behind the apparent diffidence is Eliot's matter-of-fact awareness of his ideas as things which now have an existence of their own: 'I am aware, of course, that my "objective correlative" and "dissociation of sensibility" must be attacked or defended on their own level of abstraction, and that I have done no more than indicate what I believe to have been their genesis.' (Ibid.)

Their immediate genesis *was* in Eliot's own sensibility, but one's sensibility does not develop in a vacuum. The view of literary history which the Clark Lectures set forth has roots in the European Romantic tradition, as my brief discussion of Schiller and Gourmont suggests; the aesthetic embodied in Eliot's historiography owes much, ironically, to the English Romantics, especially Keats. Eliot's development of earlier critical ideas is a particularly striking example of the fruitful interaction of tradition and the individual talent.

2
Romantic Criticism and the Golden Age

Les vrais paradis sont les paradis qu'on a perdus.
                              Proust, *Le Temps Retrouvé*

It is no longer surprising to hear Eliot spoken of as part of the Romantic tradition, but the change in perspective has been a recent one. Eliot's own 'classicizing' essays of the 1920s, which culminate in the 'Preface' to *For Lancelot Andrewes* (1928), were something of a red herring in this regard: since Eliot's sympathies were so obviously with the classical, and since neo-classicism was an important phenomenon in all of the arts at the time (Stravinsky's music, Bauhaus architecture, the criticism of Babbitt and More), it came to be presumed that Eliot was a classicist in practice as well as in sympathies. But Eliot himself wrote that 'a poet in a romantic age cannot be a "classical"poet except in tendency',[1] and the reality of the classical influence upon Eliot need not obscure the fact that the Romantic heritage is fully as important in his work.

The chief danger in asserting either influence, of course, is that the terms are so equivocal and ill-defined. Eliot's distinction between classic and romantic – the difference in focus between object and subject – is relatively narrow and precise.[2] In the terms of his own distinction, we can say that Eliot's poetry is generally classical: it aims at the 'precise realizable picture' rather than the evocation of emotion in itself.[3]

C. K. Stead was among the first commentators to establish the relationship of some of Eliot's ideas to Romantic tradition. In *The*

New Poetic: Yeats to Eliot (1964), he attempts to deal with Eliot's treatment of 'the problem of conscious direction and unconscious process in the writing of poetry', and, despite some exaggerations, he does an admirable job of demonstrating that Eliot's theory of composition is basically Romantic.[4]

> These three essays ['Tradition and the Individual Talent', 'Ben Jonson', 'Hamlet']... show how obsessively concerned Eliot was at this time with a process of poetry in which the conscious will played only the minor role of sub-editor. His remarks imply a kind of poetic composition at least as dependent on spontaneous 'imagination' and 'inspiration' as that which any of the romantic poets might have affirmed.[5]

By analysing the forms in which sections of 'The Hollow Men' first appeared – in a bewildering variety of arrangements and titles – Stead is able to show that 'the structural unity of [Eliot's] early poetry is a unity of feeling' rather than of form.[6]

Romantic attitudes are apparent in the poetry as well, and recent critics have been more willing to acknowledge them as such. It is possible to look at *The Waste Land* as a Romantic work, for example, though the multiplying ironies and perspectives of the poem make it next to impossible to establish a single point of view towards a given scene or incident. The magnificent opening of 'A Game of Chess' is a good example of the ambiguities:

> The Chair she sat in, like a burnished throne
> Glowed on the marble, where the glass
> Held up by standards wrought with fruited vines
> From which a golden Cupidon peeped out
> (Another hid his eyes behind his wing)
> Doubled the flames of sevenbranched candelabra ... (*CPP* 39)

From one point of view, Eliot's disillusion is complete. The rape of Philomel is enacted again and again in a series of vicious or trivial sexual encounters; here, the allusion to *Antony and Cleopatra* suggests that the grand passions of the past were as shallow and meaningless as those of the woman described in this passage, or those of the typist and the house agent's clerk. Elizabeth and Leicester in 'The Fire Sermon' suffer the same reduction in stature.

But the overall pattern of the poem suggests a different perspective towards Eliot's use of the past in the poem. Even when the juxtaposition is ironic at the expense of the past, there is an underlying current of nostalgia: the great ages may have been corrupt, but they had at least a sense of purpose, a belief in the significance of human actions, a standard (however often betrayed) by which to judge experience. The 'inexplicable splendour of Ionian white and gold' which characterizes Magnus Martyr is ultimately more compelling than any irony which attempts to place all civilizations on a common level of futility and venality. (*CPP* 45)

Even as he attacks Romantic solipsism, then, Eliot partakes (particularly in the Clark Lectures) of another aspect of the Romantic sensibility – the tendency to look *back* to a source of value. Blake seeks a lost innocence of vision, Wordsworth a lost unity with the natural world; Coleridge seeks to revive our sense of wonder, Yeats our reverence for 'traditional sanctity and loveliness'.[7] The same looking-back is characteristic of Romantic criticism in its different phases: the golden age of art is always somewhere in the past, a perished Eden, like Eliot's age of unified sensibility, which the critic hopes to revive. This common thread of historical myth is at the centre of Eliot's relationship to Romantic criticism.

Nostalgia is not purely a Romantic phenomenon, of course: Greece and Rome and other cultures have had their own myths of lost perfection. But it would not be difficult to show that these functioned largely as general *symbols* of the ideal and were not as historically specific as much Romantic mythography. In any case, the idea of the golden age is not central to the thought of non-romantic periods, while it can fairly be called one of the defining features of Romanticism.

Romantic Criticism and the Golden Age

Some Precursors: *Keats, Coleridge, Wordsworth and Arnold*

The most important influence on Eliot's historiography is the one which seems, at first glance, least likely – that of Keats. Among Eliot's predictably negative comments on Keats, this one is typical: 'Because we have never learned to criticize Keats, Shelley and Wordsworth (poets of assured though modest merit), Keats, Shelley and Wordsworth punish us from their graves with the annual scourge of the Georgian anthology.'[8] But Eliot acknowledges the importance of Keats in *The Use of Poetry* (1933), and had done so as early as 1920, in the essay 'Philip Massinger'. When one considers that Keats is not a romantic in Eliot's sense of the word – i.e. not self-centred – the possibility of a real influence seems worthy of exploration.

Keats's aesthetic ideas have been much discussed, but little attention has been given to the radical novelty of his view of language. It is scarcely an exaggeration to say that until Keats, no major poet or critic had suggested that the development of the English language had been anything but a steady progress in range, precision and expressive power.[9] Individual poets might be criticized, but the language itself had gained something at every stage of its history. Thus Dryden, who in this respect is typical of all the English poet-critics from Ben Jonson to Samuel Johnson, speaks of Chaucer as the poet who 'first adorned and amplified our barren tongue from the Provençal, which was then the most polished of all the modern languages'; although he 'wanted the modern art of fortifying', he cannot be harshly judged, since he lived 'in the dawning of our language' – a dawning which leads to the full noon of Dryden's own age.[10]

This meliorist view of language is challenged by Keats in his poems and letters alike. In 'Sleep and Poetry', the famous indictment of Augustan verse is preceded by a suggestion of historical crisis; the terminology, that of separation, will sound familiar to any reader of Eliot. ('This' in the first line refers to the glories of the Renaissance in England.)

> Could all this be forgotten? Yes, a schism
> Nurtured by foppery and barbarism,

> Made great Apollo blush for this his land.
> Men were thought wise who could not understand
> His glories: with a puling infant's force
> They sway'd about upon a rocking horse,
> And thought it Pegasus. Ah dismal soul'd![11]

The verse is, except for the epigrammatic last lines, almost embarrassingly bad, but the message is clear. If the language we inherit is sickly and inadequate, we must go back to its earlier stages and attempt to recover its true genius – hence, in Keats and others, the reactionary nature of the revolution: 'Let us have the old Poets'.[12]

The resemblance between Keats's sense that the language had taken a wrong turn and Eliot's awareness of the diminished power of poetry since the Renaissance is obvious enough. Less obvious, perhaps, is the parallel between Eliot's concept of tradition and Keats's view of the usefulness of the past. Both poets see past works of art not as a set of monuments, but as a continuing source of energy for the contemporary poet. Both school themselves in the tradition through reading, criticism and imitation; Eliot goes further and includes theft in the formula.[13] Keats, like Eliot, paradoxically achieves through his submission a new and highly individual style which is, at the same time, part of the tradition it alters.

The particular reasons for Keats's looking back to the poets of the Renaissance also remind one of Eliot's views. 'The ancients were Emperors of vast Provinces,' writes Keats to Reynolds in 1818; each of the moderns, on the other hand, 'like an Elector of Hanover governs his petty state, and knows how many straws are swept daily from the Causeways in all his dominions.'[14] Keats saw, more clearly than any of the other Romantics, the peculiar dangers of 'point of view' in the poetry of his time. Although Wordsworth was, at times, second only to Shakespeare in Keats's poetic affections, the 'egotistical sublime' represented a radically different kind of poetry from that which Keats himself desired to write.[15] The Wordsworthian painting of interior states was for Keats, as it subsequently proved to be for others, limiting – a 'petty state' – and perilously close to solipsism. As Bate notes in his *Burden of the Past and the English Poet*, Keats felt an uneasiness that 'this poetry of the inner life could forfeit objectivity and range'.[16]

Hence the attractiveness of the worlds of Spenser and Chapman, where the connotative and subjective have little or no place. In the bright clear images of these poets Keats found the 'material sublime' which he felt was the essence of great poetry.[17] That phrase can be read two ways: first, as a poetic inversion of 'sublime material'; secondly, and more plausibly, as a conscious oxymoron which links the sublime in poetry to its concrete embodiment – a *material* sublime as opposed to any attempted evocation of the ineffable. This demand for the union of the bodily and the discarnate emotion to which it gives rise is, in effect, an early form of the demand for an 'objective correlative': 'a set of objects, a situation, a chain of events which shall be the formula of that *particular* emotion; such that when the external facts, which must terminate in sensory experience, are given, the emotion is immediately evoked'.[18] Keats would surely have agreed with Eliot that 'the suggestiveness is the aura around a bright clear centre, that you cannot have the aura alone'.[19]

The image is not only concrete, but also gets the poet beyond the limitations of discursiveness. While argument is abstract and subject to counter-argument, the complexities and contradictions of life can be conveyed by the image in a single, simple (in the sense of unitary), non-rational effect: in the concrete details of autumn Keats gives us the paradoxes of fruition and decay, joy and sorrow, the height of life and the nearness of death.[20] Both Kermode and Stead have discussed the desire of the modernist poets, particularly Yeats and Eliot, to escape from the tyranny of statement; neither, however, has mentioned how early the means of that escape are discussed in criticism.[21] The principle is enunciated in one of Keats's most celebrated letters:

> I have not yet been able to see how any thing can be known for truth by consequitive [sic] reasoning – and yet it must be – Can it be that even the greatest Philosopher ever arrived at his goal without putting aside numerous objections – However it may be, O for a Life of Sensations rather than of Thoughts![22]

Beyer says that Keats uses 'sensations' to mean 'intuitive perceptions through the senses',[23] and this definition sounds strikingly like Eliot's concept of the undissociated sensibility, in which 'feeling' and 'thought' are simply different names for the same unified entity: Eliot speaks in 1919 of 'a quality of sensuous thought, or of the senses thinking, of which the exact formula remains to be defined'.[24]

Ideally, then, the paraphrasable content of a work of art should disappear entirely and leave only the image. Eliot says that a creation of art should not embody a philosophy but '*replace* the philosophy': one thinks of Keats's hatred of 'poetry that has a palpable design upon us'.[25] What separates the 'sensations' of art from those of quotidian life is the degree of vividness and clarity they possess. Keats declares that 'the excellence of every Art is its intensity', and this idea, too, is reflected in Eliot's criticism: 'it is not the "greatness", the intensity, of the emotions, the components, but the intensity of the artistic process, the pressure, so to speak, under which the fusion takes place, that counts.'[26]

For both Keats and Eliot, poetry should avoid the subjective and the intellectual; and the writer who finds it easiest to eliminate his personality from the *form* of his work, and to fuse idea with external reality, is the dramatist. Keats's admiration for Shakespeare is based in part upon the plays themselves – there are dozens of Shakespearian references in the letters – but also upon the perfect *objectifying* of Shakespeare's view of the world. Keats realizes that an understanding of Shakespeare does not depend upon our knowledge of his 'personality', which, as Schiller discovered to his initial frustration, is not to be found in the plays. Shakespeare is the 'chameleon poet' who 'has as much delight in conceiving an Iago as an Imogen'.[27] This capacity, discussed elsewhere in the letters as 'negative capability',[28] is similar to the ability which Eliot demands in many of his essays on drama: the ability to create a world free of the poet's voice, a world beyond his 'personality'. The praise of Shakespeare is not, obviously, a point of contact between Keats and Eliot – who has not praised Shakespeare? – but the elevation of drama to the highest place among kinds of poetry is a significant link between the two. It was Keats's ambition to achieve, in his maturity, 'the writing of a few fine Plays'.²⁹ Eliot, from the early Sweeney fragments through the West End comedies, had the same ambition, and there are dramatic elements in all of his poems.

These shared ideas about the nature and function of poetry result naturally in similar judgments on a number of writers. Keats's criticism of Milton is well known:

> The Paradise lost though so fine in itself is a corruption of our Language – it should be kept as it is unique – a curiosity. A beautiful and grand Curiosity. The most remarkable Production of the world – A northern dialect accommodating itself to greek and latin inversions and intonations ... I have but lately stood on my guard against Milton. Life to him would be death to me. Miltonic verse cannot be written but [in] the vein of art ...³⁰

Keats was not, of course, the first to criticize Milton: there is a whole anti-Milton tradition in criticism before Keats, running from Dryden (who considered Milton a great poet but not a good writer) to Samuel Johnson.³¹ But the *grounds* of Keats's disapproval are remarkably similar to Eliot's: '... we can go so far as to say that, although Milton's work realizes superbly one important element in poetry, he may still be considered as having done damage to the English language from which it has not wholly recovered.'³² He is, therefore, a bad model for poets: his highly individual style includes mannerisms which it is fatal to imitate.

For both Keats and Eliot, the preferred alternative to the Miltonic voice is Elizabethan. I have already mentioned Keats's fondness for Spenser and Chapman; Eliot, also an admirer of Chapman, always refers approvingly to the conversational tone of Elizabethan verse, a tone which he finds in even the most 'conceited' poems of Donne. The Romantic poets whom Eliot favours are those who were most influenced by the Elizabethans – Landor, Beddoes, and Keats himself.

It is apparent that the doctrine of impersonality was, for Eliot, the centrally important element in Keats's criticism. In *The Use of Poetry* (1933), he cites one of the letters with approval:

> Men of Genius are great as certain ethereal chemicals operating on the Mass of neutral intellect – but they have not any individuality, any determined character – I would call the top and head of those who have a proper self Men of Power.[33]

Eliot may have paid this passage the compliment of theft: it certainly sounds like his own description of the poet as the catalytic shred of platinum in a chemical reaction.[34] In the early 'Philip Massinger' (1920), Eliot's emphasis is also on Keats's transcendence of the personal: 'Of Shakespeare notably, of Jonson less, of Marlowe (and of Keats to the term of life allowed him), one can say that they *se transvasaient goutte à goutte*; and in England ... there are not many writers of whom one can say it.'[35]

Eliot's direct references to Keats are admittedly few in number. The affinities are nevertheless clear, though they are obscured somewhat by the different forms of expression that Keats and Eliot employ in their prose, and Eliot's praise of Keats as a critic in *The Use of Poetry* is unqualified: 'There is hardly one statement of Keats about poetry which, when considered carefully and with due allowance for the difficulties of communication, will not be found to be true....' (*UPUC* 101) Keats's influence can perhaps be reduced to this: Eliot, believing that feeling was the basis of all poetry but distrustful of subjective and uncontrolled emotion, found in Keats a theory analogous to his own, embodied in a historical myth, accompanied and supported by a finally successful, 'impersonal' practice of poetry. He was therefore encouraged in his own habit of thinking of poetry not as issuing from heart or head (for from either source it was feeling), but as focused on subject or object. Eliot's own poetry, always the best index to his preferences, contains several Keatsian echoes.[36]

In Coleridge, Eliot found the same concern with the dangers of personality and point of view expressed in more philosophical terms. Eliot's admiration for Coleridge, despite the strictures he expresses in *The Use of Poetry*, was considerable. He shared Coleridge's interest in philosophical and religious questions and, as Kojecky has shown, Coleridge's influence can be found throughout Eliot's writing on social issues; the concept of the clerisy was of particular importance.[37] The careers of the two poets are also similar in many ways, and it is apparent that Eliot even identified with Coleridge in feeling that he was 'written out' at forty-five. (*UPUC* 156)

Coleridge's influence on Eliot as a literary critic is largely the history of Eliot's reading of *Biographia Literaria*. In 'Andrew Marvell' (1921), Eliot refers to the discussion of Imagination in Chapter XIV of Coleridge's work, and in *The Use of Poetry* he takes up the celebrated distinction between imagination and fancy that occurs in Chapter XIII. (*SE* 298; *UPUC* 76–79) It seems likely that one passage in Chapter XII influenced, or at least reinforced, Eliot's critical vocabulary in the Clark Lectures.[38] In Chapter XII Coleridge, discussing the relation of subject and object, attempts to define a practical philosophical realism:

> For wherein does the realism of mankind properly consist? In the assertion that there exists a something without them, what, or how, or where they know not, which occasions the objects of their perception? Oh no! This is neither connatural nor universal. It is what a few have taught and learned in the schools, and which the many repeat without asking themselves concerning their own meaning. The realism common to all mankind is far elder and lies infinitely deeper than this hypothetical explanation of the origin of our perceptions, an explanation skimmed from the mere surface of mechanical philosophy. It is the table itself, which the man of common sense believes himself to see, not the phantom of a table, from which he may argumentatively deduce the reality of a table, which he does not see. If to destroy the reality of all, that we actually behold, be idealism, what can be more egregiously so, than the system of modern metaphysics, which banishes us to a land of shadows, surrounds us with apparitions, and distinguishes truth from illusion only by the majority of those who dream the same dream? '*I* asserted that the world was mad,' exclaimed poor Lee, 'and the world said, that I was mad, and confound them, they outvoted me.'[39]

Coleridge's own position is not mere commonsensical realism: he insists later in the chapter that any theory of perception must consider the self, the subject, and his own account of the mind involves the active union of subject and object. But his rejection of the extremes of empiricism and psychologism is clear, as is the similarity between his position and Eliot's.

Eliot appears to have found Coleridge's literary criticism rather limited. He refers in *The Use of Poetry* to Coleridge 'drugging himself with metaphysics', and it seems fair to conclude that Eliot preferred a criticism which was more directly engaged with the problems of literature and less concerned with ultimate questions. (*UPUC* 68) For Eliot himself, in the Clark Lectures, ontology was primarily a metaphor, a way of speaking about poetry.[40]

Wordsworth and Coleridge are discussed together in *The Use of Poetry*, and it would be natural to assume that Wordsworth, supremely the poet of the personal, had little influence on Eliot's criticism. In some of Eliot's later remarks on the proper language of poetry, it is true, we can discern a Wordsworthian note: 'Emotion and feeling, then, are best expressed in the common language of the people – that is, in the language common to all classes: the structure, the rhythm, the sound, the idiom of a language, express the personality of the people which speaks it.'[41] And Wordsworth is mentioned in *The Use of Poetry* as one who attempted to restore to English poetry, in a time of need, its relation to contemporary speech (*UPUC* 71); but the rest of Eliot's unexceptionable remarks do not suggest any deep familiarity with Wordsworth's ideas.

Nevertheless, Eliot says that Wordsworth's critical insight 'is enough to give him the highest place' (*UPUC* 80), and there are intriguing points of contact between the two poets – more intriguing, one might say, for being almost completely unacknowledged. I have already mentioned that the proper alternative to scepticism, in Eliot's mind, seems to be a kind of naïveté of vision; in the last chapter, I associated this with Schiller's description of 'naïve' or 'simple' poetry. Schiller's essay represents one aspect of the Romantic glorification of the unity which exists between the child, or the primitive, and nature: the same motif is apparent in Wordsworth, who is frequently educated, in his poetry, by the uneducated, particularly by children.

Unlikely as it seems in Eliot, the poet of the urban and adult worlds, the same cluster of characters appears, invested with the same powers. Poet, primitive, mystic, and child share what Eliot refers to as 'the pre-logical mentality', which, according to Lévy-Bruhl, 'persists in civilized man, but becomes available only to or through the poet'. (*UPUC* 148) This idea, most clearly expressed in *The Use of Poetry*, occurs even in Eliot's earliest essays. In his review of Wyndham Lewis's *Tarr*, for example, Eliot declares that 'the artist, I believe, is more primitive, as well as more civilized, than his contemporaries, his experience is deeper than civilization, and he only uses the phenomena of civilization in expressing it.'[42] Reviewing an anthology of North American Indian songs, he makes a similar point: '... the artist is, in an impersonal sense, the most conscious of men; he is therefore the most and the least civilized and civilizable; he is the most competent to understand both civilized and primitive.'[43] These statements are obviously important to our understanding of Eliot's poetic use of primitive ritual; they also clarify much in his theory of composition, and lend support to Stead's contention that it is largely a theory of unconscious process.

This 'primitivism' occurs in Eliot's poetry as well. The pre-logical mentality of children often appears as a kind of unfallen intellect: 'Animula' (1929), a beautiful short poem, conveys the nature of the child's perception. The 'simple soul' – *l'anima semplicetta* –

> Confounds the actual and the fanciful,
> Content with playing-cards and kings and queens,
> What the fairies do and what the servants say.
> The heavy burden of the growing soul
> Perplexes and offends more, day by day;
> Week by week, offends and perplexes more
> With the imperatives of 'is and seems'
> And may and may not, desire and control.
> The pain of living and the drug of dreams
> Curl up the small soul in the window seat
> Behind the *Encyclopaedia Britannica*. (*CPP* 71)

The innocence of the child's vision is apparent in his acceptance of fairy tales, which are as 'real' as his physical surroundings. As he learns to distinguish between imagination and reality ('is and seems'), the child becomes confused and depressed: eventually, he learns to believe only in fact. The whole understanding, the unified sensibility, is split into rational and imaginative functions, and the distinction which Basil Willey describes, between 'fact' and 'value', results in the devaluation of the poetic and intuitive.[44] The soul which issued simple – that is, unitary – from the hand of God emerges from the 'hand of time'

> Fearing the warm reality, the offered good,
> Denying the importunity of the blood,
> Shadow of its own shadows, spectre in its own gloom,
> Leaving disordered papers in a dusty room. (*CPP* 71)

The link between child and pre-dissociation poet is clear enough, but there are also references to the world of Wordsworth's 'Immortality Ode'. The quotation from Dante which begins the poem need not mislead us, for the pattern in *Purgatorio* XVI is basically the same as that of the Ode: the soul is distracted from its search for unity with God by trifling pleasures.[45] The thematic development of Eliot's poem is very much that of Wordsworth's. 'Heaven lies about us in our infancy'; education in 'facts' obtrudes upon Eliot's 'growing soul' as it does upon Wordsworth's 'growing boy'.[46] 'Animula' echoes not only the language of the Ode, but also its imagery: in both poems there is a general movement from light to darkness.[47]

The child's ability to unite disparate things – 'what the fairies do and what the servants say' – is also part of the poet's gift, and the elements which the poet brings together may seem to be as unrelated as fairies and servants:

> When a poet's mind is perfectly equipped for its work, it is constantly amalgamating disparate experience; the ordinary man's experience is chaotic, irregular, fragmentary. The latter falls in love, or reads Spinoza, and these two experiences have nothing to do with each other, or with the noise of the

typewriter or the smell of cooking; in the mind of the poet these experiences are always forming new wholes.[48]

The passage describes a situation which we encounter frequently in Eliot's poetry: the juxtaposition of situation, emotion, memory and desire in the mind of one character.[49]

Images merely stored in childhood are often the stuff of poetry. The power of these images is a recurrent theme in Wordsworth, and Eliot, too, found them crucial to the making of poetry. In *The Use of Poetry*, he mentions the experience of a child of ten – it is not difficult to guess who it is -- peering into a rock pool and finding a sea-anemone for the first time:

> the simple experience (not so simple, for an exceptional child, as it looks) might lie dormant in his mind for twenty years, and re-appear transformed in some verse-context charged with great imaginative pressure.[50]

Later in *The Use of Poetry*, Eliot's description of preconscious or subconscious association is specifically reminiscent of Wordsworth. Speaking of our attempts to recall the past visually, Eliot notes that we find in our memory only a 'few meagre arbitrarily chosen set of snapshots', 'the faded poor souvenirs of passionate moments'. (*UPUC* 148) The power of these moments is evoked by Wordsworth in Book XII of *The Prelude*:

> There are in our existence spots of time
> That with distinct pre-eminence retain
> A renovating virtue, whence, depressed
> By false opinion and contentious thought,
> Or aught of heavier and more deadly weight,
> In trivial occupations, and the round
> Of ordinary intercourse, our minds
> Are nourished and invisibly repaired.[51]

Eliot's 'spots of time' are not necessarily those which nourish and repair, but his sense of their significance is similar to Wordsworth's:

> The song of one bird, the leap of one fish, at a particular place and time, the scent of one flower, ... six ruffians seen through an open window playing cards at night at a small French railway junction where there was a water-mill: such memories may have symbolic value, but of what we cannot tell, for they come to represent the depths of feeling into which we cannot peer. (*UPUC* 148)

Once again, the passage recalls situations in Eliot's poetry – the bird in 'Burnt Norton' I, the 'Six hands at an open door dicing for pieces of silver' and the water-mill from 'Journey of the Magi'. In 'The Silurist', Eliot refers to childhood as 'something to be buried and done with, though the corpse will from time to time find its way up to the surface'.[52] This remark (a more useful gloss on the 'Stetson' lines in *The Waste Land* than any amount of vegetation ritual) suggests that the idea of unwilled memory was important to Eliot throughout his career as a poet.

One last point of resemblance between Wordsworth and Eliot is worth mentioning; though not susceptible of proof, it will perhaps reinforce the points I have been making about the relationship between the two poets. Eliot speaks in 'John Marston' (1934) of 'the kind of pattern which we perceive in our own lives only at rare moments of inattention and detachment, drowsing in sunlight'.[53] These moments of half-conscious insight are the mainspring of many of Eliot's poems: an unspoken collaboration between the scene and the sensibility of the speaker produces the quiet personal meditation, a mixture of description, thought, and memory, which characterizes 'Gerontion', 'A Song for Simeon', and the *Quartets*, to cite only a few examples. We tend to forget that Eliot's poetry is more tied up with the sense of place and the *genius loci* than that of most modern poets. The quiet tone of his 'landscape' poems surely owes much to Wordsworth, despite all the differences of temperament, belief, and style.[54]

Eliot found within the Romantic poets themselves, then, most of the ideas which he used in his critique of Romanticism. The apparent paradox is easily explained. Eliot's definition of romanticism focused, as I have said, on the confusion of subject and object: 'The Function of Criticism', with its denunciation of the 'Inner Voice', is his central essay on the topic. The less temperate essays will be found to be developments of this central idea, carried on with the help, or under the influence, of various critics whom Eliot admired and acknowledged – Irving Babbitt, Julien Benda, T. E. Hulme, Charles Maurras, and Ezra Pound are among his sources.[55] At the same time, Eliot realized that the 'Romantic' failure of objectivity could be found in earlier poets, such as Donne, and that it was not, in any case, the whole of Romanticism; he in fact found in the Romantic critics many of his own concerns. In Wordsworth's view, as in Gourmont's, the dissociative force of scepticism disrupted the primitive unity of mind in the individual; in Keats's letters – clearly the most important Romantic influence on Eliot's thought – Eliot found the same process embodied in a myth of literary history; in Coleridge he found a philosophical vocabulary applied to literary problems.

Eliot's involvement with these three critics far surpassed, in intensity and duration, his experiences with the other Romantics, who were also remarkable critics in their various ways. Eliot found Blake, for all his undoubted abilities, 'inclined to formlessness'; his ideas display 'the crankiness, the eccentricity, which frequently affects writers outside the Latin traditions'.[56] The ideas of Shelley (including, presumably, his critical ideas) seemed to Eliot 'always to be ideas of adolescence', and his admiration for Byron had nothing to do with Byron's critical sense.[57]

The various commentators who have discussed other aspects of Eliot's debt to Romantic criticism (Bornstein, for example) have included the 'rejected' Romantics, such as Shelley, as influences in Eliot's development, and they are probably right to do so. To begin with, Eliot's more extreme criticisms in themselves suggest the existence of a kinship which Eliot seeks to deny: one need not be a Freud, or even a Bloom, to see in these attacks the rejection of a father. Furthermore, as my own discussion of Eliot's historiography shows, an influence can be consciously used and remain, for reasons of literary politics, unacknowledged; it can also, of course, exist on an entirely subconscious or pre-conscious level, like the child's memory of the sea-anemone.

The current of literary nostalgia and historic myth which we have noted in Keats did not perish with the Romantics. It appears more clearly, in fact, in the writings of their Victorian successors; the pattern is particularly clear in the work of Matthew Arnold. Eliot's affinities with Arnold are frequently mentioned but seldom analysed: the complex pattern of shared ideas, influence, and opposition is most often reduced to a few generalizations about attitudes towards culture. Certainly the careers of the two men are parallel in many ways – 'the early work of esoteric and personal poetry leading to poetry of a more public character, the poetry leading to literary criticism and that in turn leading to social and religious criticism'.[58] It is, in fact, in Eliot's social criticism that Arnold's legacy is clearest. The treatment of classes and elites, the approach to the question of culture, the concern for the whole life of man, even the sanctioning of force, all have their origins in Arnold's work.[59]

In Eliot's literary criticism there are also notable similarities. In 'The Function of Criticism at the Present Time' Arnold speaks of 'a criticism which regards Europe as being, for intellectual and spiritual purposes, one great confederation',[60] and it is this sort of criticism which Eliot espouses, first in *The Sacred Wood* (1920), most elaborately in *Notes Towards the Definition of Culture* (1948). Arnold's definition of criticism might serve as a summary of all that Eliot found permanently useful in his thought.[61]

Arnold's indictment of the Romantic poets for not 'knowing enough', which Eliot singles out for praise in *The Sacred Wood*, is the natural consequence of such a criticism. (*SW* xii) Arnold's admiration for French literary standards ('Why is all the *journeyman-work* of literature, as I may call it, so much worse done here than it is in France?') clearly lies behind Eliot's call for 'second-order minds' to maintain the current of ideas in society.[62] The tone and movement of an Eliot essay are also influenced by the urbanity of Arnold's style, and the casual manner conceals, in each writer, a palpable design upon the reader's mind. Arnold aims to inculcate a 'certain temper of mind'; an Eliot essay, 'the statement of an attitude', clearly aims at the same end.[63] One could easily make out a case for Arnold as the continuing presence in Eliot's thought, both as mentor and as symbol of the tendencies in Victorian thought which Eliot most disliked. From 'The

Function of Criticism' (1923) through *Notes Towards the Definition of Culture* (1948), the titles themselves recall Arnold's work in a number of fields. Against the similarities must be set the profound differences of opinion which separate Eliot and Arnold on – for example – the value of culture as an ethical force.[64]

As interesting as these points of contact are, they constitute only one level of the relationship between Arnold and Eliot, and not the one which Eliot himself found most useful. I would like to suggest that a large part of Arnold's influence is of a rather different kind than has been supposed.

The importance of Arnold's 1853 'Preface' to his *Poems* has always been recognized, both as a stage in Arnold's career and as an important moment in critical awareness of the limitations of Romanticism. For Arnold himself the essay was, in the words of E. D. H. Johnson, 'a recantation of everything that no longer satisfied him in the content and form of his earlier poetry'.[65] It was also an expression of Arnold's dissatisfaction with the inwardness of Romantic poetry, and, as such, 'a disavowal of the life of the imagination lived in isolation from the outer world'.[66]

The essay is basically, it seems, a reassertion of the need for action in poetry. In justifying the exclusion of 'Empedocles on Etna' from the collection, Arnold appeals to the criteria of Aristotle's *Poetics*:

> What then are the situations, from the representation of which, though accurate, no poetical enjoyment can be derived? They are those in which the suffering finds no vent in action; in which a continuous state of mental distress is prolonged, unrelieved by incident, hope, or resistance; in which there is everything to be endured, nothing to be done. In such situations there is inevitably something morbid, in the description of them something monotonous. When they occur in actual life, they are painful, not tragic; the representation of them in poetry is painful also.[67]

The statement is clear enough. Warren Anderson and R. H. Super agree that Arnold's strictures are intended to apply only to epic and tragic poetry, but Arnold himself does not make this qualification.[68] The reason for his apparent negligence, I believe, is that he was actually arguing a wider issue – one which involves all poetry and the standards by which we must judge it. Consider, for example, the following passage:

> With them [the Greeks], the action predominated over the expression of it; with us, the expression predominates over the action. Not that they failed in expression, or were inattentive to it; on the contrary, they are the highest models of expression, the unapproached models of the *grand style*. But their expression is so excellent because it is so admirably kept in its right degree of prominence; because it is so simple and so well subordinated; because it draws its force directly from the pregnancy of the matter which it conveys.[69]

Here the original distinction has been transmuted, as it so often is in Arnold's prose, into something else. What began as a distinction between action and inaction has become a contrast between two ways of describing action, one external and clear, the other personal and fretful. The first is characterized by what Arnold calls, early in the essay, 'disinterested objectivity'; in the second, as in the fragments of the historical Empedocles, 'the dialogue of the mind with itself has commenced; modern problems have presented themselves; we hear already the doubts, we witness the discouragement, of Hamlet and of Faust.'[70]

What we have, in short, is something like Schiller's distinction between 'naïve' and 'sentimental' poetry. Arnold knew and admired Schiller's work, and Schiller is cited, on a different subject, in the 'Preface' itself. Unlike Schiller, who defended modern, 'sentimental' poetry, Arnold is firmly on the side of the 'naïve' or 'simple' style: the terms in which he discusses Greek tragedy show that he values highly what he calls 'a certain baldness of expression' in it.[71]

> The terrible old mythic story on which the drama was founded stood, before he entered the theatre, traced in its bare outlines upon the spectator's mind; it stood in his memory, as a group of statuary, faintly seen, at the end of a long and dark vista: then

came the poet, embodying outlines, developing situations, not a word wasted, not a sentiment capriciously thrown in: stroke upon stroke, the drama proceeded: the light deepened upon the group; more and more it revealed itself to the riveted gaze of the spectator: until at last, when the final words were spoken, it stood before him in broad sunlight, a model of immortal beauty.[72]

The simile here is vitally important in conveying Arnold's meaning. The scene or story is there, external to the poet, who brings to it nothing of his own but an ability to illuminate – *his* feelings are not conveyed to the spectator, who experiences only 'the pregnancy of the matter' through what Eliot would call an objective correlative.

The insistence upon light and clarity is the real argument of the preface: even in its first pages, Arnold declares that 'What is *not* interesting is ... that which is vaguely conceived and loosely drawn; a representation which is general, indeterminate, and faint, instead of being particular, precise, and firm.'[73] Such a statement inevitably reminds one of the passage in 'Andrew Marvell' in which Eliot compares poems by Marvell and Morris: 'The emotion of Morris is not more refined or more spiritual; it is merely more vague ... we are inclined to infer that the suggestiveness is the aura around a bright clear centre, that you cannot have the aura alone.'[74] Arnold's censure of 'the dialogue of the mind with itself' is also strikingly similar to Eliot's criticism of Donne.

The resemblances between Arnold's 'classicism' and Eliot's are notable, and are reinforced, even in the Preface, by Arnold's approach to the related question of romantic solipsism. Citing J. M. Ludlow, he attacks the inward tendency of modern literature:

> But the modern critic not only permits a false practice; he absolutely prescribes false aims. – 'A true allegory of the state of one's own mind in a representative history,' the poet is told, 'is perhaps the highest thing that one can attempt in the way of poetry.' And accordingly he attempts it. An allegory of the state of one's own mind, the highest problem of an art which imitates actions! No assuredly, it is not, it never can be so: no

great poetical work has ever been produced with such an aim.
... *Faust* itself, judged as a whole, and judged strictly as a poetical work, is defective.[75]

The poet who writes about 'the state of his own mind' has, in Eliot's terms, 'retired inside his skull'. (*CL* II:15) The poet is therefore, for Arnold, 'most fortunate, when he most entirely succeeds in effacing himself' – a statement echoed in Eliot's more startling declaration that 'poetry is ... not the expression of personality, but an escape from personality'.[76]

Arnold displayed a courage amounting to temerity in questioning, at the age of thirty-one, the poetic standards of his age; but he was sure of his ideas and repeated them whenever occasion arose. In his inaugural lecture as Professor of Poetry at Oxford, in 1857, we find him asserting that

> The predominance of thought, of reflection, in modern epochs is not without its penalties; in the unsound, in the over-tasked, in the over-sensitive, it has produced the most painful, the most lamentable results; it has produced a state of feeling unknown to less enlightened but perhaps healthier epochs – the feeling of depression, the feeling of *ennui*. Depression and *ennui*; these are the characteristics stamped on how many of the representative works of modern times![77]

In the healthier epochs, literature communicates 'the complete intelligence of its own situation' and thus achieves what Arnold calls 'adequacy'.[78] But in an age of intellectual disorder, it is virtually impossible to find 'the true point of view from which to contemplate this spectacle', and the modern artist is likely to be overwhelmed by the world's multitudinousness.[79] The poet then becomes, to use Eliot's term, 'ruminative'; the clear representation becomes sicklied o'er with the pale cast of thought.[80] Both Arnold and Eliot use Hamlet as the type of the modern introspective artist, and both see, in his refusal to act, the modern artist's turning away from the world.[81]

In such a situation, the analysis of style becomes, for Arnold and Eliot alike, a means of determining the health of the society which produced the poetry. 'The stages in literature which led up to this point of perfection, and the stages in literature which led downward from it, will be deeply interesting also', Arnold says.[82] In Lionel Trilling's words, 'whenever Arnold talks about style, he is talking about society.'[83] His attacks on 'occasional bursts of fine writing' and 'isolated thoughts and images' are part of the indictment of the age's failure to 'see life steadily and see it whole', or 'to see the object as in itself it really is'.[84]

It is here that Arnold's real legacy to Eliot lies. Not only in the Clark Lectures, but in all his major essays, Eliot seeks to determine the adequacy of language to the matter which it attempts to encompass 'with shabby equipment always deteriorating'.[85] In the essays on individual writers he focuses frequently upon isolated passages, why and how they work, what they tell us about the age; in the theoretical essays – 'Tradition and the Individual Talent', 'The Function of Criticism', the Clark and Norton lectures – he attempts to discover the animating sources of language itself. It is not, therefore, the Arnold of *Culture and Anarchy* who influences Eliot most deeply, but the Arnold of 'On Translating Homer': not simply because Eliot, too, was interested in the problems of translation, but because the problem of expression, of *rendering*, is the central problem of all art. The attempt to account for its ups and downs gives rise inevitably to what I have called historical myth: thus we have Arnold's 'epochs of concentration' and 'epochs of expansion', and Eliot's emblematic stages in the relationship of language and belief.[86]

The question of Arnold's influence upon Eliot, or of anyone else's, is essentially a side-issue. In the case of Schiller or Keats, Wordsworth or Arnold, we can establish the similarity of certain ideas and conjecture that Eliot used the earlier poet-critic in formulating his own ideas. But the real similarity is not in any supposed borrowings: it lies rather in the common perception of an issue or problem and the attempt to come to terms with it imaginatively. Like Arnold, Eliot found himself, in a Romantic age, desiring a classic clarity of expression; he was eventually to conclude that 'a poet in a romantic age cannot be a "classical" poet except in tendency'.[87] The divided consciousness gave rise in each case to a rich body of criticism in which the age could see itself, and literature, anew.

Romantic Criticism and the Golden Age

Reified Argument: The Middle Ages as Image

We have examined, so far, Eliot's relationships with various poet-critics in the Romantic tradition, and have focused on the similar problems discussed by Eliot and his predecessors. There are also similarities between the images Eliot uses in presenting his argument and the iconography of Romantic criticism as a whole. The most prominent of these, in the Clark Lectures, is an idealized picture of the Middle Ages, in which that long, complex, and various period becomes in effect a single image of order and harmony with which to compare the modern world. The view of the Middle Ages which Eliot takes up would not have been possible before the Romantic period, largely because of the myth of progress which prevailed through much of the eighteenth century. What is more interesting, for our purposes, is that this image of the Middle Ages, in altered or eccentric forms, is at the centre of twentieth-century aesthetics as well.

Alice Chandler, in *A Dream of Order*, has charted with admirable thoroughness the rise and fall of the medieval ideal in nineteenth-century English literature.[88] In the novels of Scott, ideas about the medieval world are largely implicit: there is another tradition, however, stemming from Cobbett's *History of the Protestant Reformation in England and Ireland* (1824–26), in which the attack on the modern world is forceful and explicit. Carlyle's first major work, *Past and Present* (1843), belongs to this latter tradition. So, in different ways, do Ruskin's *Stones of Venice* (1851–53) and Morris's *News from Nowhere* (1891).[89] Like any good myth, the medieval ideal is subject to a variety of interpretations: it can be used to support Carlyle's gospel of faith and work or Morris's socialism equally well. Some features common to its various manifestations suggest that medievalism was a twofold movement. As a development of the Romantic movement it was, in Professor Chandler's words, 'opposed to the Newtonian and Lockean view of the universe as a vast machine in which man was a subordinate mechanism moved by pleasure and pain'.[90] But it was also, I would suggest, a reaction against certain elements in Romanticism, particularly intellectual subjectivism.

The constant leitmotif in the major writers of the medievalist tradition is the idea of clarity, both intellectual and artistic. In *Past and Present*, for example, the high-handedness of Abbot Samson is not justified because he is a Carlylean hero; he is, rather, a hero because of his ability to see and act on the truth:

> There exists in him a heart-abhorrence of whatever is incoherent, pusillanimous, unveracious, – that is to say, chaotic, *un*governed; of the Devil, not of God.[91]

> That he was a just clear-hearted man, this, as the basis of all true talent, is presupposed. How can a man, without clear vision in his heart first of all, have any clear vision in his head?[92]

The truth which Samson sees and submits to is not the truth 'as he sees it', nor is it mere rationality. It is a perception of the living universe as it is, beyond points of view, and his clarity of vision enables Samson to impose his will upon the Abbey after its period of decadence. The same capacity on a larger scale results in a social order which is stable, harmonious, purposeful, and prosperous.

In Ruskin, too, clarity of vision becomes morally important. Much of Ruskin's work in *Modern Painters* is devoted to establishing the connection between *aesthesis* and *theoria* – between perception of the outward qualities of objects or works of art and perception of the spirit or whole moral life which is embodied in them.[93] This ambitious programme, announced in the second volume of *Modern Painters*, is best summed up by a statement from the third:

> The greatest thing a human soul ever does is to *see* something, and tell what it *saw* in a plain way. Hundreds of people can talk for one who can think, but thousands can think for one who can see. To see clearly is poetry, prophecy and religion all in one.[94]

Ruskin's own achievement of clear sight is impressive, and it is to him that we look for the first well-informed and sympathetic discussion of the ethos of Gothic architecture.

Despite the limitations of Ruskin's religious views, and the absurdities of judgment to which they led him, *The Stones of Venice* is a magnificent work, 'splendid in rhetoric, orderly in plan, based on direct observation and hard work'.⁹⁵ The contrast of medieval and modern in *The Stones of Venice* takes a particular form. In *The Crown of Wild Olive*, Ruskin says that he had 'no other aim than to show that the Gothic architecture of Venice had arisen out of, and indicated in all its features, a state of pure national faith, and of domestic virtue; and that its Renaissance architecture had arisen out of, and in all its features indicated, a state of concealed national infidelity, and of domestic corruption'.⁹⁶ Gothic architecture, to which the creative freedom of the individual worker contributes, is naturally unified; in Renaissance architecture the unity is imposed and mechanical.

I mention the arguments of Ruskin and Carlyle for two reasons. The first is to reinforce a point made in the previous chapter: that the history which Eliot is writing is of a particular symbolic type, in which figures and details are made to stand for more than themselves. John D. Rosenberg, in his study of Ruskin, raises the inevitable question of whether this sort of writing can really be considered history at all. 'The answer is unequivocally no, if one accepts the "objective" historian's position that the very best we can do is present the facts and resolutely refuse to judge them.'⁹⁷ But the selection of facts is itself an act of judgment, and objectivity remains an impossible ideal. If we attempt to classify Ruskin's kind of history, we find it to be part of a particular tradition:

> In so far as *The Stones of Venice* presents a total view of Venetian civilization, a view compounded of its people, its arts, its acts, its thought, the book is a kind of archetypal cultural history. But in its moral orientation it is as anti-modern as Shakespeare's histories or the chronicle of Israel's fate recorded by her prophets. None gives us history as such. Each subordinates events to the overriding pattern which shapes our ends, rough hew them as we will. Neither wealth nor power but Israel's false dealings with the Lord of Righteousness inexorably determine her passage from glory to the chastisement of captivity. The chronicle of tribal growth, nationhood, and dispersal has

become a fateful moral drama which reveals, under divine scrutiny, the character of its protagonists. This is essentially the kind of history Ruskin was writing, or that Shakespeare wrote when he shaped the chaos of English medieval history into a drama of punishment and expiation for the guilt of Richard's blood.[98]

Carlyle writes to demonstrate that the fortunes of a society follow its faith in the living order of the universe, Ruskin to show that a nation's art reflects its moral vigour. Eliot, too, shapes the chaos of history for a particular purpose, and he might have said with Stephen Dedalus that history was a nightmare from which he was trying to awake.[99] The shape of Eliot's history is its thesis, which, oversimplified, could be stated thus: societies, like individuals, pass through stages of perception; when they redevelop a capacity for scepticism, their art is more likely to reflect its makers than the world, and to lose much of its significance in the process. To classify Eliot's history with Carlyle's and Ruskin's is simply to say that the artist's encounter with history, like the prophet's, is of a particular kind.

There is, however, a distinct development in this kind of historiography, in which *The Stones of Venice* represents a real advance over *Past and Present*. Both works appear at first glance to work by juxtaposition – St Edmund's Abbey set against the modern mill town, Gothic set against Renaissance architecture. But in Carlyle's work, St Edmund's has its ups and downs, like England in the nineteenth century: what we see is not so much a contrast between the images themselves as a series of parallels between them, which Carlyle works out verbally. In Ruskin, on the other hand, the visual contrast is simplified to the point of being absolute. The Gothic part of the Doge's Palace, completed in 1423, represents all of the spiritual and artistic qualities of medieval Christendom; the later additions and later buildings show, more clearly than argument could, the decline of faith and art. 'The book, so carefully plotted around a series of contrasting symbols, ends with the juxtaposed images of simple Gothic tombs and ever more inane Renaissance monuments celebrating the virtues of virtueless men. Ruskin houses the body of Renaissance

Venice in an overblown, tasteless sarcophagus.'[100]

Given the premises which Ruskin has persuasively set forth, the argument itself is reified, borne *by the images* in a way that Carlyle's, by its very nature, could not be. And this brings us to the second reason for discussing the Victorian medievalists: that Ruskin's method of argument by images, and his use of the Middle Ages as a standard, anticipate much of twentieth-century literary aesthetics. It would be going too far to talk of 'medievalism' as a movement in the twentieth century: Professor Chandler, for one, has argued that the medieval ideal perished in Henry Adams's *Mont-St.-Michel and Chartres*. But in the criticism of T. E. Hulme, Ezra Pound, and W. B. Yeats, the medieval image becomes the central means of defining a new sort of classicism, and the image represents, as it did for the nineteenth century, the ideal of clarity and objectivity.

The case of Hulme, whose important critical writings are gathered in *Speculations*, is probably the clearest.[101] Hulme begins by asserting that the fundamental error of modern thought is the idea of continuity, specifically the idea that the perfection characteristic of the mathematical and physical sciences on one hand, and of transcendental and religious values on the other, likewise characterizes the intermediate sphere of human life. This fallacy, which is shared in one form or another by all philosophers since the Renaissance, is characteristic of the humanist attitude, which is fundamentally opposed to the religious. The latter insists upon original sin, upon the fact that perfection is outside the human: 'while [man] can occasionally accomplish acts which partake of perfection, he can never himself *be* perfect.'[102] Humanism, lacking the sense of values as absolute, logically develops the belief that 'life is the source and measure of all values, and that man is fundamentally good'.[103]

Renaissance and post-Renaissance art is therefore vital in the technical sense: it exploits pleasure in the reproduction of human and natural forms.

> Byzantine art is the exact contrary of this. There is nothing vital in it; the emotion you get from it is not a pleasure in the reproduction of natural or human life. The disgust with the

trivial and accidental characteristics of living shapes, the searching after an austerity, a *perfection* and rigidity which vital things can never have, lead here to the use of forms which can almost be called geometrical.[104]

It is not my purpose to demonstrate the influence of Hulme upon Eliot: I argue in the first appendix that such influences are impossible to establish. But the method of argument clearly has affinities with Eliot's. The radical simplifying of cultural history, and the use of medieval art to represent the ideal of clarity, are Ruskinian. Most of the ideas are not – Hulme uses Ruskin as an example of the romanticism he is arguing against – but the technique of argument is; in Hulme's other papers literature is discussed in similar terms.[105]

It is difficult to show, in short passages, the contribution of Ezra Pound to critical medievalism. His interest in the period is a commonplace: *The Spirit of Romance* (1910), subtitled 'An Attempt to Define Somewhat the Charm of the Pre-Renaissance Literature of Latin Europe', shows that interest but is not often explicit about the value that Pound finds in the best literature of the Middle Ages. His central aesthetic principle is best expressed by his later quotation from Stendhal, which we have already cited: 'dans ce genre, on n'émeut que par la clarté.'[106] That *clarté*, which Pound also found in the Chinese written character, is characteristic of the best of medieval writing; Pound speaks of Daniel's diction as being 'so vivid as to seem harsh in literal translation', and his praise of Dante, like Eliot's, is based on the utter lucidity of Dante's language: 'If the language of Shakespeare is more beautifully suggestive, that of Dante is more beautifully definite.'[107] Pound repeatedly comments on, or shows in translation, the robustness, directness, and clarity of the 'medieval clean line'.[108]

In Yeats we encounter the most complex and eccentric view of history to be found in any twentieth-century writer; but the central argument is similar to those we have already looked at, and Yeats's method is simply the extreme of tendencies long established in this kind of historiography. The central document is of course *A Vision* (1925; revised edition, 1937), Yeats's elaborate symbolic account of the nature of personality and the course of history. It is a very obscure book, and the difficulties it presents have as much to do with its intent as with its structure. Nevertheless, without going too deeply into the method of the book, we can arrive at some conclusions about its meaning and the nature of the tradition which Yeats carries on.

The central image of *A Vision*, that of the interpenetrating cones or gyres, represents subjectivity and objectivity and the movement from one to the other in human beings and in time itself:

> if we apply the cones to history, at the time of Christ objectivity was at its fullest expansion; the self was struggling to escape from personality, to be lost in 'otherness,' while at the time of the Renaissance subjectivity was at its fullest expansion, and great personalities were everywhere realizing themselves to the utmost. In our time history is swinging back again towards objectivity, for the cycles continue in eternal recurrence.[109]

'Unity of Being', the harmonious relationship of mind and body, individuality and otherness, is represented by the full moon of Phase Fifteen, and 'can never find direct human expression'.[110] It comes closest to doing so in the Italian painters of the fifteenth century, but Yeats is inclined to include Byzantium in Phase Fifteen as well.[111] Of all historical periods, the early Byzantine interested him most:

> I think that in early Byzantium, maybe never before or since in recorded history, religious, aesthetic and political life were one, that architect and artificers – though not, it may be, poets, for language had been the instrument of controversy and must have grown abstract – spoke to the multitude and the few alike. The painter, the mosaic worker, the worker in gold and silver, the illuminator of sacred books, were almost impersonal, almost perhaps without the consciousness of individual design, absorbed in their subject-matter and that the vision of a whole people.[112]

'Workman, noble and saint' could find their separate fulfilments in what Yeats called 'a phase of complete beauty'.[113]

Once again, the medieval order is a symbol of impersonal vision, clarity and order; Yeats takes his place as part of a continuing tradition of thought.[114] But *A Vision* brings us up against a problem in the whole tradition: in its detail and scope, Yeats's book has the appearance of a philosophy of history, but there are suggestions – despite Yeats's mention of parallels between his work and Spengler's – that it was not intended as such.[115] There is no doubt that Yeats believed in parapsychology, and he solemnly records in his Introduction various happenings which suggest the supernatural origins and authority of the work; but he suggests also that the whole system is a construction of the subconscious, 'that the communicators are the personalities of a dream shared by my wife, by myself, occasionally by others'.[116]

Perhaps this is a simple hedging of bets on Yeats's part, a precaution lest he be accused of excessive credulousness. Another part of the Introduction, however, suggests the irrelevance of the whole question of Yeats's belief in his system as a system. After several days of his wife's automatic writing, Yeats 'offered to spend what remained of life explaining and piecing together those scattered sentences. "No," was the answer, "we have come to give you metaphors for poetry." '[117] The importance of *A Vision* is therefore quite independent of the question of literal belief; in a letter written only weeks before his death, Yeats says 'It seems to me that I have found what I wanted. When I try to put all into a phrase I say "Man can embody truth but he cannot know it." '[118] A. G. Stock evaluates *A Vision* in terms which, like Rosenberg's, are equally applicable to Carlyle, Ruskin, and Eliot:

> His language about the soul begs all the questions which a metaphysician would be bound to reason out. In writing of history he does not try to investigate facts; he takes them from whatever authorities have appealed to him and interprets them by a thesis. But he creates and arranges images so as to express his sense of values, and this is the genius of mythology. A myth is a myth not because it is false to physical or historical fact but because, true or false, it offers just such an expressive image. If

we believe absolutely in its values we accept it as true, in a sense to which mere factual accuracy can only be an endorsement.[119]

C. K. Stead, in *The New Poetic*, has analysed the development of a new aesthetic in English poetry between 1900 and 1920. I will not do violence to Professor Stead's argument by summarizing it: his book is one which every student of modern poetry should read. Stead's conclusion is that the Georgians and Imagists, Yeats, Pound, and Eliot are all part of a movement away from the shortcomings of discursive poetry; they all concentrate on the clear presentation of an image or situation, and thereby express 'a level of mind deeper and more obscure than that at which conscious thought and "opinion" are supreme: where ... the mind of the individual becomes the general mind of the race'.[120] As Yeats says in the letter cited above, 'You can refute Hegel but not the Saint or the Song of Sixpence.'[121]

My point, briefly, is that a similar process occurs in the conduct of argument over a somewhat longer period. One can avoid generalization in a poem, but not in a prose argument, where some conclusion is called for; an argument, however, is subject to counter-argument. The solution is a combination of techniques which Stead comes close to describing:

> A close scrutiny of Eliot's criticism will show, I believe, ... the gradual realization of a poetic technique ... designed to bring into balance the two halves of the divided sensibility: a technique which weighs, on the one hand, that part of the poet's mind which rationalizes, constructs, and, in the rhetorician, illegitimately persuades and pleases at the expense of complex truth; and, on the other hand, that passive part of the mind which ... negatively comprehends complexity, and provides images to embody it, but fails on its own to construct, assert, or even affirm.[122]

Stead is talking here about the relationship of rational structure and unconscious process in Eliot's theory of poetic composition, but the remarks could refer to his literary criticism equally well. The variety of rhetorical techniques which Eliot employs is dazzling, and we shall examine some of them in the next chapter; but the argument which is assisted by these techniques depends finally upon image, and therefore upon the reader's imagination.[123] The Clark Lectures show the process in a particularly pure and overt form, but it is characteristic of all Eliot's criticism. The image may be a single picture of a period, or a quotation, or the whole corpus of a writer's work: in any case, it allows for a radical simplification of what the image represents. Like the x in an algebraic equation, it acquires a value from what is done with it. Donne and Cowley become emblems of the directions of poetry after them, Dante the exemplar of poetic perfection and clear sight. Eliot's argument is not spared the task of assertion, but the selection of images, and their arrangement, make the point more eloquently – and less refutably – than mere argument could.

What has evolved, then, is a kind of symbolist historiography. Frank Kermode first used this phrase in *Romantic Image* to describe literary history written in support of the Symbolist view of the image as a non-discursive kind of knowledge peculiar to poetry. Kermode's placing of Eliot in the Symbolist line was the first important discussion of the Romantic backgrounds to Eliot's thought, and Kermode uses, as I have, the examples of Yeats, Pound, and Hulme. But I am using the term 'symbolist' in a different sense (hence the lower case). I am referring to the kind of historical writing in which the period *itself* is reduced to symbolic or emblematic form for the purposes of argument. Kermode refers to Eliot's version of literary history as 'a kind of allegory', but it is in fact an arrangement of 'images' of the very kind Kermode discusses.[124]

All historians have a tendency to portray men and events as emblems of ideas and forces; they also, as a matter of professional ethics, try to guard against giving this tendency too free rein. Carlyle's *French Revolution* is a great symbolic and historical drama, but a very partial view of the Revolution. When the historian is dealing with literature, however, he is already in the realm of symbol. The men most fit to write literary history, the artists themselves, perform the same kind of ordering in their visions of the world as a whole. And – unless we deny that literature itself is a means of knowledge – these symbolic histories require no apologies or justifications, but simply a different means of approach on the reader's part.

In the Romantic critics, Eliot found sympathetic ideas and certain of the means (philosophical vocabulary, historical myth) with which to develop them. The Victorian and later writers fulfilled a similar double function: they not only reinforced Eliot's idealized picture of the Middle Ages, but showed him a way of reifying argument through the juxtaposition of symbolic images. We know that Eliot was familiar with the work of all the writers I have discussed in this chapter; we ought, however, to avoid the conclusion (which studies of influence tend to foster) that the writer influenced was the passive receiver of others' ideas. Eliot provides a corrective to this view in 'Tradition and the Individual Talent', and his historiography shows us the folly of attributing too much to a critic's ancestors. Whatever the Clark Lectures and Eliot's essays owe to the nineteenth century in their nostalgia and their use of argumentative images, they are wholly Eliot's own. I have already suggested that the question of influence is less important than the common perception of a particular problem; that the lectures belong to an identifiable tradition of historical writing serves simply, as Eliot realized, to make them accessible.

Having mentioned Eliot's use of images in argument, I have already raised the question of rhetorical strategy in his criticism. In the last chapter, I shall examine how Eliot's use of language contributes to that strategy and, in doing so, shows us another aspect of his relation to Romantic and Victorian criticism.

3
Eliot as Rhetorician

> Let us avoid the assumption that rhetoric is a vice of manner, and endeavour to find a rhetoric of substance also, which is right because it issues from what it has to express.
> '"Rhetoric" and Poetic Drama'
> (1919)

> Attempts to analyse metaphor solely to debunk an argument or suggest that it is 'nothing but' a metaphor are not to be encouraged. What is to be encouraged is the analysis itself, in which there is, I think, an activity of considerable and increasing importance for literary critics. ...
> Northrop Frye[1]

The most frequently noted feature of Eliot's prose style is that it combines assertion and reticence to a remarkable degree. Particularly in essays from Eliot's great period as a critic (roughly 1918 to 1936), one is apt to encounter the largest statements about literature and sensibility, or apparently final judgment upon this or that figure; but the logic of the argument often remains elusive. The statement is treated as self-sufficient, or becomes part of another, larger issue: there is in the prose, as Bernard Bergonzi has said, 'an effect of extreme evasiveness despite its polemical sharpness of tone'.[2]

The natural question is why. Like Johnson and Hazlitt, Eliot wrote his best criticism hurriedly, under the pressure of deadlines, since his various activities as extension lecturer, banker and editor took up most of his time. But as an explanation of the essays' logic this is not really satisfactory: Eliot had the opportunity to revise his essays when they were gathered together in books, but the changes, when they occur at all, are minor.

The answer lies rather in Eliot's attitude towards argumentation itself. Although he has certain beliefs about the relationship between sensibility and language, Eliot does not, clearly, have a theory of literature in the sense that Frye or Lukács may be said to have one. Between the fundamental points of Eliot's 'classicism' there is much *feeling* about literature, relatively articulable but not susceptible of demonstration in reasoned argument: hence the use of the symbolic images discussed in the last chapter. Criticism was, for Eliot, a branch of rhetoric rather than of philosophy; it was natural for him to treat it as an art of persuasion rather than a science of 'proof'.[3]

But there are other reasons for this attitude, which the Clark Lectures make clear. It is apparent from the historical myth of Eliot's criticism that rational argument is harder to conduct as words are treated more and more subjectively. As the background of shared belief disappears, as words come to be thought of as constructions rather than as references, the nature of argument undergoes fundamental and permanent changes. Philosophy takes on an emotional colouring in the work of Kant, Fichte, Hegel, and Schopenhauer; the same element of emotional temperature appears in the critical prose of Ruskin, Arnold, and Newman.[4]

It is possible, of course, to dismiss these ideas as being merely Eliot's opinion or 'point of view', but his ideas have been confirmed and elaborated by John Holloway in his invaluable book *The Victorian Sage*. Since part of what follows depends upon Holloway's methods, I shall summarize his argument briefly before going on. Various Victorian writers, reacting against the scientific emphasis upon matter and the philosophical stress upon logic, assert the existence of a higher kind of 'proof' of propositions. Newman's categories of 'real assent' and 'notional assent' signify the difference between two kinds of intellectual acquiescence: the latter kind of assent is sufficient for logic, science, and mathematics, but the former is required for 'a proposition of practical concern in human life'. The difference is, in Holloway's words, 'something richer, more varied, more personal; something irreducible to any mechanism or pattern'.[5] Despite his occasional criticism of Newman, Eliot referred favourably to Newman's distinction between kinds of assent: in a BBC broadcast of 1932, Eliot noted that 'towards any profound conviction one is borne gradually, perhaps insensibly over a long period of time, by what Newman called "powerful and concurrent reasons"'.[6]

The sage bears a wisdom which is basically simple but not always easily understood. 'I assume a something', says Coleridge, 'the proof of which no man can *give* to another, yet every man can *find* for himself.'[7] Expressed in abstract form, the truths of the sage are likely to seem simple in one sense or another – either obvious or foolish. The Victorian authors therefore emphasize that this knowledge is 'known by a special sense, an intuition'. It must be experienced or simply grown into: it cannot be 'proven'. Between articulable points of doctrine, the same elaborates, exhorts, gives examples, and draws conclusions, using a form of what Holloway calls 'organic thinking'.[8] Exposition takes the place of demonstration; the reader is familiarized with the feel of an idea rather than being driven to it logically.

Two of Holloway's conclusions are of particular importance for our purposes. The first is that 'we are not studying techniques of *persuasion*: not at least in one common sense of that phrase'.

> Many (by no means all) of the techniques and methods comprising rhetoric, as it used to be called, did not relate specially to the conclusions they recommended. They increased the listener's or the reader's credulity in a quite general way, and served one conclusion no better and no worse than they did others. But the methods traced here persuade because they clarify, and clarify because they are organic to a view presented not by one thread of argument alone, but by the whole weave of a book.

The second conclusion we need to bear in mind is that this kind of writing 'comes to possess a non-logical unity and compulsion like that of art in words'.[9]

These ideas are, in a modified form, applicable to Eliot's prose. First, the structure of an Eliot essay is not logical but psychological; it aims at inducing a certain temper of mind rather than persuading the reader on particular small points. And, because of its 'reticence' and non-rational structure, we are more likely to understand Eliot's critical prose if we read it as we would poetry, with attention to suggestion, nuance, and tone.

To a certain degree, of course, all criticism depends upon rhetoric and rhetorical strategy: the reasonableness of Aristotle and the apparent consistency of Johnson are both the creations of language rather than logic. But in critics before Coleridge, there is at least an identifiable thread of sequential argument (which is all that is meant by 'proof' as a critical term), and it is this which becomes less and less evident in the continuing Romantic tradition which Holloway discusses. It is with the writers of this tradition that Eliot has his most notable affinities; as a stylist, he is most often compared with Arnold, and however he may have deplored the element of 'emotional temperature' in the great Victorians, he employed devices similar to those of Ruskin, Arnold, and Newman. He did so quite consciously, and often in a humorous spirit.

There is considerable evidence, in fact, that Eliot thought of the whole business of criticism − journals, papers and lectures, disputes and reputations − as a sort of solemn game or insiders' joke.[10] The pseudonyms with which he signed his early reviews ('Crites', 'T. S. Apteryx', 'Gus Krutzsch') suggest a lack of high seriousness, and Hugh Kenner has suggested that Eliot's characteristic donnish style originated in parody. He is probably right. The weekly reviewing for journals like the *New Statesman* and the *Athenaeum* was, during the First World War, still in the hands of critical impressionists, 'men of letters' who used Pater's method but lacked his taste and intelligence; to read their work is to understand how necessary Eliot's essays on 'Imperfect Critics' were. It was in this environment that Eliot began writing criticism, and the extreme sensitivity to style apparent in his verse borrowings made it easy for him to adapt himself to the style of the *Athenaeum* or the *Times Literary Supplement*, a technique which Kenner calls 'blandly subversive'.[11]

> The rhetorical layout of essay after essay can best be described as a parody of official British literary discussion: its asperities, its pontification, its distinctions that do not distinguish, its vacuous ritual of familiar quotations and bathetic solemnities. The texture of an Eliot review is almost indistinguishable from that of its neighbours; only the argument, and the tone derived from an extreme economy of phrase, are steadily subversive.[12]

Eliot was not called 'Possum' for nothing.

If this were not enough, we have Eliot's own word that the element of 'illegitimate' persuasion in the essays is large. Writing to E. M. Forster in 1929, he put the matter bluntly: apparently responding to a comment in Forster's previous letter, Eliot acknowledges that there is an element of bluff in much of his prose, and suggests that he was aware of it from the beginning of his critical career.[13] For critics hostile to Eliot, this is evidence enough that no one need pay attention to Eliot as a critic after all. But if we attempt to dispose of 'rhetoric' entirely there will be very little criticism left. The real importance of the rhetorical element here is that it constitutes another link between Eliot and the ongoing Romantic tradition: in how he speaks as well as in what he says, he shows his nineteenth-century heritage. In analysing Eliot's prose style, we simply extend the study of his art into another area.

The necessity of some sort of analysis becomes clear if we subject one of Eliot's essays to even the most cursory rational dissection. 'The Function of Criticism', published in 1923, is one of Eliot's most influential essays and a standard anthology piece. Up to a certain point, its argument can be summarized:

1 Literature is a collection of organic wholes in relation to which individual works have their significance: the artist must surrender himself to a common inheritance and a common cause if his work is to be comprehensible and lasting.
2 Since criticism is involved with the elucidation of works of

art and is not autotelic, the critic, like the artist, ought to control his individual prejudices and seek grounds of agreement with other critics in 'the common pursuit of true judgment'. (*SE* 25)

3   Most critics, however, are violently individualistic, and we are therefore tempted to dispense with criticism altogether. But we are obliged to admit the usefulness of certain works and writers, and must therefore try to establish some principles by which to distinguish good criticism from bad.

This summary accounts for the first three pages of an eleven-page essay, but any attempt to take it further would run into great difficulty. The second section of the essay takes up the question of allegiance to something outside oneself, which Middleton Murry defines as the distinguishing feature of classicism; and the argument begins to move, it seems, in several directions at once. Individualism – listening to one's inner voice to the exclusion of everything else – is associated in short order with Romanticism, pantheism, and Whiggery. It is only in the third section that Eliot returns, circuitously, to the idea of criticism. Assuming the role of the Inner Voice, he asks

> Why have principles, when one has the inner voice? If I like a thing, that is all I want; and if enough of us, shouting all together, like it, that should be all that *you* (who don't like it) ought to want ... And we can not only like whatever we like but we can like it for any reason we choose. We are not, in fact, concerned with literary *perfection* at all – the search for perfection is a sign of pettiness, for it shows that the writer has admitted the existence of an unquestioned spiritual authority outside himself, to which he has attempted to *conform*. We are not in fact interested in art. (*SE* 29)

In its use of 'perfection' and its criticism of democratic attitudes, the passage is reminiscent of *Culture and Anarchy*. Eliot then goes on, in the final section of the essay, to the critic's qualifications.

It is the second section which presents the problem. It does not advance the argument in any paraphrasable way, but it is undeniably effective. Eliot suggests that the idea of allegiance involves corollary principles in religion and politics, and in doing so implies that the issue under discussion is at the heart of the relationship between literature and the world for which it is made.[14] A welter of references (Joan of Arc, Lloyd George, Hudibras, Catholic mysticism) reinforces one's sense of the issue's importance without becoming specific: Eliot's attitude towards each subject is clear, but the import of the whole remains obscure to anyone who has not read Eliot's critical writings *in extenso*. The essay is, in short, a prime example of the sage at work, elaborating an idea which cannot be 'proven' even in the limited sense of the word as we are using it. As Holloway says,

> a discussion may consist of what might be called 'nodal' propositions, with a far from immediately plain sense, but introduced, familiarized, made easier for the reader to grasp, by a variety of techniques that would indeed be sophistical, if their interpretation could be nothing but logical; but not otherwise.[15]

The substance of 'The Function of Criticism', then, could perhaps be written thus: 'Reliance upon one's own perceptions and ideas leads ultimately to a refusal to consider anything else; in literature and criticism it results in a form of solipsism which defeats the purpose of art as a means of communication.' This is again, of course, an Arnoldian idea: the value of true criticism, and of tradition, is that they enable us to get beyond the limitations of the individual mind. The tribute to Arnold in Eliot's essay is largely implicit; the title and one reference, in which Arnold is referred to only as 'an elder critic', are the only overt suggestions that Eliot was consciously reaffirming Arnoldian standards.

In 1930, Eliot spoke of Arnold's criticism as 'representing a point of view which is particular though it cannot be wholly defined', and the remark describes Eliot's criticism – and the activities of the sage generally – equally well.[16] In what follows, I attempt rhetorical rather than ideological definition: even a highly conscious rhetoric, however, resists analysis in categorical terms. The headings I employ are largely for the sake of convenience in classification.

Tone

In discussions of the art of persuasion, 'tone' is at once the most invoked and the least analysable element. It makes the analysis of language and style seem easy by comparison. Words like 'urbane' and 'conversational' are apt to occur without supporting evidence of their appropriateness, since they are relative as well as evaluative terms. Henry James's style was conversational, but the conversation was that of Henry James. If I say that Eliot's tone is conversational, then, it is in the hope of specifying what *kinds* of conversation it involves. That the tone varies greatly is obvious: W. H. Auden, with characteristic insight and humour, has identified at least three speakers in Eliot's work.

> First there is the archdeacon, who believes in and practices order, discipline and good manners, social and intellectual, with a thoroughly Anglican distaste for evangelical excess. ... And no wonder, for the poor gentleman is condemned to be domiciled with a figure of a very different stamp, a violent and passionate old peasant grandmother, who has witnessed murder, rape, pogroms, famine, flood, fire, everything; who has looked into the abyss and, unless restrained, would scream the house down. ... Last, as if this state of affairs were not difficult enough, there is a young boy who likes to play slightly malicious jokes. The too earnest guest, who has come to interview the Reverend, is startled and bewildered by finding an apple-pie bed or being handed an explosive cigar.[17]

Eliot was in fact an accomplished mimic as well as a parodist, and his sensitivity to conversational as well as written styles is apparent in *The Waste Land*. It is not surprising, therefore, that we encounter a great variety of 'voices' in the essays. That which is heard most often is simply fluent and assured; many of the essays open with a strong statement which the rest of the paper attempts to confirm:

> If one follows Blake's mind through the several stages of his poetic development it is impossible to regard him as a naif, a wild man, a wild pet for the supercultivated.[18]

No author exercised a wider or deeper influence upon the Elizabethan mind or upon the Elizabethan form of tragedy than did Seneca.[19]

What I have to say is largely in support of the following propositions: Literary criticism should be completed by criticism from a definite ethical and theological standpoint.[20]

Tennyson is a great poet, for reasons that are perfectly clear. He has three qualities which are seldom found together except in the greatest poets: abundance, variety, and complete competence.[21]

The value of this sort of opening is apparent. Its obvious self-confidence creates confidence in the reader, and disposes him favourably towards what follows; the directness of the statement also creates an impression of candour, and suggests that the critic has all his cards on the table. Sometimes Eliot maintains this positive tone throughout an essay – as he does in ' "Rhetoric" and Poetic Drama' – but more frequently he varies it for interest's sake. Thus the straightforward discourse of a given essay may be interrupted by an epigram:

When a theory of art passes it is usually found that a groat's worth of art has been bought with a million of advertisement.[22]

Poetry is 'capable of saving us,' he says; it is like saying that the wall-paper will save us when the walls have crumbled.[23]

Or lightened by a low pun:

... when an Elizabethan hero or villain dies, he usually dies in the odour of Seneca.[24]

Eliot's fondness for lower-class speech, fed by the music-hall during his early years in London, is another means of providing contrasts which are both startling and comic:

Only the pure in heart can blow the gaff on human nature as Machiavelli has done.[25]

Poetry is not a career, but a mug's game. (*UPUC* 154)

Usually, of course, the language is more decorous; occasionally, it becomes so decorous as to constitute parody. In 'Johnson as Critic and Poet', for example, we find this Johnsonian passage:

> Now it is generally observable of mankind, that in the elation of success in some course which we have set ourselves, we can be oblivious of many things which we have been obliged to resign in the accomplishment of it. We do not take kindly to the thought that, in order to gain one thing, we may have to give up something else of value. With these lost values the path of history is strewn and always will be: and perhaps a purblindness to such values is a necessary qualification, for anyone who aspires to be a political and social reformer. The improvement of the language, which the eighteenth century had achieved, was a genuine improvement: of the inevitable losses only a later generation could become aware.[26]

This capacity for parody appears likewise in Eliot's use of allusion. In altering a well-known line for his own purposes, Eliot displays his erudition in a small way, achieves ironic distance from his subject, and makes his point.

> [Sacheverell Sitwell] tends in his weaker moments to fly off like a beautiful but ineffectual aeroplane, beating its propeller vainly in a tree. ...[27]

> Mr. Clive Bell, lingering between two worlds, one dead, is in some respects the Matthew Arnold of his time. ...[28]

> And each essay is rounded by a bibliography.[29]

> Those who hunger and thirst after righteousness, and are not

> satisfied with a snack-at-the-bar, will want a great deal more
> [than respectability]. ...[30]

> Heaven and Earth shall pass away, and Mr Arnold with them,
> and there is only one stay. (*UPUC* 119)

In these cases the effect is relatively simple; in others, the reference itself helps to suggest the inadequacy of a certain point of view.

> But Wordsworth had no ghastly shadows at his back, no
> Eumenides ... he went droning on the still sad music of
> infirmity to the verge of the grave. (*UPUC* 69)

Here the play on Wordsworth's 'still, sad music of humanity', reinforced by Eliot's reminder of the passions that animate Greek drama, conveys a criticism of Wordsworth's limited emotional range. Similarly, the statement that 'we must witness of Professor Murray ere we die that these things are not otherwise but thus' turns the voice of Euripides' chorus against the inadequacies of his translator.[31]

By these means Eliot establishes rhetorically the scale by which his subjects are to be measured. He accomplishes a similar end in his use of an object or setting which fixes the subject's 'real' stature or, occasionally, his 'real' vocation.

> Thomas Woolner was a sculptor whose works and celebrity fully
> entitle him to the reward of a biographical volume; though the
> present is a very large one.[32]

> Mr. Bell will survive not as an individual, but as the
> representative of a little world of 1914.[33]

> We can criticize his [George Wyndham's] writings only as the
> expression of this peculiar English type, the aristocrat ... riding
> to hounds across his prose, looking with wonder upon the world
> as upon a fairyland.[34]

> ... their instinct turned to shows and circuses, as does that of the

later race which created the Commedia dell'Arte, which still provides the best puppet shows, and which gives a home to Mr. Gordon Craig.[35]

With Woolner and Bell it is simply a matter of proportion. In the cases of Wyndham and Craig, Eliot creates a sense of comic displacement: Craig doing set designs for Punch and Judy, or Wyndham riding to hounds across a real meadow, would presumably be all right. Another form of reductive irony is that of damning by faint praise, a technique which allows Eliot to acknowledge his subject's greatness and set it on its ear at the same time:

> Tennyson had a brain (a large dull brain like a farmhouse clock) which saved him from triviality. The subject given (airy fairy Lillian) he took it lightly, but as a serious study in technique.[36]

> That so little material as appears to be employed in *The Triumph of Time* should release such an amazing number of words, requires what there is no reason to call anything but genius.[37]

The irony of these remarks at least suggests something of the shortcoming Eliot sees in each figure. His more exasperating attacks are unanswerable because they imply that a certain writer is beneath consideration without suggesting why. The slighting remarks about Milton are there long before Eliot actually argues an anti-Miltonic position,[38] and Eliot speaks of Meredith in *The Sacred Wood* as if admiration for him were in itself a sign of defective intelligence:

> And the suspicion is in our breast that Mr. Whibley might admire George Meredith.[39]

> The Charles Louis Philippes of English literature are never done with, because there is no one to kill their reputations; we still hear that George Meredith is a master of prose, or even a profound philosopher.[40]

It is difficult to argue with criticism like this when each sentence is the only mention of Meredith in the essay.[41]

Eliot sometimes gives the reader a little set-piece by way of introduction to the matter at hand. These appear mostly in the uncollected criticism, and it is easy to see why Eliot was wary of including such material in his collections of essays. The passage below, for example, looks very much like the sort of impressionistic criticism that Eliot was opposed to. The technique is, to use Kenner's term, 'subversive':

> In the days when prosperous middle-class chimney-pieces were decorated with overmantels and flanked by tall jars of pampas grass; when knowing amateurs began to talk of Outamaro and Toyakuni; in the days when Mrs. Pennell's friends found source of laughter in feeding peacocks with spongecake soaked in absinthe; when Mr. George Moore was wearing a sugarloaf hat with a flat brim; then, or perhaps a little later ... in the long-forgotten Nineties when sins were still scarlet, there appeared a little book called *Pastels in Prose*.... This book introduced to the English reader the Prose-Poem.[42]

By evoking the arty milieu in which prose-poems were written and read, and by associating the volume with fashions as short-lived as those of interior decoration, Eliot anticipates his conclusion that the idea of prose-poetry is the creation of dilettantes: the best work which appears at first glance to be part of the genre (Rimbaud's *Illuminations*, Claudel's *Connaissance de l'est*) is identifiably, by its rhythms, prose or poetry, not a mixture of the two. 'Then, or perhaps a little later' suggest that the volume was slightly *passé* even when it appeared; 'in the days when' implies the 'once upon a time' of fairy tales, and encapsulates the 1890s as a period of childish things. The pampas grass, Outamaro, and absinthe are foreign affectations, and much of the article will be devoted to French writing; the contrast between scarlet sins and prose pastels constitutes a criticism of the vagueness and mistiness of the worst of 1890s writing. Before the argument even begins, the prose poem has been made to look ridiculous by association. Eliot has succeeded in using one genre of the 1890s – critical impressionism – as a destructive tool against another.

In the same way, he can use detail from a work to suggest the faults of the whole. After Eliot's discussion of the shortcomings of Georgian verse, a few words from each poet in turn are enough to damn him.

> Mr. Squire slips in, referring to a house as a 'mean edifice.' Mr. Nichols effects a rhetorical balance:
> Whose voice would mock me in the mourning bell,
> Whose face would greet me in hell's fiery way.
> ... Mr. Gibson asks, 'we, how shall we ...' etc. Messrs. Baring and Asquith, in war poems, both employ the word 'oriflamme.' Mr. Drinkwater says 'Hist!'[43]

The pretensions of a writer on the future of English are exposed by his reliance upon cliché:

> The quality of Mr. de Selincourt's style may be judged from the following: 'What, then, do we wish to be? A fundamental question that ... Language is a branch of the tree of life ... merest tyro ... What is the future of the English language? The problem is evolutionary ... Everyone feels in Chaucer the joyous expansiveness of youth, in Hardy the sombre introspection of old age ... secluded by-path ... In Celtic, with its tenderness and wild glamour, we feel the mountain and the valley, the rocks and the rain; in the mellow vowels of Italian the blue of the Mediterranean and its cloudless skies. ... The French call love "amour" ... The salient feature of our age. ...'[44]

The tone here is that of the jaded *boulevardier*, with undertones of Prufrock ('I have known them all already') – a tone not easily kept up, and one which Eliot seldom resorts to.

His more characteristic manner in attack is one of donnish asperity, frequently expressed in flurries of questions:

> We quite agree that poetry is not a formula. But what does Mr. Gosse propose to do about it? If Mr. Gosse had found himself in the flood of poetastry in the reign of Elizabeth, what would he

Eliot as Rhetorician

have done about it? Would he have stemmed it? What exactly is this abyss? and if something 'has gone amiss with our standards,' is it wholly the fault of the younger generation that it is aware of no authority that it must respect?[45]

Any question asked in the course of a written argument is naturally rhetorical. A series of questions *en masse* has, or ought to have, a double effect: it creates the impression of rigour on the critic's part, and of almost wilfully flabby thought on the part of his opponent. Eliot uses this means of attack in his disputes with John Middleton Murry and the English Association.[46] When the questions are dispersed, they serve as neat turning-points. The 'Matthew Arnold' lecture in *The Use of Poetry* is built around this technique: each question summarizes Eliot's criticism of an Arnoldian idea and enables him to move swiftly to his own conclusion.[47] The technique is one which Arnold himself used expertly, and it is, as Eliot said of Bradley's treatment of Arnold, 'a great delight to watch when a man's methods, almost his tricks of speech, are thus turned against himself'.[48]

The donnish manner is also apparent in Eliot's sudden expressions of puzzlement. In the midst of an analysis, Eliot admits that he is baffled:

> We are told on the wrapper that the 'main thesis' of the book is that Swift was *a man without a soul*. Mr. Leslie makes the same observation at one point inside the book. He does not develop it explicitly; but if it is indeed the main thesis, it is incapable of explaining anything. And I cannot see what such an assertion means.[49]

> But why creative newness, or organic novelty as we might call it, should *be* Value I cannot puzzle out.[50]

> I do not understand Mr. Murry's attitude towards 'faith,' or his theory of reason. ...[51]

These comments not only create a disarming impression of frankness, but also suggest strongly that the writer under discussion cannot think very clearly. In his review of Edmund Blunden's book on Vaughan, for example, Eliot cites Blunden's description of Vaughan's 'solar, personal, flower-whispering, rainbow-browed, ubiquitous, magnetic Love' and adds dryly 'I am unable to attach any meaning to this incoherent chain of adjectives.'[52]

The technique, which is clearly a form of attack, is another which Eliot appears to have borrowed from F. H. Bradley. In the 1927 essay on Bradley, he mentions the philosopher's 'polemical irony and his obvious zest in using it, his habit of discomfiting an opponent with a sudden profession of ignorance, of inability to understand, or of incapacity for abstruse thought'.[53] That essay provides a good summary of what Eliot found to be of permanent value in Bradley, and suggests much about the influence of Bradley's personality on Eliot's style — an influence which was, according to Eliot's own account, crucial.[54]

The question of personality is central, for it is, finally, our awareness of Eliot as a reasonable and sensitive reader of literature which determines much of our response to his critical prose. 'We must learn to take literature *seriously*', he says at the end of an early review;[55] but he was aware that the 'high seriousness' which Arnold demanded of literature need not be — as it occasionally was in Arnold's own work — solemn. There is a large element of sheer panache in the essays: Eliot, like the original narrator of *The Waste Land*, 'do the police in different voices', and takes obvious pleasure in his virtuosity.[56] The voice of the essays is protean. Whimsical and serious, precise and obscure, insouciant, arch, and admonitory by turns, it also strikes 'the occasional note of arrogance, of vehemence, of cocksureness or rudeness'.[57] But in the best of Eliot's criticism, 'the cool outsider's gaze and the poised intellectual gaiety' which Bergonzi noted are always evident.[58]

Forms of Statement

Declarative sentences, like happy families, are in one sense all alike. But, depending upon its form and its position in the whole argument, a statement may invite assent in different ways, and the writer's means of introducing major statements are among his most useful devices. Within the atmosphere established by the tone or tones of an essay, Eliot employs a wide variety of forms of statement.

It is in part by what he takes for granted that we 'know' any critic, and some of Eliot's assumptions, at least, are straightforwardly stated. After listing the qualifications of the perfect critic, for example, Eliot adds that 'we assume the gift of a superior sensibility', thereby introducing, quite casually, the most crucial elements of all – maturity of mind and sensitivity to the ways in which words are used: what is often called 'taste'.[59] In a true critical *system*, taste has little or no place. *Lucky Jim* fits as well into Northrop Frye's structure as *The Odyssey* or *Madame Bovary*; a sentence from a government report is as susceptible to structuralist analysis as a sentence from Ruskin or Newman. But Eliot, like other major critics of our century (Leavis and Richards, for example), does not have a system, and it would be a mistake to think of his central ideas, preoccupations or historic mythography as vehicles of judgment. The animating principle, the central assumption, is that of taste.[60]

The point may seem too obvious to require stating, but we are inclined to overlook how deeply criticism is influenced by sensibility, and how seldom that influence is acknowledged in the *form* of critical statements. Eliot writes that 'Swinburne's judgment [of Elizabethan drama] is generally sound, his taste sensitive and discriminating.'[61] In form, this is a statement of fact; in fact, it is in itself a judgment based on taste.

Many of Eliot's conclusions in the earlier essays become assumptions in later ones. These central ideas are so frequently and so lightly invoked that the reader who goes through much of the criticism is apt to be unaware of how much else depends upon them: like axioms in geometry, they are the essential elements for more complicated exercises. The importance of tradition, the necessity of clear images, the objectifying of point of view, the concern with the slight alteration from the expected which constitutes great poetry – these leitmotifs constitute such unity as the essays have.

Eliot as Rhetorician

They also serve to clarify Eliot's *pronunciamentos*, those single-sentence judgments with which the early criticism abounds. Many of these are extraordinary, and seem designed as affronts to the reader's sense of things; they are at the same time mysterious, for they appear without supporting argument. When we read of George Eliot, 'who could write *Amos Barton* and steadily degenerate', we are inclined to dismiss the remark as a misunderstanding of George Eliot's art, a sentence dashed off before the week's deadline.[62] But similar remarks occur twice in the carefully edited *Sacred Wood*:

> How astonishing it would be, if a man like Arnold ... had shown his contemporaries exactly why the author of *Amos Barton* is a more *serious* writer than Dickens, and why the author of *La Chartreuse de Parme* is more serious than either?[63]

> Mr. More has, it seems to me, in this sentence just failed to put his finger on the right seriousness of great literary art; the seriousness which we find in Villon's *Testament* and which is conspicuously absent from *In Memoriam*; or the seriousness which controls *Amos Barton* and not *The Mill on the Floss*.[64]

In the context of Eliot's criticism as a whole, these remarks are comprehensible. We know that Eliot requires clarity. He also values irony as an indication that the author can look at his characters' situation, or his own, from the outside; and irony is apt to be mistaken by the imperceptive for a lack of seriousness. Villon and Stendhal are serious without being heavy and portentous: neither could have written the death of Little Nell, or the more earnest conversations in *The Mill on the Floss*, without introducing a bit of reductive irony.[65] In this case, as in others, one element of Eliot's judgment (the basis on which it has been made) is suppressed, and the conclusion stands alone, dramatic in its isolation.[66]

Such extreme critical ellipsis becomes rarer after *The Sacred Wood* and is, in any case, never used in discussion of the essay's main subject. As he approaches that subject in many of the essays, Eliot suggests an idea which the reader can entertain – take on approval, almost – while the discussion is going on. By stating his conclusion at the beginning, Eliot appears to be straightforward, without palpable designs on the reader's mind; but at the same time he sets up the terms of discussion. Even if the reader does not agree that 'Seneca had as much to do with [the] merits and ... progress [of Elizabethan tragedy] as with its faults and delays', he has been forced to think of Elizabethan tragedy in Senecan terms.[67] If the central statement occurs late in the essay, it crystallizes Eliot's argument by providing a sudden persuasive focus to the discussion of the preceding pages:

> It is, in fact, the word that gives [Swinburne] the thrill, not the object.[68]

> But the weakness of [Blake's] long poems is certainly not that they are too visionary, too remote from the world. It is that Blake did not see enough, became too much occupied with ideas.[69]

> The artistic 'inevitability' lies in this complete adequacy of the external to the emotion; and this is precisely what is deficient in *Hamlet*.[70]

The theoretical essays also frequently revolve around a single point.

In these instances the rest of the essay either elaborates or builds to the central statement. But there are many statements in the essays which are not really susceptible of elaboration. These usually concern the texture of a poet's verse or the feel (there is no more precise word) of his work as a whole. Eliot's technique here is a direct appeal to the reader's experience of literature.

> If we look at the work of Jonson's great contemporaries, Shakespeare, and also Donne and Webster and Tourneur ... have a depth, a third dimension, as Mr. Gregory Smith rightly calls it, which Jonson's work has not. Their words have often a network of tentacular roots reaching down to the deepest terrors and desires. Jonson's most certainly have not. ...[71]

Eliot as Rhetorician

Like any *aperçu*, this cannot be argued. Quotation out of context – and quotation is out of context almost by definition – would not convey this dimension of drama: the observation is one which we immediately feel to be true (or not true), and which no amount of demonstration would prove to us otherwise.

Particularly in the Elizabethan essays, most of which are general approaches to the work of individual playwrights, Eliot is prone to this sort of statement. The following are typical:

> In spite of all the long-winded speeches, in spite of all the conventional Italianate horrors, Bianca remains, like Beatrice in *The Changeling*, a real woman; as real, indeed, as any woman in Elizabethan tragedy.[72]

> Heywood's is a drama of common life, not, in the highest sense, tragedy at all; there is no supernatural music from behind the wings.[73]

> as we familiarize ourselves with the play we perceive a pattern behind the pattern into which the characters deliberately involve themselves; the kind of pattern which we perceive in our own lives only at rare moments of inattention and detachment, drowsing in sunlight.[74]

What enables him to succeed with these judgments is not only the justice of the remarks themselves, but Eliot's knowledge of reader psychology. He knows, for example, that literature can delight us in unlikely, even bizarre, ways, and can therefore appreciate the grotesquerie of Crashaw's 'Tear', which we quoted earlier:

> Fair drop, why quak'st thou so?
> 'Cause thou streight must lay thy head
>   In the dust? O no,
>   The dust shall never be thy bed;
> A pillow for thee will I bring,
> Stuft with down of Angels wing.

Eliot remarks in his 1927 essay that

Crashaw's images, even when entirely preposterous – for there is no warrant for bringing a pillow (and what a pillow!) for the *head* of a *tear* – give a kind of intellectual pleasure – it is a deliberate conscious perversity of language, a perversity like that of the amazing and amazingly impressive interior of St. Peter's.[75]

The reader usually agrees with Eliot, I believe, when the *aperçu* can be tested against his own nerve endings or his own experience. The technique backfires, however, when this sort of validation is not possible. Some of Eliot's more portentous historical generalizations fail simply because, in unelaborated form, they have the look of 'mysteries' in the theological sense – that is, articles of faith beyond rational comprehension.

> The history of every branch of intellectual activity provides the same record of the diminution of England from the time of Queen Anne. It is not so much the intellect, but something superior to the intellect, which went for a long time into eclipse; and this luminary, by whatever name we may call it, has not yet wholly emerged from its secular obnubilation. (*UPUC* 62)

In the Clark Lectures, such a statement might be possible; we would, at least, have a context of general historical argument in which to place it. Here, in *The Use of Poetry* (1933), it is simply a stumbling-block. 'This luminary' is never given a name: it might be the soul, or the unified sensibility, or the sense of an all-encompassing divine order. The Latinate stiffness of Eliot's diction suggests that he was somewhat uneasy in making so sweeping a statement. The *magnum mysterium* is best confined to theology.

In other areas, Eliot's use of generalizations is more successful. He is inclined, like Matthew Arnold, to generalize about English and European attitudes towards culture. Both men begin with a point of view best expressed in 'The Function of Criticism at the Present Time', where Arnold speaks of 'a criticism which regards Europe as being, for intellectual and spiritual purposes, one great confederation, bound to a joint action and working to a common result; and whose members have, for their proper outfit, a knowledge of Greek, Roman, and Eastern antiquity, and of one another.'[76] One natural result of such a criticism is the attack on English provincialism which characterizes much of the best work of both Arnold and Eliot. Arnold believed that the life of the mind was respected in France, that a certain standard was insisted upon in French prose.[77] We find these ideas echoed in Eliot's opinion that 'the French in the year 1600 *had already a more mature prose*' than the English.[78] In 'The French Intelligence', a note on Julien Benda, Eliot uses Arnold's contrast of England and France to criticize Arnold himself:

> Almost the only person who has ever figured in England and attempted a task at all similar to that of M. Benda is Matthew Arnold.... But what an advantage a man like M. Benda has over Arnold. It is not simply that he has a critical tradition behind him, and that Arnold is using a language which constantly tempts the user away from dispassionate exposition into sarcasm and diatribe, a language less fitted for criticism than the English of the eighteenth century. It is that the follies and stupidities of the French, no matter how base, express themselves in the form of ideas – Bergsonism itself is an intellectual construction, and the mondaines who attended lectures at the Collège de France were in a sense using their minds. A man of ideas needs ideas, or pseudo-ideas, to fight against. And Arnold lacked the active resistance which is necessary to keep a mind at its sharpest.[79]

The contrast also includes generalizations about English and European attitudes towards form in art. Arnold speaks of the impatience of the Celt with *architectonice*, and this criticism is a recurrent motif in his comments on English literature as compared with European; similarly, Eliot remarks in 'William Blake' on 'that more Mediterranean gift of form'.[80] The essential difference is between professional and amateur: Arnold saw professionalism embodied in the French Academy, and Eliot finds that professionalism slighted in *The Times*.

the writer engages our sympathy by charging the worst lines of
Milton and Wordsworth to professionalism. Here are two of his
statements:
   Professionalism is a device for making things easy.
   Decadence in art is always caused by professionalism.
An attitude which might find voice in words like these is behind
all of British slackness for a hundred years and more: the dislike
of the specialist. It is behind the British worship of inspiration,
which in literature is merely an avoidance of comparison with
foreign literatures, a dodging of standards. It goes to explain,
for instance, why in English literature there are so few really
well-written novels.[81]

Generalizations are easily challenged, but there is little likelihood
that they will cease to be made: some irresistible impulse towards
simplification will keep them in production indefinitely. What
matters, for our purposes, is not the justice of the opposition
which Eliot (or Arnold) sets up between Briton and European, but
the fact that such generalizations serve a variety of rhetorical
functions. They create a sense of the critic's wide scope of inquiry;
combined with the brilliance of example for which both critics are
celebrated, they secure the reader's agreement on immediate
points; and they reinforce the central principles of each man's
criticism. When, for example, Eliot speaks of 'England, which has
produced a prodigious number of men of genius and
comparatively few works of art', he is invoking the central idea of
'Tradition and the Individual Talent' – that individual genius is of
little account without the shaping power and discipline of
tradition as a countervailing force.[82]

Eliot's definitions are another important aspect of his use of
statement, but a difficult one to discuss. Eliot speaks in *The Sacred
Wood* of 'the tendency of words to become indefinite emotions',
and we know from *Four Quartets* that he almost despairs of precise
language.[83] In such circumstances, 'definition is a labor of
creation rather than of criticism'.[84] Since definitions are
inevitable, Eliot's own are frequently constructed simply to
forestall others which might be worse: 'Poetry is a superior
amusement. I do not mean an amusement for superior people. I

call it an amusement *pour distraire les honnêtes gens*, not because that is a true definition, but because if you call it anything else you are likely to call it something still more false.'[85] Occasionally the result is merely arbitrary, a demarcation rather than a definition – 'When I say the Renaissance, I mean for this purpose the period between the decay of scholastic philosophy and the rise of modern science.'[86] The true definitions are a different matter.

The most famous of these have had a mixed success. 'Objective correlative' has made its way in the world: it is a just term for an entity which Eliot describes precisely, and it is difficult to think of a term which would do the same job as concisely.[87] 'Dissociation of sensibility' has not passed into general critical use, though there has been enough ink spilled in discussion of it, because the phenomenon it attempts to name is, in Eliot's published criticism, too vaguely described. 'The auditory imagination', discussed in *The Use of Poetry*, is less well-known than the terms above, but still noteworthy.

What is interesting in these instances, and what makes them difficult to talk about as definitions, is the fact that Eliot reverses the normal order of definition. He does not begin with a term the meaning of which he seeks to pin down, but with an observed phenomenon for which he seeks a name – an example of the modernist reaction against abstraction. Eliot strives to avoid 'the tendency of words to become indefinite emotions' by beginning with bodily experience; his practice is therefore in keeping with his belief that sensibility is more inclusive than the rational mind. In this reversal of the defining process Eliot once again shows his Arnoldian heritage. John Holloway has noted how Arnold's discussions of terms 'do not suggest, as [Newman's and Carlyle's] did, that investigating senses is a kind of discovery. He is really finding a single convenient *name* for a complex of features plainly listed.'[88]

A similar technique is apparent in some of the essays when Eliot introduces an unexpected term into the discussion. In 'Ben Jonson' – an essay so fine that it is difficult to set bounds to one's quotation from it – Eliot's discussion of the characteristics of Jonson's drama culminates in the finding of an unforeseen but suggestive analogy:

His characters are and remain, like Marlowe's, simplified characters; but the simplification does not consist in the dominance of a particular humour or monomania. That is a very superficial account of it. The simplification consists largely in reduction of detail. ... This stripping is essential to the art, to which is also essential a flat distortion in the drawing; it is an art of *caricature*, of great caricature, like Marlowe's. It is a great caricature, which is beautiful; and a great humour, which is serious ... Jonson did not get the third dimension, but he was not trying to get it.[89]

The word 'farce' emerges in 'Christopher Marlowe' with much the same effect of surprised assent on the reader's part.[90]

The technique remained a congenial one for Eliot throughout his career. *Notes Towards the Definition of Culture* (1948) suggests the method in its title – concept before word – and the central chapters show, as Raymond Williams has said, 'that brilliance and nervous energy of definition which distinguishes Eliot's literary criticism'.[91] The book is Eliot's *Culture and Anarchy*, built upon the Arnoldian pillars of definition and the ironic exposure of opponents by means of their own remarks.

Related to definition is the technique of distinguishing among terms, which creates a favourable impression of the critic's acuity and also allows the argument to advance by breaking general terms into useful particular meanings. Eliot's distinction between 'unity' and 'conformity', between poetic and intellectual lucidity, and his distinguishing of three senses of culture, all show the device at its simplest.[92] Occasionally the distinction results in a neat reversal, as when Eliot compares the 'surface' quality of Jonson's work with the apparent 'evocative quality' of Beaumont and Fletcher's: after citing passages from the latter, Eliot remarks that

> Detached from its context, this looks like the verse of the greater poets; just as lines of Jonson, detached from their context, look like inflated or empty fustian. But the evocative quality of the verse of Beaumont and Fletcher depends upon a clever appeal to emotions and associations which they have not themselves

grasped; it is hollow. It is superficial with a vacuum behind it; the superficies of Jonson is solid.[93]

The least clear and therefore the most controversial of Eliot's distinctions is that between 'feeling' and 'emotion'. 'Feeling' is a problematic term in Eliot's early essays, as we have seen; in 'The Metaphysical Poets' it suggests both sense-perception and sensibility.[94] In the earlier 'Tradition and the Individual Talent' (1919), the celebrated analogy of the platinum filament is followed by this passage:

> The experience, you will notice, the elements which enter the presence of the transforming catalyst, are of two kinds: emotions and feelings. The effect of a work of art upon the person who enjoys it is an experience different in kind from any experience not of art. It may be formed out of one emotion, or may be a combination of several; and various feelings, inhering for the writer in particular words or phrases or images, may be added to compose the final result. Or great poetry may be made without the direct use of any emotion whatever: composed out of feelings solely. (SE 18)

It is suggested here that emotion is generic (Love, Anger, Sadness) and feeling specific, the latter being tied up with the writer's sensibility and the associations of certain events and things. But in the rest of *The Sacred Wood* the two words seem to be used interchangeably to indicate emotion as we commonly think of it.[95] The resulting confusion has led to a number of gallant and doomed attempts to codify Eliot's usage in terms of Bradley's philosophy or other schemata.

The most convincing explanation is that of C. K. Stead, who finds that 'feeling' and 'emotion' are part of a series of opposed terms in Eliot's criticism:

'impersonal' ...	'personal'
'unconscious' ... (conscious)	'mind'
'feelings' ...	'emotions'
'images, phrases' ...	'structure'
'detail' ...	'design'[96]

On the left are elements of the life which exists below the level of consciousness, intense, confused, and unarticulated; on the right, those elements which shape feeling into an artistically apprehensible form. The distinction is not, clearly, the common one between form and content: Stead uses Ransom's terms 'structure' and 'texture', but I think that 'Dionysian' and 'Apollonian' are really more useful terms. Both represent kinds of energy, but the latter is energy with direction, discipline, and aesthetic form.

There is much in Eliot's criticism to support Stead's point. Eliot uses the expression 'art-emotion' or 'artistic emotion' repeatedly, and many of Eliot's comments on works of art fit Stead's conclusions.[97] The distinction is not, then, as it seemed to be above, simply between generic 'emotion' and individual 'feeling', but between inner feeling and the proper objectifying of it which characterizes the successful work of art. We are left with the odd situation of Stead's having made a distinction of Eliot's rather clearer than Eliot himself managed to do – evidence, if such were needed, that Eliot's control of rhetoric was not invariably effective.[98]

One can say generally of Eliot's statements that, in the earlier criticism at least, they are extremely concise. Particularly at the beginning of an essay, Eliot is likely to slice through masses of material for a few salient points:

> Three conclusions at least issue from the perusal of Swinburne's critical essays: Swinburne had mastered his material, was more inward with the Tudor-Stuart dramatists than any man of pure letters before or since; he is a more reliable guide to them than Hazlitt, Coleridge, or Lamb; and his perception of relative values is almost always correct. Against these merits we may oppose two objections: the style is the prose style of Swinburne, and the content is not, in an exact sense, criticism.[99]

None of these assertions is positively demonstrated in the pages that follow, but Eliot is not guilty of evading the issue. Particularly in discussing a writer's whole *oeuvre*, Eliot really is obliged to deal with vast amounts of material in a short space. He therefore often writes in such a way as to combine fact and judgment, and the combination is informative even when the judgments are not elaborated on.

> [Marston's *Sophonisba*] has a good plot, is well constructed and moves rapidly. There are no irrelevances and no comic passages; it is austere and economical. The rapidity with which the too-scheming Carthaginians transfer their allegiance from Massinissa to Syphax ... is not implausible. ... The scene in which the witch Erictho takes on the form of Sophonisba in order to induce Syphax to lie with her, is by no means what Bullen would have it, a scene of gratuitous horror ... it is integral to the plot of the play; and is one of those moments of a double reality, in which Marston is saying something else, which evidence his poetic genius. And the memorable passages are not, as in his earlier plays, plums imbedded in suet; they may be taken as giving a fair taste of the quality of the whole play. ...[100]

There is a directness and terseness about the style of passages like this which – even more than the verbal echoes mentioned earlier – recall Dr Johnson, and Eliot is, in his moments of quick and candid assessment, closer to Johnson in practice than to any other of the English poet-critics. The two share an easy authority and a disinclination to argue the point.

Eliot often succeeds with these *dicta* because he puts forth even the most arbitrary connections so suggestively:

> *Avez-vous observé que maints cerceuils de vieilles*
> *Sont presque aussi petits que celui d'un enfant?*

Those lines are the work of a man whose verse is as magnificent as Dryden's, and who could see profounder possibilities in wit, and in violently joined images, than ever were in Dryden's mind. For Dryden, with all his intellect, had a commonplace mind. His powers were, we believe, wider, but no greater, than Milton's ... He bears a curious antithetical resemblance to Swinburne.[101]

Eliot as Rhetorician

There is surely no other critic who could suggest that Milton, Dryden, Baudelaire and Swinburne form a useful group for comparison. It is unlikely that any reader will take the whole passage at face value, but the juxtaposition of Baudelaire and Dryden is oddly effective. A more extended comparison would probably not be as striking.

Conciseness is not, of course, invariably a virtue in criticism. We have already seen one example of ambiguity resulting from it, and it is not difficult to find other instances: the brevity of Eliot's early remarks about the dissociation of sensibility, for example, resulted in a good deal of controversy not only about whether Eliot was right, but also about just what he meant.

I have dealt with seven forms of statement that appear frequently in Eliot's prose, and have given some of them, for the purposes of discussion, rather arbitrary names – assumption, *pronunciamento*, suggested idea, *aperçu*, generalization, definition, and distinction. These are obviously not the only possible categories, and I cannot claim to have analysed even these aspects of Eliot's use of statement with any completeness. The variety of forms, and Eliot's resourcefulness in using them, should nevertheless be apparent.

Tactics and Metaphors

Eliot imposed no overall structure upon his essays: the shape of each was determined largely by the material under review and the nature of the points he wanted to make. Within the essays, however, certain patterns recur as means of placing and evaluating literary figures.

The largest of these patterns is the historical survey, which is worked out in some detail in the Clark Lectures. This simplification of literary history – and, as I have suggested, any ordering of literary history is a simplification – often places the writers in an almost programmatic relationship to each other. Eliot begins the seventh of the Clark Lectures, for example, with a bit of emblematic summary: Donne and Crashaw become symbols of the emergence of modern Europe, Cowley a symbol of the transition from seventeenth- to eighteenth-century England.[102] In the Norton Lectures of 1932–3 a similar technique is employed. Sidney, Jonson, and Dryden appear as stages in the growth of the capacity for independent critical analysis; Addison and Coleridge represent stages in the decline of the concept of imagination after Dryden.[103]

A single essay obviously cannot generate this sort of perspective, but a reading of all of Eliot's essays suggests that it was never far from his mind. Nor is the perspective always historical: occasionally it appears as the grouping, across centuries and even arts, of artists with similar visions of human experience. Eliot was interested, for example, in what he defines as Marlowe's 'farce', 'which secures its emphasis by always hesitating on the edge of caricature at the right moment'.[104] Eliot perceives the same spirit in the work of Ben Jonson, and suggests in the Marlowe essay that a history of this 'old English humour, the terribly serious, even savage comic humour', could be traced down to Dickens.[105]

Fragments of this history appear here and there in Eliot's essays over a five-year period. Massinger is discussed as a representative of the Old Comedy, and compared with Marlowe and Jonson: 'the more farcical comedy was the more serious'.[106] In one of his 'London Letters' for the *Dial*, Eliot discusses the 'mordant, ferocious' wit of the music-hall comedians, the greatest of whom is Marie Lloyd; later in the same letter he remarks that some of H. M. Bateman's caricatures 'continue the best tradition from Rowlandson to Cruikshank. They have some of the old English ferocity.'[107] Both here and in a later essay this ferocity is also seen as characteristic of Hogarth and Wyndham Lewis.[108] The tradition which was in Eliot's mind and clearly *implied* in individual essays is revealed piecemeal in the prose over several years. A similar affinity across centuries and cultures links Laforgue and Baudelaire to the English metaphysicals: they share 'the same essential quality of transmuting ideas into sensations, of transforming an observation into a state of mind'.[109]

Eliot is not talking here about influence; the method, if one can talk of a method governing such scattered remarks, is that which Eliot espoused in 'Tradition and the Individual Talent' – writing about a work of art with the sense that 'the whole of the literature of Europe from Homer and within it the whole of the literature of his own country has [sic] a simultaneous existence and composes a simultaneous order.'[110] Such a view appears to imply that ahistorical, 'decontextualized' study of poetry which has become such a feature of American universities since the Second World War; but Eliot suggests his approach as part of the historical sense rightly considered.

> The existing monuments form an ideal order among themselves, which is modified by the introduction of the new (the really new) work of art among them. The existing order is complete before the new work arrives; for order to persist after the supervention of novelty, the *whole* existing order must be, if ever so slightly, altered; and so the relations, proportions, values of each work of art toward the whole are readjusted; and this is conformity between the old and the new. (*SE* 15)

Ulysses conforms to the epic tradition, which it illuminates and alters; the tradition retains its vitality by being reborn in twentieth-century Dublin. Wyndham Lewis likewise alters the tradition of 'farce' which renders him comprehensible.

Despite the fact that his perspective is usually wider, Eliot does use the idea of influence for his own purpose, which is often to imply an evaluation by placing a writer in a certain line of descent. Given Eliot's high opinion of Baudelaire, it is not difficult to see the intent of a passage like this:

> Since the generation – the *literary* generation – of Mr. Symons and the 'nineties, another generation has come and gone – the *literary* generation which includes Mr. Bernard Shaw, and Mr. Wells, and Mr. Lytton Strachey. This generation, in its ancestry, 'skipped' the 'nineties: it is the progeny of Huxley, and Tyndall, and George Eliot, and Gladstone. And with this generation Baudelaire has nothing to do; but he had something to do with the 'nineties, and he has a great deal to do with us.[111]

Similarly, Gilbert Murray's place in the development of 'a

Freudian-social-mystical-rationalistic-higher-critical interpretation of the Classics' is a considerable blot on his credentials as a translator.[112]

Often, of course, Eliot simply mocks the whole idea of influence as a kind of bootless pedantry. In the Clark Lectures, the tone of the send-up is suitably solemn: Eliot traces a complex genealogy in which Baudelaire, mated this time with various other writers, produces offspring as varied as Huysmans and the surrealists, Mallarmé and Blaise Cendrars, Corbière and Cocteau.[113]

This technique damns (or praises) by association. The contrary technique, that of setting up a foil, can accomplish similarly 'critical' results. The comparison of Jonson's and Beaumont and Fletcher's verse, already referred to, is an example of the technique; the comparison of Dryden and Milton is another.[114] Eliot's boldest use of the technique is to contrast styles from different centuries. Morris is pitted against Marvell, Milton against James, Shelley against Crashaw, Tennyson against Dante.[115]

One's first impulse is to protest against comparisons which take no account of different conditions, genres, or types of ability. But, again, the method is in keeping with Eliot's view of all literature as simultaneous, and he contrasts only works which share significant features. A poem of Morris attempts to evoke the same feeling as Marvell's 'Nymph and the Fawn', but without the latter's clarity of image; it fails. The syntactic complexity of Henry James is due to his 'determination not to simplify', while Milton's is determined by 'the musical significance ... rather than by the attempt to follow actual speech or thought'. (*OPAP* 142) One of Eliot's neatest touches is to display as opponents a translator, who is presumably trying to be faithful to his material, and the original author. Gilbert Murray 'has interposed between Euripides and ourselves a barrier more impenetrable than the Greek language'; Arthur Symons's translation of Baudelaire envelops the poet in 'the Swinburnian violet-coloured London fog of the 'nineties'.[116]

Even when the distinction is not one of quality, the opposition can still help to isolate the personal element in writing which interests Eliot. The sermons of Lancelot Andrewes have little in common with those of Donne, but discussion of one illuminates the other.[117] The recurrent pairing of Dante and Shakespeare in

Eliot's essays provides a fruitful contrast between the poet who finds a world-view ready-made and the poet who must construct at least a part of his own; or, in other instances, a contrast between bare and mannered styles in poetry.[118]

The vehicle of these comparisons is quotation, and no reader of Eliot's criticism can fail to be impressed by his almost unfailing ability to choose lines which reinforce his point and which, once heard, stick in the memory. As M. C. Bradbrook says,

> Against his reserved and restricted style they stand out, exactly chosen to make the point towards which he has been engaging the reader – but making it because the reader too is compelled to work over these particular lines, to respond actively to them, to relate to them all his past experience of the writer under discussion.[119]

Quotation is, in fact, the fine pivot upon which many of the essays turn, and Eliot's principles of selection are interesting. In 'Milton II' he says that there are two types of poet who can be of use to a later writer: those who suggest something new to be done, or a different way of doing the same thing, and those who 'teach us what to avoid, by showing us what great poetry can do without – how *bare* it can be.'[120] Eliot's quotations generally illustrate one of these two types: the innovative or the bare and Dantesque.

The Dantesque is, for Eliot, the summit of poetry. It is clear expression of even the most spiritual emotions, and Dante is the ideal model for the young poet, since he has no vices of style.[121] To assert this quality is one thing, but to discern it in poets other than Dante is a real contribution to criticism. Eliot finds this starkness in the Sophoclean bareness of Middleton's

> Can you weep Fate from its determined purpose?
> So soon may you weep me.[122]

It also characterizes parts of *In Memoriam* which are 'economical of words' and which show 'a universal emotion related to a particular place',[123] and (a triumph of objectivity on Eliot's part, given his antipathy to Shelley) *The Triumph of Life*.[124] Dante is not always mentioned by name in Eliot's analyses of these passages, but what Eliot clearly values in them is the eloquent plainness – what he calls, in his essay on Murray's translations of Euripides, 'the Greek brevity'.[125]

The second category of quotations is the larger, and includes those passages which exhibit 'that perpetual slight alteration of language, words perpetually juxtaposed in new and sudden combinations, meanings perpetually *eingeschactelt* into meanings, which evidences a very high development of the senses.'[126] Eliot's desire to isolate the essential, the personal, in poetry is related to his interest in the 'slight alteration'; it is a desire to assess the extent of individual contributions within the tradition.

Occasionally the contribution can be defined. Marlowe, for example, 'gets into blank verse the melody of Spenser, and he gets a new driving power by reinforcing the sentence period against the line period.'[127] More often – and it is here that the device of quotation becomes central to the process of argument – the distinctive contribution of the poet is less palpable. 'Every writer', Eliot notes in 'Christopher Marlowe', 'who has written any blank verse worth saving has produced particular tones which his verse and no other's is capable of rendering.' (*SE* 119) Thus Eliot finds a 'distinct personal rhythm' in the verse of John Ford and other Renaissance dramatists; in attempting to define an author's distinctiveness he often cites passages which display 'that combination of intelligibility and remoteness'[128] that we find in Shakespeare:

>   See, a carbuncle
> May put out both the eyes of our Saint Mark;
> A diamond would have bought Lollia Paulina,
> When she came in like star-light, hid with jewels. ....[129]
>
>   (Jonson)

> I that am of your blood was taken from you
> For your better health; look no more upon't,
> But cast it to the ground regardlessly,
> Let the common sewer take it from distinction.
> Beneath the stars, upon yon meteor,

Ever hung my fate, 'mongst things corruptible;
I ne'er could pluck it from him; my loathing
Was prophet to the rest, but ne'er believed.[130]

                                              (Middleton)

Does the silkworm expend her yellow labours
For thee? For thee does she undo herself?
Are lordships sold to maintain ladyships
For the poor benefit of a bewildering minute?[131]

                                              (Tourneur)

These passages have a complexity and suggestiveness which make them useful in different contexts, and it is not surprising that Eliot uses some of his examples repeatedly.[132] Many of the 'stolen' lines which figure in Eliot's poetry also appear in the criticism.[133]

Many of the lines are what Arnold called 'touchstones', and Eliot's use of them is often discussed with reference to Arnold's. It is a fairly easy matter, however, to show that Arnold's touchstones are chosen less for their perfection of form or language than for their *tone*, which Vincent Buckley has rightly characterized as 'a sad magnanimity, a composed sense of the finality (not, of course, the uselessness) of human experience.'[134] Hamlet's dying words to Horatio –

> If thou didst ever hold me in thy heart,
> Absent thee from felicity awhile,
> And in this harsh world draw thy breath in pain
> To tell my story –[135]

are great poetry, but they are one of Arnold's touchstones because they reflect Arnold's own sense of life. To set these lines beside Eliot's favourite passage from Chapman

> fly where men feel
> The cunning axletree, or those that suffer
> Under the chariot of the snowy Bear...[136]

is to see the difference between doctrinal and purely poetic standards of selection.[137]

Eliot's use of this kind of quotation shows his awareness of the evocative aura which can surround plain statement, but his own use of language in criticism relies more upon clear analogies to evoke the desired response in the reader. The first and largest category of these could be called simply *mots justes*, metaphors and similes which – in keeping with Eliot's ideas about clarity of image – convey with vivid physicality his sense of the question at hand.

> In the preceding passage Massinger had squeezed his simile to death, here he drags it round the city at his heels. ...[138]

> Of all authors Montaigne is one of the least destructible. You could as well dissipate a fog by flinging hand-grenades into it.[139]

> Mr. Wyndham Lewis ... often squanders his genius for invective upon objects which to everyone but himself seem unworthy of his artillery, and arrays howitzers against card houses. ...[140]

> Whether decent or indecent, their drollery is as far from mirth-provoking as can be: a continuous and tedious rattle of dried peas.[141]

> Poetry is 'capable of saving us,' he says; it is like saying that the wall-paper will save us when the walls have crumbled.[142]

> There are, of course, two futures: there is the future of the present, the future which we are actually working upon, and there is the future of the future, the future beyond our power, the future of the housemaid's dream of marriage.[143]

These figures of speech do their work quickly and authoritatively, and it is most often a work of destruction. But Eliot occasionally uses the same tropes to positive effect, particularly in discussing poetry. In Shakespeare, the right image rises 'like Anadyomene from the sea'; in free verse, 'the ghost of some simple metre should lurk behind the arras ... to advance menacingly as we doze, and withdraw as we rouse'.[144]

The second category includes two metaphors which Eliot uses repeatedly, and which reveal much about his aesthetic. The first is the metaphor of life, which in many writers is merely a cliché: we have heard too often of 'living literature' and 'vital treatment'. Eliot's use of the organic metaphor for the imagination or the work of art shows us another aspect of his relationship to Romantic tradition. When Eliot speaks of 'the sudden irruption of the germ of a new poem', he is carrying on the tradition – associated with Romanticism generally and Coleridge in particular – which affirms that the work of art develops according to an internal logic of its own and is not subject to 'rules'.[145] When he speaks of literatures as 'organic wholes' he asserts the living relationship between past and present and the necessity of an understanding deeper than that of consciousness, particularly individual consciousness, alone.[146]

Since life encompasses body and mind, the life-metaphor is an ideal image of the unified sensibility.

> When a poet's mind is perfectly equipped for its work, it is constantly amalgamating disparate experience; the ordinary man's experience is chaotic, irregular, fragmentary. The latter falls in love, or reads Spinoza, and these two experiences have nothing to do with each other, or with the noise of the typewriter or the smell of cooking; in the mind of the poet these experiences are always forming new wholes.[147]

As a living thing, the poet's mind can create a non-mechanical unity out of diverse, even contradictory, elements: Coleridge found this ability to reconcile 'opposite or discordant qualities' to be the characteristic power of the living imagination.[148] In the Clark Lectures the life-metaphor is once again explicit: Eliot speaks of the 'inorganic' reassociation of sensibility effected by the Romantics, and of the 'revivification' of technique in nineteenth-century French verse. (CL VI: 15–16)

The other persistent metaphor in this category is that of light. In 'Dante' (1929) Eliot praises the poet's 'masterly use of that imagery of *light* which is the form of certain types of mystical experience' (*SE* 267), and in his own poetry the metaphor recurs with a variety of meanings: Godhead, knowledge, awareness, hope. In the criticism, Eliot's use of light metaphors is based not, as we might expect, on the Romantic image of the work of art as a lamp, but on the ideal of classical clarity enunciated in 'Andrew Marvell': '... we are inclined to infer that the suggestiveness is the aura around a bright clear centre, that you cannot have the aura alone.'[149] It is natural that Eliot should indicate approval or disapproval with metaphors of light and clarity:

> One gets the impression of a large but cosy society ... deriving its intellectual illumination from the dispersed radiance of Great Men rather than from the inter-polar sparks of intelligence.[150]

> Some writers appear to believe that emotions gain in intensity through being inarticulate. Perhaps the emotions are not significant enough to endure full daylight.[151]

> *Hamlet*, like the sonnets, is full of some stuff that the writer could not drag to light, contemplate, or manipulate into art.[152]

> And if it is real poetry it will convey this experience in some degree to every reader who genuinely feels it as poetry. Instead of being obscure, it will be pellucid.[153]

The third category of metaphors is thematically related to the idea of clarity. Although Eliot's concept of poetry centres on the idea of unconscious creative process, he views the finished artefact – 'edited' by the conscious mind – as a sort of precision mechanism, exact in its effects upon the reader's sensibility. He expresses this sense of the work in analogies drawn from the physical sciences. A term like 'objective correlative' is pseudo-scientific, and its definition reveals Eliot's desire for an analysable cause-and-effect relationship in literature: 'in other words, a set of objects, a situation, a chain of events which shall be the formula of that *particular* emotion; such that when the external facts, which must terminate in sensory experience, are given, the emotion is immediately evoked.'[154]

As an observer and recorder of phenomena, the poet is a sort of scientist: '... it is just as absurd for [a poet] not to know the work of his predecessors or of men writing in other languages as it would be for a biologist to be ignorant of Mendel or De Vries.'[155] Donne becomes, in the Clark Lectures, a radiologist using bismuth to determine the position of the intestine on an X-ray screen; Dante's *Vita Nuova* is compared to a scientific report on the use and transformation of emotions. (CL II: 20, IV: 1) In speaking of Swinburne, Eliot mentions the 'critical solvents' which we employ 'to break down the structure of his verse'. Even the impersonality of the poet is expressed in radically scientific terms: he becomes merely the catalytic shred of platinum which triggers the conversion of experience into art.[156]

Eliot's use of these metaphors was highly conscious: in 'The Perfect Critic' (1920), he mentions 'that familiar vague suggestion of the scientific vocabulary which is characteristic of modern writing'. (*SW* 2) It is tempting to speculate on the sources of this kind of imagery. It may derive from the Futurist and Vorticist glorification of the mechanical, from Marinetti or Wyndham Lewis. It may represent an aspect of Pound's critical influence, for we find the same kind of language in his criticism. In his desire to convince us that 'the touchstone of an art is its precision', Pound often employs metaphors as radical as Eliot's: he speaks of writers as 'the voltometers and steam-gauges' of a nation's intellectual life, and of the arts as a form of science like chemistry.[157] And it is possible that both Pound and Eliot derived this type of metaphor from Gourmont, who refers to the dissociation of ideas in terms of chemical analysis.

This rough anatomy of Eliot's means of persuasion distorts the techniques in question by isolating them, and the accumulation of examples is likely to make Eliot's use of any single trope seem excessive. But in almost any given essay, tone, statement, and metaphor are united in a style which is both smooth and persuasive. 'Andrew Marvell' (1921) is a particularly good example of the artfulness of Eliot's argumentation.

The essay is not easily summarized, for, like 'The Function of Criticism', it does not ultimately depend upon rational argument. It contains, moreover, three distinct (though interdependent) themes:

1   the definition of 'wit' and its place in poetry;
2   an evaluation of Marvell as a poet;
3   the breaking-up of the seventeenth-century sensibility.

These themes are not so much developed as related to each other in the course of the essay. The governing device, if one can speak of a 'governing' device in an essay which employs so many, is that of wide historical perspective. Thirty-seven poets from Homer to Hardy are named or cited in the essay, more than twenty in its first two pages. By grouping these poets as representatives of different kinds of poetic excellence, Eliot establishes that the quality which distinguishes Marvell's verse is 'a quality of a civilization, of a traditional habit of life'. (*SE* 292)

This quality is not named at first; Eliot goes instead to a bit of summary history. 'Out of that high style developed from Marlowe through Jonson ... the seventeenth century separated two qualities: wit and magniloquence.' (*SE* 293) This generalization – immediately qualified, but used throughout the essay – leads to the definition of wit as 'a tough reasonableness beneath the slight lyric grace'; this definition in turn becomes the entertained idea which is amplified in the following pages. (Ibid.)

The sense of wit which Eliot evokes emerges in part from his appeal to the reader's literary experience. The names of La Fontaine, Gautier, Herrick, Waller, and Catullus are invoked before Eliot settles down to analyse Marvell's 'Coy Mistress'; quotations from the poem itself lead to further literary parallels and an amplification of the original definition. 'This alliance of levity and seriousness (by which the seriousness is intensified) is a characteristic of the sort of wit we are trying to identify.' (*SE* 297) Then, rather suddenly, we come upon the *mysterium*, the dissociation:

[Wit] is a quality of a sophisticated literature; a quality which expands in English literature just at the moment before the English mind altered. ... When we come to Gray and Collins, the sophistication remains only in the language, and has disappeared from the feeling. Gray and Collins were masters, but they had lost that hold on human values, that firm grasp of human experience, which is a formidable achievement of the Elizabethan and Jacobean poets. (*SE* 297)

Eliot's purpose in introducing a large historical statement at this point is not immediately apparent, for he goes on to criticize Marvell's excesses, to use Morris as a foil for Marvell's virtues, and to insist on the need for clarity in poetry. When Eliot returns to 'wit and magniloquence' several pages later, the dissociation is reintroduced through a contrast in which two poets become symbolic images of literary trends: 'Dryden was great in wit, as Milton in magniloquence; but the former, by isolating this quality and making it by itself into great poetry, and the latter, by coming to dispense with it altogether, may perhaps have injured the language.' (*SE* 301) Marvell is thus placed at the Great Divide of English literature. His peculiar achievement in a period of fragmentation is 'an equipoise, a balance and proportion of tones, which, while it cannot raise Marvell to the level of Dryden or Milton, extorts an approval which these poets do not receive from us.' (*SE* 302) It is this balance which makes of Marvell a classic.

The themes of the essay converge and separate around the figure of Marvell and passages from his poetry. The comparisons with French and Latin verse, displaying Eliot's customary ingenuity of example, contribute to the large statements about wit which occur in the latter part of the essay. The various techniques (I have not named all of them) are unobtrusive, since they are employed in a style which remains conversational despite its erudition and authoritative tone. The whole critical tradition is implied but not belaboured: Eliot's references to Johnson's *Life of Cowley* and Coleridge's definition of Imagination suggest the scope of the argument and its importance to poetics as a whole. The essay moves easily between particular and general subjects – the success and limitations of Marvell's imagery on one hand, the 'alteration' of the English mind on the other – in search of a quarry which, Eliot concludes, 'we have patently failed to define'. (*SE* 304)

But definition is not, after all, the highest activity of the critic. He is not, despite Eliot's metaphors, a scientist: he deals with a subject as complex, as defiant of categories and pigeonholes, as man himself. His task is to convey an elusive *sense* of works which retain their power over us by being simply stories and songs. He is almost inevitably, then, a 'sage' in Holloway's sense, a rhetorician seeking to familiarize us with ideas which are indemonstrable and at times almost inexpressible.

Eliot's major essays are, strictly, *essais* – attempts – and, despite their firm tone, they retain a tentativeness which is part of their charm. Eliot himself expressed some qualms about his critical work, but the best of it, including some still uncollected material, constitutes the most impressive body of general literary criticism written in English during this century. It is eloquent testimony to the fact that the poet-critic is still, in an age of academic criticism, our best guide to the tradition.

Conclusion

I

To summarize: although Eliot does not have a critical system, his criticism is suffused with certain ideas about the relationships among belief, sensibility, and language. These ideas are embodied in a view of literary history which is sketched in several early essays, but not fully developed until the Clark Lectures of 1926. As literary history, or as critical commentary on metaphysical poetry, the lectures are not very satisfying; but as an argument for certain standards, and as a definition of what Eliot considers a proper work of art to be, they are clearer than much of his published criticism, and constitute an essential part of his work. The Clark Lectures clarify Eliot's developing thought about Donne, and explain much about his regard for poets as diverse as Dante and Laforgue. More importantly, they suggest a considerable Romantic influence in Eliot's criticism.

Eliot's relation to the Romantic tradition suggests at least a partial answer to one of the perennial questions about the literature of our century: whether modernism was in fact a new movement or largely a continuation and development of Romantic ideas. Frank Kermode and C. K. Stead have contributed solid evidence to support the latter view, and George Bornstein has added to their findings. The first chapter of Bornstein's book is a good review of the whole dispute.[1] It should be obvious that my conclusions are compatible with theirs, though I have approached the subject from a different angle. We are still far from being able to write a definitive history of modernism; we still, in fact, have some difficulty in defining it. Much work remains to be done on the moderns' sense of their relation to Romantic tradition, and the results cannot fail to aid us in developing a more comprehensive view of what modernism really was.

The Clark Lectures contribute to that view by clarifying the relationship of modernism and Romanticism in Eliot's criticism. Less guarded in expression than Eliot's published essays, they suggest that Eliot found, in the Romantics and their Victorian successors, various ideas which were central in the making of his own modernist aesthetic. These ideas are related, and in fact overlap somewhat; they can be summarized, in the order of their importance, as follows.

1   The value of historical myth as a way of embodying literary and aesthetic values (cf. Schiller, Keats, Arnold, Ruskin);
2   The importance of perception by the whole mind rather than an isolated intellectual faculty (cf. Schiller, Keats, Wordsworth);
3   The necessity of clear (objective) sight as a means of avoiding solipsism (cf. Keats, Arnold, Ruskin, Hulme, Pound);
4   The inadequacy of poetry which reflects primarily the intellect and which becomes, as a result, overtly philosophical or 'ruminative' (cf. Keats, Arnold).

A constant element in these points of doctrine – the factor which unites the various points and links the Victorian and Edwardian writers with their Romantic predecessors – is nostalgia. Schiller and Arnold look back to the Greeks, Keats to the Renaissance, Ruskin, Hulme, and Pound to the Middle Ages: all find in the language and outlook of particular periods that combination of qualities which modern literature needs. Eliot looks back in various essays and lectures to the Greeks, to Dante, and to the metaphysicals – but most often, and most consistently, to Dante.

Eliot also learned a good deal about the conduct of argument from the Romantics and their nineteenth-century successors. The use of historical myth is in itself, of course, as much an argumentative technique as it is an idea. Eliot's other borrowings can be summed up under the following headings:

1   The use of medieval art and thought as a standard by which

Conclusion

to judge the modern (cf. Ruskin, Hulme, Yeats, Pound);

2   The reifying of argument through the juxtaposition of symbolic images (cf. Ruskin's use of Gothic and Renaissance monuments to represent the ethos of each period with Eliot's use of Donne and Crashaw as types or images of promiscuous Thought and Feeling, his conscious simplifying of literary periods, his placement of writers in diagrammatic relationship to each other, etc.);

3   The sophisticated use of a variety of rhetorical strategies, developed most fully by the Victorians, which depend less on sequential argument than acquainting the reader with the 'feel' of an idea through control of tone, implication, metaphor, etc.

Here again there is a unifying motif – in this case the Romantic concern with the idea which, ineffable or indemonstrable in itself, can yet be conveyed persuasively through the Image. Kermode has traced the development of this idea from the Romantics through Yeats and Eliot; but the idea can be seen at work not only in Eliot's poetry and theory of poetry, but also in his *practice* of criticism, which is at least partly 'negative' in Keats's sense: it works as much through embodied ideas as through 'legitimate' argument. As Yeats says, summarizing not only his work but the whole tradition, 'Man can embody truth, but he cannot know it.'[2]

Eliot was familiar with all of the earlier critics I have mentioned, and wrote about several of them. This fact and smaller points of similarity (such as the philosophical vocabulary and organic analogies which Eliot shares with Coleridge) suggest that Eliot's use of Romantic criticism was deliberate, almost systematic; but, as I have already said, the question of influence is secondary. If the tradition was consciously or unconsciously used, Eliot's critical achievement remains original and profound. If it were not so used, Eliot's place in that tradition would nevertheless be established, simply by the similarity of his ideas and methods to those of the Romantics. The probable mixture of tradition and innovation, whatever the exact proportions may be, shows Eliot as the ideal Janus of 'Tradition and the Individual Talent'.

Why was Eliot not identified long ago as a Romantic critic? There are several reasons, the most notable being that his affinities with the Romantic tradition, though pervasive, are few and specific: Eliot can hardly be considered a Romantic critic at all if Blake, say, is considered definitive of Romanticism. Secondly, Eliot's own attacks on Romanticism and the romantic sensibility muddied the waters for quite a while. These attacks were, as we have seen, never as thoroughgoing as they sometimes appeared to be, and there were literary-political reasons for such severity as there was. It would hardly have done for Eliot to damn certain Romantic doctrines and tendencies while praising others. Romanticism, however vaguely defined, was one thing in the popular mind, and had to be taken or left as a whole.

But, of course, it never was one thing in fact, and the *word* 'Romantic' itself was the greatest obstacle to sorting out the mixture of good and bad, often contradictory ideas which the period left us. Eliot defined 'Romantic' fairly precisely in his own criticism, and attacked only the confusion of subject and object which he saw as a growing tendency in English literature from the time of Donne. He could do nothing with prevailing, imprecise usage. A letter to the *Times Literary Supplement* in 1920 indicates his frustration:

> I suggest that the difficulties which veil most critics' theories of Romanticism (and I include such writers as Pierre Lasserre and Irving Babbitt) are largely due to two errors. One is that the critic applies the same term 'romantic' to epochs and to individual artists, not perceiving that it assumes a difference of meaning; and the other is that he assumes that the terms 'romantic' and 'classic' are mutually exclusive and even antithetical, without actually enforcing this exclusiveness in the examination of particular works of art.[3]

For Eliot himself, the terms were obviously not mutually exclusive. Keats was thoroughly 'classical' in Eliot's sense, since he sought to transcend subjective, individual perception.[4] Eliot, in turn, was 'Romantic' in his concern with the non-discursive Image. 'It would perhaps be beneficial', he concluded in the letter already referred to, 'if we employed both terms as little as possible, if we even forgot these terms altogether, and looked steadily for

Conclusion

the intelligence and sensibility which each work of art contains.'[5]

Still, in some ways, an attractive idea; but even less possible today than it was in 1920, and perhaps no longer really desirable. Eliot's definition of 'Romantic' was an early example of critical responsibility in the use of the term. In the years since his early essays – beginning, perhaps, with Lovejoy's essay 'On the Discrimination of Romanticisms' – scholarly criticism has broadened and deepened our sense of what Romanticism was.[6] It is now taken for granted that any critic discussing the subject will specify what he means by the term, and such specificity is no doubt the best we can hope for in the fallen world of language.

II

I have explained some of Eliot's ideas and attempted to fill in some of the necessary background, but I have not 'defended' those ideas for a variety of reasons. To begin with, Eliot's version of literary history is mythic and not, therefore, subject to the kind of argument and counter-argument which we bring to discussions of the fall of the Roman Empire. A second reason is that the tradition to which Eliot's historical criticism belongs constitutes a kind of defence in itself: any idea which has appealed to minds as diverse as those of Keats and Ruskin, Hulme and Yeats, has a kind of strength we must come to terms with, even if we disagree with the argument itself.

When we analyse Eliot's historiography, we find a congeries of metaphors, a skilful use of rhetoric, and a central, unproven assertion, and we are tempted to suppose that, through our analysis, we have shown Eliot's ideas to be merely rhetorical or sophistical. But, as Northrop Frye says in the passage cited earlier, the attempt to debunk an argument by suggesting that it is ' "nothing but" a metaphor' is not to be encouraged.[7] The premise which lies behind such an attitude is that metaphors are by nature fictional: the older faith, expressed by Emerson in the 'Language' section of *Nature*, is that literature is significant because metaphors are a means of perceiving order, not of creating it *ex nihilo*.

We are not obliged to share that faith, of course, but we seem to be afflicted with a kind of critical schizophrenia. We take ideas about history seriously enough when they are presented symbolically in a novel or poem; we are willing to read great amounts of solemn exegesis in the hope of understanding those ideas; we believe, in one way or another, that literature contains truths which are unavailable to mere reason. When it comes to *literary* history, however, we become so many Gradgrinds insisting on Facts. We live in an age of scholarly and academic criticism, and often suppose that non-academic criticism is somehow unsound – charming and interesting, no doubt, but unsound. An argument which is not supported by stout columns of footnote and buttressed with flying quotations is not, to our minds, really an argument at all.

I am perhaps belabouring an obvious point, but it seems that we are in danger of losing our sense of imagination as a real power of the mind – of the critical as well as the creative mind, since the two are not really separable. We accept the imagination *in its place*; we have inherited what Basil Willey calls 'the cleavage ... between what you *felt* as a human being or as a poet, and what you *thought* as a man of sense, judgement and enlightenment.'[8] So divided, we are not likely to judge any of the English poet-critics, from Sidney to Arnold, favourably. One suspects, however, that Sidney's *Apologie* and Shelley's *Defence* will somehow survive, as vindications not only of poetry but of a faculty which we exclude from criticism at our peril.

Eliot's historiography is not a means of generating judgments; a writer is not evaluated according to his position on one side or the other of the supposed dissociation. Eliot's praise of poets as diverse as Baudelaire, Tennyson, and Yeats shows that he was not a critical dogmatist. His version of literary history is essentially an aesthetic writ large, a pattern consciously simplified for the sake of vividness. In his essay on Ben Jonson, Eliot describes this kind of simplification, noting that it consists

> largely in reduction of detail, in the seizing of aspects. ... This

Conclusion

stripping is essential to the art, to which is also essential a flat distortion in the drawing; it is an art of caricature, of great caricature, like Marlowe's.[9]

Eliot's comments apply to his historical generalizations uncannily well — so well that I have altered appropriately his advice on how to read Jonson.

> If we approach [Eliot] with less frozen awe of his learning, with a clearer understanding of his 'rhetoric' and its applications, if we grasp the fact that the knowledge required of the reader is not archaeology but knowledge of [Eliot], we can derive not only instruction in two-dimensional life — but enjoyment ... There is a brutality, a polished surface, a handling of large bold designs in brilliant colours. ...[10]

To turn an author's words on himself in this way is, perhaps, a bit of sharp practice, but these remarks are surely appropriate to the 'two-dimensional' history which Eliot gives us. That it is, in its present form, two-dimensional cannot seriously be questioned; Eliot himself realized that a fuller account of his ideas (the ambitious three-volume history of Renaissance thought and literature mentioned in the preface to the Clark Lectures) would necessarily involve him in qualifications and reservations. Scholarly criticism, with its 'ifs' and 'buts' and 'maybes', would have engaged Eliot in an enterprise not merely larger in scope than the lectures, but also, as I suggested in Chapter 1, fundamentally different in kind. And it is perhaps for this reason that Eliot chose not to embark on the larger project, and to leave the lectures, which were bound to be mistaken for a kind of history they did not pretend to be, unpublished.

The Clark Lectures can help us to learn to read Eliot's criticism for what it is — not a particularly easy task. Bornstein, for example, is severe on Eliot's criticism of the Romantics, and with some justice; but, like many of Eliot's critics, he does not take into account the particular kind of criticism Eliot was writing. Bornstein praises Harold Bloom's *Anxiety of Influence*, while acknowledging that it 'belongs to mythology in the best sense

Conclusion

rather than to literary scholarship'. But he is unwilling, it seems, to see Eliot's criticism of the Romantics as similarly mythological.[11] Bornstein's difficulty arises from the fact that Eliot behaves, at times, like a conventional critic. We tend to see him as being all of a piece, and to ignore the fact that his criticism is an artful patchwork of 'real' argument and rhetoric, particular comments and general principles, genuine insights and occasionally extreme judgments. We must learn to distinguish these elements in the prose so as not to confuse Eliot at his most Procrustean with Eliot the permanently valuable critic. Eliot's defenders have proven no more willing than his detractors to make these distinctions.

The historical myth is an essential part of Eliot's criticism in that we cannot see the shape of the whole without it, but Eliot's real greatness as a critic lies elsewhere – in his formulations of modernist aesthetics; his ability to delineate the essence of an author's genius in half a dozen quotations, perfectly analysed or used simply as examples; his unerring distinctions between living language and dead; his independence of mind, which led him to disagree not only with received opinion but also with his own earlier judgments; and his ability to find delight and worth in poetry quite unlike that of his own models. He is not a critic with whom one can agree all the time, but no critic of worth is. Eliot is that rarer thing, a man whose criticism can be read for the sheer pleasure of contact with a highly civilized mind.

III

At the end of Chapter 1, I mentioned some of the ways in which Eliot's historiography formed a suggestive account of the crisis of modern literature and its tendency towards solipsism. The years since Eliot's criticism of poets who 'retire into their skulls' have not seen any reversal of the tendency to talk about oneself and, in many cases, largely to oneself. The truth in Eliot's myth now seems truer than ever: what Virginia Woolf referred to as 'the cramp and confinement of personality' now seems to be taken for

Conclusion

granted as the only possible arena of discourse. The results, with some few exceptions, have not been heartening. Anthony Hecht, reviewing a volume of poetry by Richard Wilbur, has observed that 'in this poetic era of arrogant solipsism and limp narcissism – when great, shaggy herds of poets write only about themselves, or about the casual workings of their rather tedious minds – it is essential to our sanity, salutary to our humility, and a minimal obeisance to the truth to acknowledge, with Wilbur ... the vast alterity, the 'otherness' of the world, that huge corrective to our self-sufficiency.'[12]

This is delightfully overstated, but not far off the mark. Essentially the same point is made by Wilbur in a poem called 'The Eye', which Hecht cites. Invoking St Lucy, the poet asks her to

> Forbid my vision
> To take itself for a curious angel.
> Remind me that I am here in body,
> A passenger, and rumpled. ...
>
> Correct my view
> That the far mountain is much diminished,
> That the fovea is prime composer,
> That the lid's closure frees me.
>
> Let me be touched
> By the alien hands of love forever,
> That this eye be not folly's loophole
> But giver of due regard.[13]

And it is not in poetry alone that the lid's closure has freed men into isolation. Critical movements usually lag behind their poetic counterparts; it is, therefore, only in the last twenty years that critical solipsism has developed a theoretical structure. It has, in fact, developed a number of such structures, which share a belief in the impossibility of determining the meaning of literary texts. E. D. Hirsch, Jr, the most trenchant and informed critic of the 'cognitive atheists' (his term), summarizes the consequences of their beliefs:

> since genuine knowledge of an author's meaning is impossible, all textual commentary is therefore really fiction or poetry. Emancipated by this insight, we can face the *écriture* of the past without illusion, as representing no stable or accessible meaning. We can write about writing with new-found creativity and freedom, knowing that we ourselves are creating a new fiction which will itself be fictionalized by those who read us. The challenge is to make these fictions creatively, interestingly, valuably.[14]

The standard defence of such a position is that it is inevitable, that, as post-Kantians, we are obliged to admit the relativity of experience to mind. The passage from F. H. Bradley cited earlier makes the same point: '... my experience falls within my own circle, a circle closed on the outside; and, with all its elements alike, every sphere is opaque to the others which surround it. ...'[15] But, as Hirsch points out, the metaphors of 'perspective' and 'point of view' which arise from this theoretical base do not dispose of the object. They suggest the difficulty of determining meaning, but do not, despite the arguments of the cognitive atheists, affirm the impossibility of doing so. Thus Eliot and others can subscribe to the truth of the Bradleyan position and yet retain a commonsense belief in the possibility of communication and therefore of a valid hermeneutics.

The consequences of the extreme relativist position are both funny and frightening. We have, on the one hand, the relativist critic who becomes indignant when *his* writings are misconstrued – the comic spectacle of the double standard, the meaning of which seems to escape the critic himself.[16] More seriously, the relativists themselves do not seem to have faced all of the implications of the relativist view. The case of a critic who has faced most of them – Harold Bloom – is of particular interest.

Bloom's status as a relativist should be apparent. His approach to criticism centres upon poets' 'misreadings' of earlier poets. The act of misreading itself is inevitable; the forms misreading takes

are the poets' means of defence against the danger of being
overwhelmed by their predecessors. Bloom has worked out the
theoretical details of this paradigm with admirable thoroughness
in four books.[17] In doing so, he has reduced the history of modern
poetry to a single theme – the struggle of poets against their
'fathers'. All writing, for Bloom, is about the struggle to write. As
Denis Donoghue has noted,

> Bloom presents literary history since the Enlightenment as one
> story and one story only, a struggle of gods and demiurges; the
> character of the struggle issues from obsession, trespass,
> defense, and revenge. ... The story has nothing to say of time,
> history, the world, society, manners, morals, chance.[18]

Poems are literally or nominally about other things, but Bloom
discerns the same pattern underlying them all; 'the center of his
interest is the self, the poet, the psychic drama disclosed in the
poem.'[19] This drama is inevitably the poet's own: our very
attempts to understand it involve us in misprision and revision.
The poem remains a hermetic experience, a means of self-defence
for the poet but not, certainly, a form of knowledge for the reader.
Blake misreads Milton and we misread Blake – Bradley's closed
circles again.

We tend to feel, of course, that we *can* understand earlier poets,
but Bloom, relentlessly working out his ideas, insists that there is
really nothing to understand. In *Kabbalah and Criticism*, he lists the
'four largest illusions that we tend to have about the nature of a
poem'.

1   There is the *religious* illusion, that a poem possesses or creates
a real *presence*.
2   There is the *organic* illusion, that a poem possesses or creates
a kind of *unity*.
3   There is the *rhetorical* illusion, that a poem possesses or
creates a definite *form*.
4   There is the *metaphysical* illusion, that a poem possesses or
creates *meaning*.[20]

Bloom is not, obviously, talking about illusion in the traditional sense (that art is a kind of trick, a fiction made to convey a truth), but in a radical sense: imagination, once conceived of as a means of perceiving truth, is now seen simply as a capacity for self-deception on the part of the poet and his reader alike. 'Poetry', Bloom asserts, 'is poems speaking to a poem, and is also that poem answering back with its defensive discourse.'[21] Literature becomes a set of funhouse mirrors reflecting each other in distorted ways, but not reflecting the external world at all.

One cannot argue with Bloom. His theory is, given its premises, unexceptionable. That it reduces literature and criticism to elaborate forms of autism is a fact which Bloom appears to face: 'Some of the consequences of what I am saying dismay even me.'[22] He nevertheless remains obstinately cheerful at the end of *Kabbalah and Criticism*, encouraged by the thought that some illusions, some misreadings, are 'stronger' than others. Blake's misreading of Milton's Satan is stronger than C. S. Lewis's; Eliot's misreading is 'pitifully weak'.[23] Bloom's ideas preclude evaluation, but he naturally retains the desire to evaluate. The traditional terms of judgment therefore undergo a sea-change, and the result – covertly evaluative vocabulary in a system which denies the possibility of evaluation – is what might be called Muscular Criticism.

With interpretation and evaluation disposed of, there is little left for criticism to do. Adherents of the view that criticism is really fiction or poetry should, Hirsch suggests, label their works appropriately, indicating that any resemblance between their work and the author's intentions is purely coincidental.[24] Despite the philosophic pretensions and exotic vocabulary of the new schools, the idea of criticism as a purely individual, 'creative' response to literature has been around for a long time. It is the central premise of critical impressionism, which Eliot argued against in 'The Perfect Critic', and, for all the differences between them, Roland Barthes has much in common with Walter Pater. Barthes is, by his own admission, not interested in what Racine meant; nor was Pater, contemplating the Mona Lisa, interested in what Leonardo meant.

We need not return, of course, to the idea of authorial intention as the basis of 'true' criticism. But if criticism is to have any meaning, it must aim at knowledge: this point would be too obvious to require stating if it were not under attack by the Know-Nothing party of contemporary letters. In 1923, Eliot could presume that 'no exponent of criticism ... has ... ever made the preposterous assumption that criticism is an autotelic activity.'[25] But times change, and we must choose between just such a view and the concept of criticism as part of the larger enterprise of humane learning, which looks outward and seeks to understand the world. To reject that world – the characteristic *gran rifiuto* of contemporary criticism – is to invite sterility. While we distrust, rightly, criticism which evaluates literature by non-literary standards, we cannot act as if nothing existed outside our minds. Eliot, F. R. Leavis, and Yvor Winters (to name three critics who did not agree on many things) share the belief that literature can be judged, and that it must be judged with reference to the world which the artist shares with his readers. They are perhaps the last of the major critics to see criticism as a moral activity.

Eliot, too, had his moments of doubt about the efficacy of language, and the meditations on language in *Four Quartets* show that those doubts never left him. For the poet,

> each venture
> Is a new beginning, a raid on the inarticulate
> With shabby equipment always deteriorating
> In the general mess of imprecision of feeling,
> Undisciplined squads of emotion.[26]

For the poet, and the critic,

> There is only the fight to recover what has been lost
> And found and lost again and again: and now, under conditions
> That seem unpropitious.[27]

To take for granted the impossibility of understanding, however, is a counsel of despair: 'For us, there is only the trying. The rest is not our business.'[28]

Conclusion

In the 'trying' – a word Eliot uses with almost all of its multiple meanings – the tradition is a sustaining force.[29] With its help, some poets manage to create that combination of movement and stillness which characterizes Eliot's Chinese jar, Yeats's lapis lazuli, and Keats's Grecian urn – the impossible union of life and death, speech and silence, real and ideal form. Without faith in the possibility of comprehending their success, we ensure that the literature of the past will be merely 'old stones that cannot be deciphered'.[30] Eliot's historical metaphor for the growth of 'psychologism' is therefore more than an *entrée* to his criticism or a way of accounting for the impasse of postmodernism: it implies a critique of the cognitive atheists and suggests the need for a thoroughgoing revaluation of modern critical theory. The results of that revaluation, if we have the courage to undertake it, will determine the course and quality of criticism in the years ahead; and, as Eliot and Arnold knew, the state of critical discourse has much to tell us about the health of our society as a whole.

In fact, Eliot's diagnosis of our malaise implies the possibility of sociological as well as literary treatment. His own sociological essays, written long after the Clark Lectures, do not approach the problem of solipsism and are in any case, as I suggested at the beginning, beyond the scope of this study. But the importance of Eliot's ideas in the analysis of social issues is apparent in the work of writers who arrived independently at similar conclusions. In *The Revolt of the Masses* (1930), Ortega y Gasset discusses the 'hermeticism of soul' which characterizes mass-man; Christopher Lasch, in *The Culture of Narcissism* (1978), analyses the failures and dangers of American culture as symptoms of the preoccupation with self; and it would not be difficult to trace a particular tradition of social commentary which links Eliot, Ortega y Gasset, Lasch and others.[31]

The Clark Lectures invite us, then, to a new conception both of the unity of Eliot's work in various fields and its relation to the traditions from which it grew. I have confined myself to a single tradition of historiography and rhetoric, and have avoided theoretical questions (about the nature of mythography in historical writing, for example) as much as possible. We are still far from attaining that whole view of Eliot, in himself and in the

Conclusion

tradition, which is the ideal, but recent studies of Eliot's work take for granted a far wider range of contexts than did critics twenty years ago.[32] We have made some progress, and, to conclude with Eliot's own words,

> the end of all our exploring
> Will be to arrive where we started
> And know the place for the first time.[33]

Appendix A
Eliot, Pound and Modernist Criticism

In *Romantic Image*, Frank Kermode shows how Yeats arrived at a Symbolist aesthetic through his study of Blake, long before he was familiar with the French Symbolists: facing a particular aesthetic problem, Yeats arrived independently at conclusions strikingly similar to those of his contemporaries in France. Similarity of ideas does not, then, necessarily indicate influence. Poets of the Romantic tradition, which modernism develops and modifies, are bound to display certain family features, even if (as in the cases of Hulme and Eliot) the critical stance is one of apparent hostility to Romantic ideas.[1]

With Eliot, as I have suggested, the question of influence is also secondary. Eliot began his critical career with the perception of a problem – the relation of subject and object in poetry. In his attempt to create a style both individual and adequate, and to discover what was most useful to him in the European past, he developed an aesthetic which is, as Kermode shows, partly Symbolist. It is also partly Romantic, in the senses I have defined; it is also, for want of a better term, Thomist – based upon a 'realist' conception of language, at least as a metaphor – and, in its prolonged working-out, wholly Eliot's own.

In refraining from asserting influence, I may seem to be arguing against Eliot himself. Certainly the man who said 'Immature poets imitate; mature poets steal'[2] was willing to acknowledge his debts, and the role of tradition described in 'Tradition and the Individual Talent' is that of a helpful and liberating force, not that of the father-with-shears described by Bloom. Whichever view is closer to the truth, our attempts to define the influence of the tradition are, in the absence of 'hard' evidence, often rather speculative. The discussion of *contemporary* influence is still more speculative, and the problems involved in it can best be illustrated by the question of Pound and Eliot as mutual critical influences.

Valerie Eliot's publication of the complete, original *Waste Land* has raised again the question of Pound's influence upon Eliot.[3] That the influence existed has never been in doubt: Eliot's dedication to the

Conclusion

tradition, which is the ideal, but recent studies of Eliot's work take for granted a far wider range of contexts than did critics twenty years ago.[32] We have made some progress, and, to conclude with Eliot's own words,

> the end of all our exploring
> Will be to arrive where we started
> And know the place for the first time.[33]

Appendix A
Eliot, Pound and Modernist Criticism

In *Romantic Image*, Frank Kermode shows how Yeats arrived at a Symbolist aesthetic through his study of Blake, long before he was familiar with the French Symbolists: facing a particular aesthetic problem, Yeats arrived independently at conclusions strikingly similar to those of his contemporaries in France. Similarity of ideas does not, then, necessarily indicate influence. Poets of the Romantic tradition, which modernism develops and modifies, are bound to display certain family features, even if (as in the cases of Hulme and Eliot) the critical stance is one of apparent hostility to Romantic ideas.[1]

With Eliot, as I have suggested, the question of influence is also secondary. Eliot began his critical career with the perception of a problem – the relation of subject and object in poetry. In his attempt to create a style both individual and adequate, and to discover what was most useful to him in the European past, he developed an aesthetic which is, as Kermode shows, partly Symbolist. It is also partly Romantic, in the senses I have defined; it is also, for want of a better term, Thomist – based upon a 'realist' conception of language, at least as a metaphor – and, in its prolonged working-out, wholly Eliot's own.

In refraining from asserting influence, I may seem to be arguing against Eliot himself. Certainly the man who said 'Immature poets imitate; mature poets steal'[2] was willing to acknowledge his debts, and the role of tradition described in 'Tradition and the Individual Talent' is that of a helpful and liberating force, not that of the father-with-shears described by Bloom. Whichever view is closer to the truth, our attempts to define the influence of the tradition are, in the absence of 'hard' evidence, often rather speculative. The discussion of *contemporary* influence is still more speculative, and the problems involved in it can best be illustrated by the question of Pound and Eliot as mutual critical influences.

Valerie Eliot's publication of the complete, original *Waste Land* has raised again the question of Pound's influence upon Eliot.[3] That the influence existed has never been in doubt: Eliot's dedication to the

Appendix A

'miglior fabbro', his praise of Pound, and his letters to the 'cher maître' put it beyond question.[4] The fact that Pound edited *The Waste Land* has created the impression in many readers' minds that Eliot was dependent upon Pound's criticism; this in turn 'confirms' the idea, which one hears on occasion, that Eliot's essays merely develop ideas which appear first in Pound's writings. Hence Yvor Winters concludes his essay on Eliot with a suggestion of conspiratorial collaboration:

> And when one seeks closely to find the features of the divinity, the primal spirit of the age to whose will surrender is required, one may well be appalled; for behind the shadows thrown by veil after veil of indeterminate prose one will find, if one is patient, the face of Ezra Pound in apotheosis.[5]

The fact that Pound was involved with so many writers at crucial times in their careers has led more than one critic to see in him the *fons et origo* of modernism; even Hugh Kenner's often admirable book *The Pound Era* creates this impression.[6]

But the history of ideas is seldom this clear. Pound himself said that Eliot had 'trained himself *and* modernized himself *on his own*',[7] and the early poems preserved in the Berg Collection of the New York Public Library confirm that he had. One finds in them echoes of Byron, Browning, and Swinburne, more or less subtly incorporated into the whole, but there is also a distinctive note quite unlike that of any other poetry of the period. These poems were written in 1909 and 1910; Eliot did not meet Pound until 1914.

We cannot, however, simply dismiss the whole matter of influence. The great moderns – Yeats, Lewis, Pound, and Eliot – knew and were influenced by one another.[8] The historian's problem is therefore to discriminate between small points of particular influence (Pound telling Eliot to read Gourmont, for example) and, on the other hand, the 'spirit of the age', which, being a spirit, is not subject to anatomization.

We speak vaguely of an idea's being 'in the air' at a certain time, and deplore our vagueness in doing so; but even the most scrupulous scholar has considerable difficulty in being more precise. The attempt to trace an idea's movement most often leads the investigator in circles. We have, for example, cited numerous passages which show Eliot's concern with the clear image in poetry. The following example (the reader may well be tired of it by now, as I am) can stand for many others: '... the suggestiveness is the aura around a bright clear centre ... you cannot have the aura alone.'[9] This statement, written in 1921, is reminiscent of declarations in Pound's prose: 'Go in fear of abstractions', or this from 'A Retrospect': modern poetry 'will not try to seem forcible by rhetorical din, and luxurious riot. We will have fewer adjectives impeding the shock and stroke of it.'[10] Does Eliot, then, whose 'precise realizable pictures'

Appendix A

Pound praised in his review of *Prufrock and Other Observations*, derive part of his poetic theory of practice from Imagism?[11] Perhaps. And perhaps we can trace Pound's ideas back to Hulme:

> The essence of poetry to most people is that it must lead them to a beyond of some kind. Verse strictly confined to the earthly and the definite (Keats is full of it) might seem to them to be excellent writing, excellent craftsmanship, but not poetry. So much has romanticism debauched us, that, without some form of vagueness, we deny the highest.[12]

And Eliot, we know, refers favorably to Hulme, so the genealogy Hulme – Pound – Eliot seems easily established.

But Eliot had written 'Prufrock' before meeting Pound, and Pound had extolled the directness and clarity of medieval verse (in *The Spirit of Romance*) before meeting Hulme.[13] The tidiness of the chronology is somewhat sullied. If we recall that this is also the period of Futurism, of Expressionism, of Dada, we can study the general upheaval in the arts without recourse to the invidious idea of who said what first. What we can look for is a general clarification of doctrine as time goes on. 'Modernism' begins with the simple perception that certain forms are outmoded, that traditional devices in poetry will no longer encompass and express the experience of men in the twentieth century: its origins are negative. A particular method such as 'des images' is the *last* step in a process of analysis which begins as unanalysed dissatisfaction. The 'classic' statements of modernist criticism are not, therefore, those which were written first.

The hunting of sources among modern critics is the result of a false belief: that poets, being dealers in words, are influenced primarily *by* words. It should be obvious that modernism is best studied across 'disciplinary' lines, but no general study has yet been made, for example, of the relationship between modernist poetry and modern painting. Wyndham Lewis and e. e. cummings actually were painters; William Carlos Williams, Gertrude Stein, and Wallace Stevens maintained lifelong interests in contemporary painting; Apollinaire was a 'poète fondé en peinture'; Marinetti influenced both painting and poetry. One link between these arts is the modern poet's desire to escape from the tyranny of statement into the purity of physical sensation. When Pound writes, in 'L'Art, 1910',

> Green arsenic smeared on an egg-white cloth,
> Crushed strawberries! Come, let us feast our eyes,[14]

we are not supposed to ask what arsenic and strawberries are doing on the same tablecloth: it would be as foolish to ask why the half-peeled

Appendix A

orange in a Dutch still-life was not eaten. The poem exists to convey the starkness of three pure colours juxtaposed.

The relationship of literature to music is similarly worthy of exploration. Pound knew Antheil and Dolmetsch, and wrote a setting of Villon's *Testament*; Eliot was fascinated both by the music-hall and by the new classicism of Stravinsky. It is said on occasion that the image of the dancer in 'Little Gidding' II is out of Yeats, and some such allusion is no doubt intended, but Eliot's articles on the Russian ballet tell us more about the significance of the metaphor in Eliot's mind.[15] Poets do not simply read poetry, and art is too complex a matter to emerge merely from past art: as obvious as this idea is, it must be reiterated in the face of those modern critics who see specifically *literary* influence everywhere.

C. K. Stead, whose arguments we have already invoked, has constructed a tentative but convincing history of the emergence of the modern poet's preoccupation with technique as a means of escape from opinion and didacticism. The Georgians, Yeats and Eliot all have their places in the development of a purer poetic speech; none of them is less original for having taken part in a movement which included them all. Pound, forestalling critics who might relate his work to that of Spire and Arcos, wrote that

> I do not think that I have copied their work, and they certainly have not copied mine. We are contemporary and as sonnets of a certain sort were once written on both sides of the channel, so these short poems depicting certain phases of contemporary life are now written on both sides of the channel; with, of course, personal differences.[16]

Eliot says very much the same thing: 'A common inheritance and a common cause unite artists consciously or unconsciously: it must be admitted that the union is mostly unconscious. Between [sic] the true artists of any time there is, I believe, an unconscious community.'[17] Newton and Leibniz discovered calculus at about the same time, and we do not discuss their 'influence' upon each other.

Given 'the spirit of the age', the general cultural climate within which Pound and Eliot worked, we still have the problem of establishing what we can about Pound and Eliot as mutual critical influences. Even the casual reader of Pound's criticism comes across phrases and ideas which call to mind the generally better-known formulations of Eliot. When he reads this passage in Pound's 'Retrospect' – 'Be influenced by as many great artists as you can, but have the decency either to acknowledge the debt outright, or try to conceal it'[18] – he is likely to think of Eliot's epigrammatic 'Immature poets imitate; mature poets steal.'[19] Pound asserts that

> when Italians were writing excellent and clear prose – in the time of

Appendix A

Henry VIII – Englishmen could scarcely make a clear prose formulation even in documents of state and instructions to envoys; so backward were things in this island, so rude in prose the language which had been exquisite in the lyrics of Chaucer.[20]

And, we recall, Eliot declares that 'the French of Montaigne is a mature language, and the English of Florio's living translation is not.'[21]

In these cases, Pound's statement is the first to appear; in other instances, Eliot is the apparent originator. The concept of 'comparison and analysis' and 'a sense of fact' dominate Eliot's definition of proper, practical criticism from the beginning of his career. We find Pound, in the 1930s, asserting that education in criticism can profit from 'the parallels of biological study based upon EXAMINATION and COMPARISON of particular specimens', and that criticism should be based upon 'an inexorable demand for the facts'.[22] In a third category, there are ideas which both Pound and Eliot recur to constantly – that the health of a language depends upon its poets, that the serious writer must immerse himself in the poetry of the past and of other languages.

I submit these examples as evidence, almost randomly chosen from a multitude of possibilities, of the practical difficulties involved in the search for sources. In a creative relationship of such intimacy (Pound editing the *Waste Land* manuscripts, Eliot criticizing the early *Cantos*) the study of ontogenesis is not particularly useful.[23]

There remain, however, several small areas in which comparisons are illuminating. There are, for example, the authorities whom Pound and Eliot share. At least two of these, Gourmont and James, are clearly Pound's enthusiasms at the beginning; he refers to Gourmont in his letters as early as 1913, and Eliot acknowledges the influence of Pound in getting him to read both writers.[24] Both Eliot and Pound refer to Gautier, Corbière, and Laforgue with approval; Gautier was, of course, the inspiration for the revival of quatrain form in the work of both poets.[25] They are agreed, too, that Dante is the ideal model for beginning poets, since he has no vices or eccentricities of style; other saints in the calendar of style are Flaubert and Stendhal.[26]

The convictions represented by these figures result naturally in similar judgments of works of literature. Neither Eliot nor Pound liked Goethe, though Eliot was obliged to pretend that he did when he received the Hanseatic Goethe Prize in 1955.[27] Eliot's supposed dislike of Milton created an uproar in the 1930s, but Pound was far more intemperate in denouncing 'the abominable dogbiscuit of Milton's rhetoric'.[28] In the general condemnation of the Romantics in which both men indulged, Landor alone escapes: he is extolled by both, Eliot calling him 'an undoubted master of verse and prose' and Pound pronouncing him – with the exaggeration which makes much of his criticism a delight to

Appendix A

read – 'the only complete and serious man of letters ever born in these islands.'[29]

The same ideas about the rise and fall of language are apt to appear in Eliot's and Pound's prose. Eliot asks us to

> Compare a medieval theologian or mystic ... with any 'liberal' sermon since Schleiermacher, and you will observe that words have changed their meanings. What they have lost is definite, and what they have gained is indefinite.[30]

Pound asserts that

> What the renaissance gained in direct examination of natural phenomena, it in part lost in losing the feel and desire for exact descriptive terms. I mean that the medieval mind had little but words to deal with, and it was more careful in its definitions and verbiage.[31]

There is the same exasperated sense of England's unconquerable provincialism:

> Whenever one attempts to demonstrate the difference between serious and unserious work, one is told that 'it is merely a technical discussion.' It has rested at that – in England it has rested at that for more than three hundred years. [Pound][32]

> An attitude which might find voice in words like these ['Decadence in art is always caused by professionalism'] is behind all of British slackness for a hundred years and more: the dislike of the specialist. [Eliot][33]

There are similarities of critical technique, too, despite the marked differences between Pound's style and Eliot's. A prominent feature in both is a certain evasion of argument. Eliot was inclined to circumvent 'proof' by the means of rhetorical persuasion we have examined; Pound, impatient with the imperceptive, is apt to say 'I would rather play tennis. I shall not argue.'[34] He states his views with a candid dogmatism. The reader can take them or leave them.

At the heart of Pound's breezy critical essays is a judicious use of quotation. Pound's eye for the perfect example is nearly as good as Eliot's, and the range of literatures referred to is even more varied. In 'The Serious Artist', for example, Pound ranges over all of Europe to gather examples of the 'passionate simplicity which is beyond the precisions of the intellect'. These four quotations occur on a single page:

Appendix A

Perch'io non spero di tornar già mai
Ballatetta, in Toscana;

S'ils n'ayment fors que pour l'argent,
On ne les ayme que pour l'heure;

The fire that stirs about her, when she stirs;

Ne maeg werigmod wryde withstondan
ne se hreo hyge helpe gefremman:
forthon domgeorne dreorigne oft
in hyra breostcofan bindath faeste.[35]

Any reader of Eliot is familiar with the technique; in 'Andrew Marvell', Eliot cites Horace and Catullus, Gautier and Villon, Jonson and Dryden in support of his points about 'wit'.[36]

Quotation nevertheless serves different ends for the two critics. Eliot works short passages, followed by his own comments, into the texture of a shaped and controlled argument. Pound is inclined to quotation at length: despite his blasts at the uninformed public, he seems to have considerable faith in the reader's ability to see for himself how good the material is. Pound's essays on Lionel Johnson, Gourmont, and Henry James make little comment on the long passages he transcribes; the essay on Arnaut Daniel is almost wholly given over to transcription of Daniel's poems and Pound's translations.[37] This confidence in the reader's perception allows for little distortion on the critic's part, but it likewise allows him little scope for the development of his own ideas.

The differences in taste between Eliot and Pound are as interesting as the similarities in judgments and choice of exemplars. They differ strongly on Swinburne, for example, whose *Triumph of Time* Pound found 'full of sheer imagism, of passages faultless'; Eliot found the same poem almost comic in its separation of sound and sense.[38] These contrary views of Swinburne reappear in the two critics' difference of opinion over the Greek dramatists. Pound finds the Greeks, apart from Homer, to be 'rather Swinburnian', and defends Swinburne's translations accordingly; Eliot, on the other hand, condemns Gilbert Murray's translation of *Medea* because 'Greek poetry will never have the slightest vitalizing effect upon English poetry if it can only appear masquerading as a vulgar debasement of the eminently personal idiom of Swinburne.'[39]

The differences between the two men when they define 'the tradition' are indicative not so much of profoundly opposed views of literature as of differing needs in the writing of poetry. Pound needed Confucius, Homer, and Arnaut Daniel much as Eliot needed Dante, the Elizabethan dramatists, and Laforgue. It is a measure of great criticism that, written frequently for immediate and personal ends, it nevertheless achieves

Appendix A

insights which prove to be of permanent value in our perception of the past. Both Pound and Eliot were concerned primarily with the renewal of poetry in their time, but the critical 'by-product' – Eliot's term – has proven to have a value of its own.

Appendix B
Eliot and Philosophical Aesthetics

Everything is what it is, and not another thing.
                                                    Bishop Butler

I have not discussed Eliot's relation to philosophy in the body of this book for several reasons, the most obvious being that the subject is beyond the scope of my study. I have suggested at various points that 'ontology', and other philosophical terms in Eliot's criticism, were primarily metaphors for the general problem of subject and object in poetry, and in Chapter 3 I suggested that criticism itself was, for Eliot, a branch of rhetoric rather than of philosophy. There is much in Eliot's comments on his own work to support these contentions, quite apart from the case I have made for them. Eliot claimed to have no capacity for abstruse thought, and said that his philosophical studies had left him with no more than a sense of three philosophers' styles.[1] He wrote to Paul Elmer More that he was not a systematic thinker, if he was a thinker at all, and admitted to E. M. Forster that the essays' apparent logic concealed an element of bluff; when his dissertation on Bradley was published in 1964, Eliot claimed that he could no longer understand it.[2]

There is nevertheless a considerable body of work devoted to tracing the links between Bradley and Eliot, and it is too important to ignore. The first important document is Anne C. Bolgan's essay, 'The Philosophy of F. H. Bradley and the Mind and Art of T. S. Eliot: An Introduction', published in 1971. This and the fuller treatment in Professor Bolgan's book *What the Thunder Really Said* established the case for Bradley as the decisive influence in Eliot's intellectual development.[3] The argument for a Bradleyan interpretation of Eliot's literary criticism has been set forth in various places, most notably in Lewis Freed's second book and the Mowbray Allan volume referred to earlier.

There is, moreover, much in Eliot's philosophical writing which appears to bear directly on the issues we have discussed. The dissertation includes a chapter on 'Solipsism', for example, and Bradley's declaration that 'the union in all perception of thought with sense ... is the one foundation of truth' is no doubt related in some way to the concept of dissociation of sensibility.[4] One can understand why more than one critic has been led to see in Bradley the 'onlie begetter' of Eliot's criticism. It is necessary, however, to make some distinctions.

(a) Eliot's general indebtedness to Bradley is beyond question, but the particular relation of Eliot's literary criticism to Bradley's philosophy remains problematic. I am inclined to agree with Richard Wollheim, who concludes a discussion of Eliot's theories of tradition and literary history with the observation that they are 'only marginally grounded in philosophy'.[5] There is a great difference between *an article of belief in epistemology* and *a statement of value in aesthetics*. The subject-matters of metaphysics and epistemology – the nature of reality and the means by which we know it – give rise inevitably to questions about the role and validity of sense-perception in cognition. But to affirm the central place of sense-perception in poetry is not to endorse a philosophic position, and an aesthetic formulation does not necessarily derive from an epistemology. As my discussion of Eliot's criticism shows (and as Kermode and Stead have shown in different ways), his aesthetic is comprehensible in purely literary terms, without recourse to the *minutiae* of any philosophical system. Ockham's razor is applicable here: attempts to explain the criticism with reference to Eliot's philosophy are, in literary terms, supererogatory, although they are undoubtedly useful in suggesting relationships among Eliot's various activities. There will certainly be resemblances between the philosophy and the criticism as products of a single mind and personality, but they are not the same thing.

I do not, then, oppose philosophical explications of Eliot so much as the tendency to confuse them with the particular value of his criticism. There are critics in whose work philosophy plays a greater role than it does in Eliot's. Writing about Coleridge, for example, J. R. de J. Jackson notes 'how closely the leading themes of Coleridge's practical and theoretical criticism are linked to a metaphysical structure of an elaborate and unfamiliar kind.' But even in the case of Coleridge, the only real philosopher-critic in our literature, 'it is important ... that we avoid mistaking the philosophical background of Coleridge's criticism for his special contribution.'[6]

We would do well to keep this distinction in mind as we read Eliot's criticism. None of the commentators I have mentioned goes so far as to equate the value of Eliot's criticism with its supposed philosophical content, and all of them make interesting points. But the general tendency of this sort of analysis is to locate the greatness of Eliot's criticism in its supposedly systematic nature, in theory rather than practice, and to give the criticism a *kind* of unity which Eliot never claimed for it. The most devoted exegesis of Eliot's thought cannot make

Appendix B

him into more than a derivative and eclectic philosopher – a secondhand Bradley – but he is a great and original critic within the tradition that he modifies and carries on. He is not of the company of Kant, Schelling and Croce: that is, he is not primarily a theoretician. In his criticism, Eliot belongs rather to a tradition of specifically literary thought which begins in England with Sidney (practically speaking) and which is the only thing necessary to render him comprehensible. That tradition is neither inferior to philosophy nor dependent upon it, but *another thing*.

(b) The desire to relate Eliot's criticism to his philosophical work is prompted not only by the vocabulary and concerns common to them both, but by the facts of chronology. Eliot's philosophical work (the dissertation on Bradley and a number of articles and reviews) was done during the years 1913–18, and was followed immediately by the period of Eliot's greatest criticism.[7] *Post hoc, ergo propter hoc*. But the preoccupations which appear in Eliot's philosophical studies, his criticism and his poetry predate, as Lyndall Gordon has shown, his serious work in any one of these disciplines – a fact which accounts for the variety of Eliot's interests and his tendency to relate them. It is therefore impossible to assert the priority of philosophy among Eliot's concerns: the study of philosophy was one manifestation of interests which were ultimately – even in Eliot's undergraduate years – religious.

(c) Even if the concept of dissociation of sensibility were derived from Bradley and only from Bradley, the myth of literary history in which it is embodied, and without which it would remain at a very high level of abstraction, could only have been derived from literary criticism – specifically, as I have suggested, the historical mythography of the Romantic poets. It is general knowledge, if not quite a commonplace, that the Romantics were also interested in the relation of subject and object in poetry; it seems plausible to suppose, then, that Eliot's ideas about literature came primarily from literary sources, while his vocabulary and analogies were influenced by his philosophical reading. His relation to Keats, Coleridge and Victorian historiography (as well as his use of Gourmont, which has been noted by several commentators) is substantive. His relation to Bradley, though it may have been philosophically decisive, is, in terms of literary significance, slight.

(d) Finally, it is worth noting that Bradley is not the only 'source' whose philosophic influence on Eliot has been argued. Various academics have maintained that Eliot's criticism is based upon, or best understood with reference to, the philosophy of Aristotle, Kant or Collingwood.[8] Without entering into the complexities of these arguments, we can draw at least two conclusions from them: (i) These accounts of Eliot's philosophy are incompatible. Unless we broaden terms to the point of meaninglessness, Eliot cannot be an Aristotelian and a Bradleyan, an adherent of Kant's aesthetics and Collingwood's. (ii) If Eliot's criticism is ambiguous enough

Appendix B

to allow of such radically different readings, its philosophical basis is clearly too slight to be analysed without recourse to Eliot's other writings – a procedure which is, as I suggested earlier, not really a contribution to our knowledge of the *criticism* at all.

These are, of course, simply marginal notes in a discussion which has already generated a number of books and articles. I make these four points because, in our desire to see the unity of Eliot's mind, we sometimes overlook the *differentiae* of various disciplines. That the unity is there is unquestionable, and I suggested, at the end of Chapter 1, some of the ways in which Eliot's literary, religious and political views are related: but the parts exist as certainly as the whole, and we overlook the distinctions at our peril. Eliot produced his most unsatisfactory work of criticism, *After Strange Gods*, when he combined religious, social and literary criticism in a single discussion. Even when the connections can be traced, as they can between Eliot's philosophical vocabulary and his literary criticism, we must be careful not to *transpose* the criticism into philosophical terms, as a pianist might transpose an orchestral work for his own instrument. Such a procedure leads, at best, to a form of the genetic fallacy (B comes from A, and is therefore really A in disguise), at worst, to a real misreading of the texts.

I have spoken so far, for clarity's sake, largely as if the philosophical and literary accounts of Eliot's criticism were incompatible alternatives. They are not, of course, and my fifth point might well be the obvious statement that one kind of influence does not preclude others. As A. D. Nuttall has shown, solipsistic fear has haunted western literature since the eighteenth century.[9] Philosophy and literature have nourished each other – or, as Eliot would contend, have corrupted each other – to the point at which it is difficult to sort out literary and philosophical influences, much less to discount one group in favour of the other. As I said in the Introduction (I seem, in Eliotic fashion, to have ended where I began), I have followed what seem to me the most direct lines of descent.

Our picture of Eliot's intellectual development is already fairly detailed. With the publication of the remaining unpublished lectures, and of his letters, including those in presently restricted collections, that picture will be very nearly complete, and a number of controversies will be laid to rest. In the meantime, there is surely room in the world for a certain amount of creative disagreement about the sources of Eliot's thought.

Notes

Introduction

1 'John Donne', *Nation and Athenaeum*, XXXIII:10 (9 June 1923), p. 328.
2 See R. P. Blackmur, *The Lion and the Honeycomb* (New York: Harcourt, Brace, 1955), pp. 162–75. Other good treatments are Muriel Bradbrook, 'Eliot's Critical Method', in B. Rajan, ed., *T. S. Eliot: A Study of His Writings by Several Hands* (London: Dobson, 1947), pp. 119–28, and Stanley Edgar Hyman, 'T. S. Eliot and Tradition in Criticism', in *The Armed Vision* (New York: Knopf, 1948), pp. 73–105; see also John Chalker, 'Authority and Personality in Eliot's Criticism', in Graham Martin, ed., *Eliot in Perspective: A Symposium* (London: Macmillan, 1970), pp. 194–210. Several of the specialized essays in David Newton-de Molina, ed., *The Literary Criticism of T. S. Eliot: New Essays* (London: Athlone, 1977) are excellent.
3 'The Frontiers of Criticism' (1956), *OPAP* 106; 'To Criticize the Critic' (1961), *TCTC* 16.
4 'The Local Flavour' (1919), *SW* 37.
5 'To Criticize the Critic', *TCTC* 14.
6 'The Possibility of a Poetic Drama' (1920), *SW* 61; 'Swinburne as Poet' (1920), *SE* 323.
7 Bernard Bergonzi, *T. S. Eliot* (New York: Macmillan, 1972), p. 58.
8 'The Perfect Critic' (1920), *SW* 11.
9 See *TLS* 985 (2 December 1920), 795, for comment on the 'malice' that occasionally leads Eliot 'into a practice contrary to those excellent principles which he states so well'.
10 'Swinburne as Critic' (1919), *SW* 21–22.
11 Bradbrook, op. cit., p. 127.
12 *SE* 297.
13 'Reflections on *Vers Libre*' (1917), *TCTC* 187.
14 Lyndall Gordon, *Eliot's Early Years* (New York: Oxford, 1977), pp. 15–36, 58.

15 The sense in which the word 'myth' is used in this study is explained in Chapter 1.
16 'Baudelaire' (1930), *SE* 424.
17 George Bornstein, *Transformations of Romanticism in Yeats, Eliot, and Stevens* (Chicago: University of Chicago Press, 1976).
18 'Preface', *SW* viii.
19 See John D. Margolis, *T. S. Eliot's Intellectual Development, 1922–1939* (Chicago: University of Chicago Press, 1972); Roger Kojecky, *T. S. Eliot's Social Criticism* (New York: Farrar, Straus, 1972); William M. Chace, *The Political Identities of Ezra Pound and T. S. Eliot* (Stanford: Stanford University Press, 1973); Lyndall Gordon, op. cit.; G. H. Bantock, *T. S. Eliot and Education* (New York: Random House, 1969).
20 Bornstein, op. cit., p. 104.
21 '... I am certain of one thing: that I have written best about writers who have influenced my own poetry'. ('To Criticize the Critic' [1961], *TCTC* 20.)
22 Bradbrook, op. cit., p. 122.

1 History and Poetry

1 Hugh Kenner, *The Invisible Poet: T. S. Eliot* (London: Methuen, 1960), p. 82.
2 *Metaphysical Lyrics and Poems of the Seventeenth Century: Donne to Butler*, ed. H. J. C. Grierson (Oxford: Clarendon, 1921).
3 'A Sceptical Patrician', *Athenaeum* 4647 (23 May 1919), p. 362. Lyndall Gordon in her book, *Eliot's Early Years* (New York: Oxford, 1977) records that Eliot, walking in Boston one day in 1909 or 1910, 'saw the streets suddenly shrink and divide' (p. 15) – a 'metaphysical' experience which had a profound effect on his life, and which surely lies behind his conviction that the most intense awareness encompasses more than the intellect.
4 'Philip Massinger' (1920), *SE* 209–10.
5 'Swinburne as Critic' (1919), *SW* 23.
6 'The Metaphysical Poets' (1921), *SE* 287.
7 Ibid. 288.
8 See D. E. S. Maxwell's discussion of this poem in *The Poetry of T. S. Eliot* (London: Routledge & Kegan Paul, 1952), pp. 74–6.
9 Frank Kermode, *Romantic Image* (New York: Vintage, 1957), p. 142.
10 See C. S. Lewis, *'De Descriptione Temporum'*, in *They Asked For a Paper* (London: Bles, 1962), pp. 9–25.
11 *HJD* 9. The other papers were 'Andrew Marvell' and 'John Dryden', also written in 1921.
12 Bernard Bergonzi, *T. S. Eliot* (New York: Macmillan, 1972), p. 69.
13 The lectures were delivered in the Hall of Trinity College between

26 January and 9 March 1926; the general title is *Lectures on the Metaphysical Poetry of the Seventeenth Century, with special reference to Donne, Crashaw and Cowley*. Although the lectures themselves have never been published, a translation of the third lecture by Jean de Menasce appeared in *Chroniques* 3 (Paris, 1927), pp. 149–73 (*Le roseau d'or*, 14), under the title 'Deux attitudes mystiques: Dante et Donne'. The translation differs in some minor respects from the original.

Each lecture is between twenty-one and twenty-six pages in length. The text is a fair, double-spaced typescript with emendations in Eliot's hand. Eliot gave this fair copy to John Hayward, who had it bound: the volume is now part of the Hayward Bequest at King's College, Cambridge, where Hayward had been an Exhibitioner. In the classification of A. N. L. Munby, late Fellow and Librarian of King's College, the lectures are Item P6 in the Hayward Bequest.

The lectures will be referred to parenthetically in the text by means of the initials CL, a Roman numeral for the lecture number and an Arabic numeral for the page within the lecture, e.g. CL VII: 12.

14 Samuel Johnson, 'Life of Cowley'.
15 Eliot's definition is also reminiscent of Coleridge's concept of the imagination, which can reconcile 'opposite or discordant qualities' (*Biographia Literaria*, Chapter XIV). The relevant passage is cited in Eliot's 1921 essay on Andrew Marvell, *SE* 298.
16 'An Italian Critic on Donne and Crashaw', *TLS* 1248 (17 December 1925), p. 878.
17 Clark Lectures II: 17. I have inserted 'variant': the typescript has 'different' and Eliot apparently forgot to type in a noun.
18 'A Commentary', *Criterion* XI, 43 (January 1932), p. 274; 'To Criticize the Critic' (1961), *TCTC* 20–1.
19 Lewis Freed analyses Eliot's criticism in philosophical terms in *T. S. Eliot: The Critic as Philosopher* (West Lafayette, Indiana: Purdue University Press, 1979), which largely supplants his earlier *T. S. Eliot: Aesthetics and History* (La Salle, Illinois: Open Court, 1962). Mowbray Allan makes use of Eliot's dissertation in *T. S. Eliot's Impersonal Theory of Poetry* (Lewisburg, Pa.: Bucknell University Press, 1974). Allan and Freed both attempt to deal with Eliot's philosophy as such; I am more concerned with Eliot's use of philosophical terms as metaphors. See Appendix B, 'Eliot and Philosophical Aesthetics'.
20 Etienne Gilson, *History of Christian Philosophy in the Middle Ages* (New York: Random House, 1955), p. 499.
21 F. C. Copleston, *History of Philosophy: Volume II, Medieval Philosophy from Augustine to Scotus* (Westminster, Maryland: Newman, 1953), p. 139.
22 Swift – to mention just one further example – also deals with the decay of language. The unfallen Houyhnhnms in *Gulliver's Travels*

embody reason, and their language naturally reflects reality; it does not include a word for 'lie'. Much of *Gulliver's Travels* is a comedy about corrupt language and abortive attempts at its reform, such as those proposed by the Grand Academy of Lagado. Eliot called the 'Voyage to the Houyhnhnms' 'one of the greatest triumphs that the human soul has ever achieved' ('Ulysses, Order, and Myth', *Dial* LXXV, 5 (November 1923), p. 481).

23 Basil Willey, *The Seventeenth Century Background: Studies in the Thought of the Age in Relation to Poetry and Religion* (Harmondsworth: Penguin, 1972), pp. 83–4. Cf. Karl Stern's study of the conflict between the rational and intuitive faculties, *The Flight from Woman* (New York: Farrar, Straus, 1965), which includes an interesting chapter on Descartes.
24 The significance of Ockhamism as the beginning of a change in the European mind as a whole is remarked on by Josef Pieper: 'Inexorably, and justified by reasons on both sides, divorce was taking place between *fides* and *ratio* – to whose conjunction the energies of almost a thousand years had been devoted. What was taking place, in short, was the end of the Middle Ages' (*Scholasticism: Personalities and Problems of Medieval Philosophy* (New York: Pantheon, 1960), pp. 150–1).
25 Cited in Willey, p. 85.
26 Pound, too, was fascinated by what he called 'the keenly intellectual mysticism of Richard of St. Victor': see *The Spirit of Romance* (New York: New Directions, 1952), p. 22.
27 The phrase 'point of view' in Eliot's criticism usually suggests that the point of view in question is rather limited. An anthology of Eliot's prose, edited by John Hayward in 1941, was entitled *Points of View* – one of Possum's jokes.
28 A myth is the imaginative expression of some great truth in symbolic or fabulous form; the contemporary meaning of the word – a 'purely fictitious narrative' – is in itself an indication of the fallen state of poetry in the world.
29 'The Perfect Critic' (1920), *SW* 9.
30 Clark Lectures II: 25. The implications of Lockean psychology in the arts are fully developed in Ernest L. Tuveson, *The Imagination as a Means of Grace: Locke and the Aesthetics of Romanticism* (Berkeley: University of California Press, 1960). The rise of aesthetic subjectivism is also treated in Samuel Holt Monk, *The Sublime: A Study of Critical Theories in Eighteenth-Century England* (Ann Arbor: University of Michigan Press, 1960).
31 'Mr. Read and M. Fernandez', *Criterion* IV, 4 (October 1926), p. 753.
32 'Three Reformers', *TLS* 1397 (8 November 1928), p. 818. Jacques Maritain's *Three Reformers*, the subject of Eliot's review, is a study of Luther, Descartes, and Rousseau – the same representatives of

individualism mentioned by Eliot in the Clark Lectures II: 19.
33 Clark Lectures IV: 17. Eliot does not, of course, take into account the dramatic element in Donne's poetry; one can maintain plausibly that the speaker in some of Donne's poems does not express Donne's ideas any more than Edmund's 'naturalism' expresses Shakespeare's view of morality.
34 Clark Lectures V: 10, IV: 11, IV: 10. The reference to Praz is from *Secentismo e Marinismo in Inghilterra* (Florence: La Voce, 1925). On 'that borderland of fading and change', cf. J. B. Leishman: 'Donne seems to be continually distracted from the object of his contemplation by a kind of mental *tic*, a "concupiscence of wit" (to borrow his own phrase), a restless, itching ingenuity which cannot fully occupy itself or identify itself with anything. ...' (*The Monarch of Wit: An Analytical and Comparative Study of the Poetry of John Donne*, 3rd edn. (London: Hutchinson, 1957), p. 100.)
35 *The Complete Poetry of John Donne*, ed. John T. Shawcross (New York: Anchor, 1967), pp. 277–8.
36 In so far as one can establish reasons for such a change, the greatest single influence on Eliot's thought about Donne seems to have been the Mario Praz volume mentioned above; parts of the Clark Lectures are reminiscent of Praz's work. See Eliot's review, 'An Italian Critic on Donne and Crashaw', *TLS* 1248 (17 December 1925), p. 878.
37 'Donne in Our Time', in Theodore Spencer, ed., *A Garland for John Donne, 1631–1931* (Cambridge, Mass.: Harvard University Press, 1931), p. 8. Cf. 'Shakespeare and the Stoicism of Seneca' (1927), *SE* 139.
38 Spencer, op. cit., p. 9; my italics. Cf. Eliot's remarks on the unity of Dante's thought in 'Dante' (1929: *SE* 237–77) and the shorter essays on the poet written in 1920 ('Dante', *SW* 159–71) and 1950 ('What Dante Means to Me', *TCTC* 125–35).
39 Eliot reviewed the Martin edition for the *Dial* in 1928; the review appears in *FLA* as 'A Note on Richard Crashaw'.
40 A theme which Eliot himself would develop in *Four Quartets*.
41 Clark Lectures VI: 8. The preceding paragraph is a summary of Clark Lectures VI: 4–8.
42 An interesting study of St Theresa, Bernini, and Crashaw is Robert Petersson's *The Art of Ecstasy* (New York: Atheneum, 1970).
43 Discussing Chaucer's *Troilus and Criseyde* in *TLS* 547 (19 August 1926), Eliot remarks on the absence of emotion in the narrative:
> Nothing is more striking than the difference between the Troilus of Chaucer and the Troilus of Shakespeare. The latter is the passing fury of a prodigious and for the moment irresponsible Titan. ... The former is the sober statement of a man who was a member of a spiritual community. ... In Chaucer's poem there is

no moral judgment either upon Criseyde or upon Troilus, or upon Pandarus; only a high dispassionate view of the place of these persons in a fixed and firm moral order.

The comparison of Tennyson's Ulysses with Dante's (*SE* 250, 331) makes the same point. The earlier poets are objective and allow the story its own effect, to which their feelings add nothing; the later are emotionally excessive, cynical, or sentimental.

44 See 'A Note on Richard Crashaw' (1928), *FLA* 96, where the same passage is cited and analysed.
45 Clark Lectures VII: 2. Cf. Eliot's remarks on Addison, 'a symptom of the age which he announced', in *UPUC* 59–63; Addison's place in the development of Lockean aesthetics is discussed by Tuveson, op. cit.
46 'Four Elizabethan Dramatists', *SE* 116.
47 *SE* 54. Eliot uses almost exactly the same words in 'Shakespeare and the Stoicism of Seneca' (1927), *SE* 132.
48 *Dial* LXXXIII, 3 (September 1927), p. 263.
49 'Milton II' (1947), *OPAP* 168.
50 'Dante' (1929), *SE* 240; cf. Clark Lectures VI: 15.
51 'Kipling Redivivus', *Athenaeum* 4645 (9 May 1919), p. 298.
52 'The Romantic Generation, If It Existed', *Athenaeum* 4655 (18 July 1919), p. 616.
53 'Contemporary English Prose', *Vanity Fair* XX, 5 (July 1923), p. 51.
54 Ibid.
55 John Holloway, *The Victorian Sage: Studies in Argument* (New York: Norton, 1965), p. 3.
56 My summary and elaboration of Eliot's argument in the Clark Lectures must suggest what any careful reader of Eliot's prose already knows: that Eliot is himself a 'sage' in Holloway's sense, seeking to convey an elusive *sense* of literary history rather than to construct a logically compelling case. Eliot's means of persuasion are dealt with in Chapter 3.
57 Eliot's interest in Laforgue dates from 1909; see Lyndall Gordon, *Eliot's Early Years* (New York: Oxford, 1977), p. 29.
58 Eliot's frequent references to Stendhal and Flaubert, particularly in the uncollected prose, suggest that he valued their irony for its 'metaphysical' qualities: see 'Beyle and Balzac', *Athenaeum* 4648 (30 May 1919), pp. 392–3, and articles listed in Donald Gallup (*T. S. Eliot: A Bibliography*, revised and extended edition (New York: Harcourt, Brace, 1969)) as C23, C41, C46a, C54, C68, C73a, C77, C82, C85, C134, C147, C154, C180; see also *SW* xiii, 15, 34, 68; *FLA* 78; *SE* 63, 137, 152, 178, 202, 217–18, 297, 462, 502; *TCTC* 12.
59 Eliot did, of course, write an appreciative essay on *In Memoriam* in 1936.
60 Clark Lectures VIII: 10. Eliot's dispute with I. A. Richards on the nature of our belief in poetic statement, which Richards calls

'pseudo-statement', is considerably clarified even by the outline history which Eliot provides. Richards's interests in linguistics and psychology led him to conclude that words have no 'real' relation to the world, but serve to organize our feelings – a modern nominalism. See Eliot's remarks on Richards, *UPUC* 123–40; also 'A Note on Poetry and Belief', *Enemy* I (January 1927), pp. 15–17, and 'Literature, Science and Dogma', *Dial* LXXXII, 3 (March 1927), pp. 239–43.

61 'Ulysses, Order and Myth', *Dial* LXXV, 5 (November 1923), p. 483.
62 'Gerontion', *CPP* 22.
63 Eliot cites Pater on the subject of 'that inexhaustible discontent, languor, and home-sickness ... the chords of which ring all through our modern literature' ('Arnold and Pater' (1930), *SE* 443).
64 Eliot discussed this accord – I can find no more precise word – in a BBC broadcast on David Jones, in the course of which he cited Jones's own words: 'There have been culture-phases in which the maker and the society in which he lived shared an enclosed and common background, where all the terms of reference were common to all. It would be an affectation to pretend that such was our situation today.'
65 The relationship of F. H. Bradley to Eliot's use of the term is discussed in Richard Wollheim, 'Eliot and F. H. Bradley: An Account' in Graham Martin, ed., *Eliot in Perspective: A Symposium* (London: Macmillan, 1970), pp. 188–9; see also the Lewis Freed book (1979) referred to above.
66 For Eliot's acknowledgment, see *SW* viii; for references to Gourmont, see 'Charles Péguy', *New Statesman* VIII, 183 (7 October 1916), p. 20; 'Observations', *Egoist* V, 5 (May 1918), p. 70; 'Studies in Contemporary Criticism I', *Egoist* V, 9 (October 1918), p. 114; 'Grammar and Usage', *Criterion* V, 1 (January 1927), p. 121; 'The Twelfth Century', *TLS* 1332 (11 August 1927), p. 542; 'Commentary', *Criterion* XIII, 52 (April 1934), p. 451; 'Philip Massinger' (1920), *SE* 217–18.
67 Glenn S. Burne, *Remy de Gourmont: His Ideas and Influence in England and America* (Carbondale: Southern Illinois University Press, 1963), p. 132.
68 'To Criticize the Critic' (1961), *TCTC* 17; Burne, op. cit., pp. 131–48.
69 Eliot uses 'dissociation' in this sense only once, in 'Beyle and Balzac', *Athenaeum* 4648 (30 May 1919), p. 393.
70 *Promenades Littéraires*, tome 3: *Le Symbolisme* (Paris: Mercure de France, 1963), p. 89.
71 See F. W. Bateson, 'Contribution to a Dictionary of Critical Terms: "Dissociation of Sensibility"', *EC* I: 3 (July 1951), pp. 302–12.
72 'The Local Flavour' (1919), *SW* 35; 'The Function of Criticism' (1923), *SE* 28; *UPUC* 53.
73 Clark Lectures II: 15; cited above.

Notes to pp. 46–51

74 Schiller, 'On Simple and Sentimental Poetry', in W. J. Bate, ed., *Criticism: The Major Texts* (New York: Harcourt, Brace, 1952), p. 409; an anonymous nineteenth-century translation.
75 Schiller, op. cit., p. 409.
76 Ibid., p. 411.
77 To be discussed in Chapter 2.
78 'Hamlet' (1919), *SE* 145.
79 Cited by Ezra Pound in 'The Serious Artist' (1913); see *Literary Essays of Ezra Pound*, ed. T. S. Eliot (New York: New Directions, 1968), p. 54.
80 'Andrew Marvell' (1921), *SE* 299.
81 Ibid., 300.
82 Ibid.
83 'Milton I' (1936), *OPAP* 143–4.
84 1919; *SE* 21.
85 'Thomas Middleton' (1927), *SE* 167; 'John Ford' (1932), *SE* 193, 199; 'John Marston' (1934), *SE* 229; 'Ben Jonson' (1919), *SE* 156; 'Cyril Tourneur' (1930), *SE* 184.
86 'John Ford' (1932), *SE* 203.
87 'London Letter', *Dial* LXXIII, 3 (September 1922), p. 331. Eliot's use of the same word to indicate a good quality and a bad was bound to create some confusion; see, for example, James Smith's often petulant but entertaining discussion of the question in 'Notes on the Criticism of T. S. Eliot', *EC* XXII, 4 (October 1972), pp. 333–61, especially pp. 351–4. Ezra Pound solved a similar problem by using the word 'virtue' (*virtù*) to indicate a poet's particularity: see 'On Virtue' in *Selected Prose 1909–65*, ed. William Cookson (New York: New Directions, 1973), pp. 28–31.
88 'Cyril Tourneur' (1930), *SE* 189.
89 Ibid., 190.
90 'Philip Massinger' (1920), *SE* 220.
91 Cf. Eliot on the ideal of 'poetry so transparent that we should not see the poetry, but that which we are meant to see through the poetry, poetry so transparent that in reading it we are intent on what the poem *points at*, and not on the poetry, this seems to me the thing to try for. To get *beyond poetry*, as Beethoven, in his later works, strove to get *beyond music*.' Cited by F. O. Matthiessen in *The Achievement of T. S. Eliot: An Essay on the Nature of Poetry*, 3rd edn. (New York: Oxford, 1958), p. 90.
92 'The Three Voices of Poetry' (1953), *OPAP* 102.
93 James Joyce, *A Portrait of the Artist as a Young Man* (New York: Viking, 1964), p. 215. Stephen's phrase is taken from a letter of Flaubert.
94 Eliot himself lends some support to this school of thought: in a letter to Paul Elmer More, he wrote 'I am not a systematic thinker, if indeed I am a thinker at all. I depend upon intuitions and perceptions. ...' Cited in John D. Margolis, *T. S. Eliot's Intellectual*

Development, 1922–1939 (Chicago: University of Chicago Press, 1972), p. xv.
95 'Ben Jonson' (1919), *SE* 155.
96 Grover Smith, *T. S. Eliot's Poetry and Plays: A Study in Sources and Meaning* (Chicago: University of Chicago Press, 1960), p. 255.
97 Gordon, op. cit., p. 53. Cf. Eliot's concern with Bergson's idea of the contrast between our discontinuous perceptions and the inferred unity behind them (Ibid., p. 41).
98 Gordon states (p. 125) that Eliot first felt a serious impetus towards the Church of England in 1923. Other commentators confirm the importance of the years 1923–5; see, e.g., Margolis, op. cit., especially pp. 33–68.
99 See above, p. 24. Eliot uses the multiple meanings of 'word' to great effect, particularly in the *Quartets*, where the themes of poetry and divinity are related.
100 Eliot refers in *The Use of Poetry*, 137 *et seq.*, to Abbé Henri Brémond's *Prayer and Poetry*, a work which attempts 'to establish the likeness, and the difference of kind and degree, between poetry and mysticism'. A good work on a related subject is William F. Lynch's *Christ and Apollo: The Dimensions of the Literary Imagination* (New York: Sheed & Ward, 1960).
101 On a different level, Yeats's interest in the occult is comprehensible in poetic terms as a desire to assert the 'magical' relationship between language (incantation, spells, etc.) and the world – i.e. to affirm the significance of the poetic act.
102 'The Literature of Politics' (1955), *TCTC* 139.
103 *Dial* LXXV, 5 (November 1923), pp. 480–3.
104 This problem is well discussed by Wayne Booth in *The Rhetoric of Fiction* (Chicago: University of Chicago Press, 1961), pp. 377–98.
105 'How It Strikes a Contemporary', *The Common Reader: First Series* (New York: Harcourt, Brace, n.d.), pp. 243–4.
106 'Tradition and the Individual Talent' (1919), *SE* 21.
107 'Bantams in Pine Woods'.
108 Clark Lectures, unnumbered prefatory page.
109 *FLA* 7. *After Strange Gods*, when it appeared in 1934, was subtitled *A Primer of Modern Heresy*.
110 Clark Lectures, unnumbered prefatory page.
111 Paul Valéry, 'Preamble' to *The Art of Poetry*, trans. Denise Folliot (New York: Bollingen, 1958), p. 7.
112 'Milton II', *OPAP* 161.
113 Ibid., 152–3.
114 1928; *SW* viii.

2 Romantic Criticism and the Golden Age

1 'Baudelaire' (1930), *SE* 424.
2 Jacques Barzun's fine *Classic, Romantic and Modern* (New York: Anchor, 1961) includes 'A Sampling of Modern Usage' of the word 'romantic' which shows, as Eliot would say, 'the tendency of words to become indefinite emotions' ('The Perfect Critic' (1920), *SW* 9). In my usage, the capitalized forms ('Romantic', 'Romanticism') refer to the historical period, the lower-case forms to the general phenomenon of romanticism.
3 The phrase is from Ezra Pound's 'T. S. Eliot' (1917); see *Literary Essays*, p. 419.
4 C. K. Stead, *The New Poetic: Yeats to Eliot* (Harmondsworth: Penguin, 1967), pp. 125-46.
5 Ibid., p. 131.
6 Ibid., p. 170.
7 'Coole Park and Ballylee 1931'.
8 'Observations', *Egoist* V, 5 (May 1918), pp. 69-70.
9 Hurd's *Letters on Chivalry and Romance* (1762) and Thomas Warton's *History of English Poetry* (1774-1781) discussed the neglected values of Renaissance and pre-Renaissance poetry long before Keats; but Hurd and Warton are minor figures, and it is in any case easy to overestimate their criticism of contemporary poetry, or to see 'Romantic' ideas in their works.
10 'Preface to the Fables', in W. P. Ker, ed., *Essays of John Dryden* (Oxford: Clarendon, 1926), II, pp. 249, 256. Eliot notes this belief in the progress of language as one of Samuel Johnson's critical limitations: see 'Johnson as Critic and Poet' (1944), *OPAP* 184-222.
11 'Sleep and Poetry', ll. 181-7.
12 *The Letters of John Keats, 1814-1821*, ed. Hyder Edward Rollins (Cambridge, Mass.: Harvard University Press, 1958), I, p. 225.
13 'Immature poets imitate; mature poets steal'. ('Philip Massinger' (1920), *SE* 206.)
14 Keats, *Letters*, I, p. 224.
15 Ibid., I, p. 387.
16 W. Jackson Bate, *The Burden of the Past and the English Poet* (New York: Norton, 1972), p. 124.
17 'Epistle to John Hamilton Reynolds', l. 69.
18 'Hamlet' (1919), *SE* 145.
19 'Andrew Marvell' (1921), *SE* 300.
20 See Earl R. Wasserman, *The Finer Tone: Keats' Major Poems* (Baltimore: Johns Hopkins, 1967) for a discussion of Keats's use of oxymoron.
21 Kermode discusses *Hyperion* as an expression of Keats's doctrine, but avoids the more direct statements in the letters.
22 Keats, *Letters*, I, p. 185.

23 Ibid., fn. 9.
24 'Swinburne as Critic' (1919), *SW* 23.
25 Eliot, 'The Possibility of a Poetic Drama' (1920), *SW* 66; Keats, *Letters*, I, p. 224.
26 Keats, *Letters*, I, p. 192; Eliot, 'Tradition and the Individual Talent' (1919), *SE* 19.
27 Keats, *Letters*, I, p. 387.
28 Ibid., I, p. 193.
29 Cited in Bate, op. cit., p. 79.
30 Keats, *Letters*, II, p. 212.
31 See Dryden, 'Preface to the Fables', in Ker, op. cit., II, p. 258; Johnson, 'Life of Milton'. Cf. Eliot, 'Milton II' (1947), *OPAP* 157.
32 'Milton I' (1936), *OPAP* 145.
33 Keats, *Letters*, I, p. 184; cited by Eliot in *UPUC* 101. Cf. *Letters*, I, p. 387: 'A Poet is the most unpoetical of any thing in existence; because he has no Identity. ...'
34 See 'Tradition and the Individual Talent' (1919), *SE* 17–18.
35 *SE* 218; cf. 'The Metaphysical Poets' (1921), *SE* 288: '... in the second *Hyperion* there are traces of a struggle toward unification of sensibility.'
36 See Grover Smith, *T.S. Eliot's Poetry and Plays: A Study in Sources and Meaning* (Chicago: University of Chicago Press, 1960), pp. 88, 254, 266.
37 See Roger Kojecky, *T. S. Eliot's Social Criticism* (New York: Farrar, Straus, 1972), *passim*, especially pp. 19–25. In 1961, Eliot spoke of his admiration for Coleridge in a pair of interviews; see Kathleen Coburn's 'Introduction' to *Coleridge: A Collection of Critical Essays* (Englewood Cliffs, New Jersey: Prentice-Hall, 1967), pp. 1–2, in which the date of the interview is given incorrectly as 1964.
38 The word 'reinforce' is important, for it seems clear that Eliot's use of philosophical vocabulary in criticism owes a good deal to sources other than his study of Coleridge's *Biographia*: his work on Bradley, his personal metaphysical preoccupations, and his poetic capacity for analogical thinking are all involved. The attribution of anything in Eliot's thought to a single source is probably an oversimplification.
39 *Biographia Literaria*, ed. J. Shawcross (2 vols.; London: Oxford University Press, 1907), I, pp. 178–9. This passage is, as Shawcross notes, taken from Schelling's *Abhandlung*. Cf. E. D. Hirsch's attack on psychologistic accounts of meaning in *Validity of Interpretation* (New Haven: Yale University Press, 1967), p. 37: 'My perception of a visible object like Coleridge's table or of a nonvisible object like a phoneme can vary greatly from occasion to occasion, and yet what I am conscious of is nevertheless the same table, the same phoneme.'
40 These few paragraphs on Coleridge's influence on Eliot's literary

criticism do not pretend to be exhaustive; that influence is particularly difficult to analyse since it can be seen *generally* in a great deal of Eliot's criticism, and specifically almost nowhere. See George Bornstein, *Transformations of Romanticism in Yeats, Eliot, and Stevens* (Chicago: University of Chicago Press, 1976), pp. 120–4.

41 'The Social Function of Poetry' (1945), *OPAP* 19.
42 '*Tarr*', *Egoist* V, 8 (September 1918), p. 106.
43 'War Paint and Feathers', *Athenaeum* 4668 (17 October 1919), p. 1036. Lévy-Bruhl is mentioned in this review, as he is in Eliot's review of *Group Theories of Religion and the Religion of the Individual*, by Clement C. J. Webb, *International Journal of Ethics*, XXVII, 1 (October 1916), pp. 115–17. Eliot speaks in this review (p. 116) of the 'mystical mentality' which, 'though at a low level, plays a much greater part in the daily life of the savage than in that of the civilized man'.
44 Cited above, p. 22.
45 See D. E. S. Maxwell, *The Poetry of T. S. Eliot* (London: Routledge & Kegan Paul, 1952), p. 72.
46 'Ode: Intimations of Immortality', ll. 67, 69.
47 In asserting these similarities, I am uneasily aware of the splendid job of destructive criticism performed by Irving Babbitt upon the Romantic cult of the child (in *Rousseau and Romanticism*, 1919). But Babbitt is only one of the influences upon Eliot, and I find, as Stead does, a greater Romantic inheritance in Eliot's work than most critics have acknowledged.
48 'The Metaphysical Poets' (1921), *SE* 287.
49 Eliot's description of the poet's mind is, of course, reminiscent of Coleridge's: see Chapter 3. Eliot's description of ordinary experience as 'chaotic, irregular, fragmentary' is strikingly similar to his description of romanticism as 'fragmentary ... immature ... chaotic' ('The Function of Criticism' (1923), *SE* 26).
50 *UPUC* 79. Eliot again uses the Keatsian criterion of 'intensity', as he did in 'Tradition and the Individual Talent'; see note 26 above.
51 *The Prelude*, Book XII, ll. 208–15.
52 *Dial* LXXXIII, 3 (September 1927), p. 261.
53 *SE* 232. The very phrasing of this passage recalls several situations in Eliot's poetry: 'Gerontion' is an obvious example, but the closest verbal parallels occur in 'A Song for Simeon' ('Dust in sunlight and memory in corners', *CPP* 69) and 'The Dry Salvages': 'the moment in and out of time,/The distraction fit, lost in a shaft of sunlight' (*CPP* 136).
54 See James Benziger, *Images of Eternity: Studies in the Poetry of Religious Vision from Wordsworth to T. S. Eliot* (Carbondale: Southern Illinois University Press, 1962), pp. 246, 248. Bornstein mentions (op. cit., p. 130) that 'Prufrock' is a form of the 'Greater Romantic Lyric' defined by Abrams.

55 See, e.g., 'The Idea of a Literary Review', *Criterion* IV, l (January 1926), p. 5.
56 'Blake' (1920), *SE* 320, 321–2. Cf. 'The Mysticism of Blake', *Nation and Athenaeum* XLI, 24 (17 September 1927), p. 779.
57 See *UPUC* 89 and 'Byron' (1937), *OPAP* 223–39. See also Alice Levine, 'T. S. Eliot and Byron', *ELH*, 45, 3 (Fall 1978), 522–41.
58 Ian Gregor, 'Eliot and Matthew Arnold', in Graham Martin, ed., *Eliot in Perspective: A Symposium* (London: Macmillan, 1970), p. 268.
59 For this last, see Raymond Williams, *Culture and Society, 1780–1950* (Penguin, 1961), p. 133. The best account of Eliot's writings on social issues is Kojecky's; Chace's more specialized study is also good.
60 Matthew Arnold, *Lectures and Essays in Criticism*, ed. R. H. Super (Ann Arbor: University of Michigan Press, 1962), p. 284.
61 Seán Lucy provides, with the necessary *caveats*, a list of ideas which Arnold and Eliot have in common: see *T. S. Eliot and the Idea of Tradition* (London: Cohen & West, 1960), pp. 30–1.
62 Arnold, 'The Literary Influence of Academies', *Lectures*, pp. 241–2; Eliot, *SW* xiv.
63 The phrases cited are from John Holloway, *The Victorian Sage: Studies in Argument* (New York: Norton, 1965), p. 203, and George Watson, *The Literary Critics: A Study of English Descriptive Criticism* (Harmondsworth: Penguin, 1962), p. 179.
64 See 'Arnold and Pater' (1930), *SE* 431–43.
65 E. D. H. Johnson, *The Alien Vision of Victorian Poetry* (Princeton: Princeton University Press, 1952), p. 181.
66 Johnson, p. 184.
67 Matthew Arnold, *On the Classical Tradition*, ed. R. H. Super (Ann Arbor: University of Michigan Press, 1960), pp. 2–3.
68 Warren D. Anderson, *Matthew Arnold and the Classical Tradition* (Ann Arbor: University of Michigan Press, 1971), p. 52; Super, *Classical Tradition*, p. 218.
69 Arnold, *Classical Tradition*, p. 5.
70 Ibid., p. 1.
71 Cf. Eliot on 'the Greek brevity', in 'Euripides and Professor Murray' (1920), *SE* 61.
72 Arnold, *Classical Tradition*, p. 6.
73 Ibid., p. 2. F. O. Matthiessen uses these lines as the epigraph to his chapter on 'The "Objective Correlative" ': see *The Achievement of T. S. Eliot: An Essay on the Nature of Poetry*, 3rd edn (New York: Oxford, 1958), p. 56.
74 (1921); *SE* 300.
75 Arnold, *Classical Tradition*, p. 8.
76 Ibid. Eliot, 'Tradition and the Individual Talent' (1919), *SE* 21.
77 'On the Modern Element in Literature', *Classical Tradition*, p. 32.
78 Ibid., pp. 21, 28.

79 Ibid., p. 20.
80 'The Metaphysical Poets' (1921), *SE* 288.
81 Arnold, 'Preface', *Classical Tradition*, p. 1; Eliot, 'Hamlet' (1919), *SE* 141–146.
82 Arnold, *Classical Tradition*, p. 31.
83 Lionel Trilling, *Matthew Arnold* (Cleveland: World, 1955), p. 154.
84 Preface, *Classical Tradition*, p. 7; 'To a Friend' (poem), l. 12; 'On Translating Homer', *Classical Tradition*, p. 140.
85 'East Coker' V, *CPP* 128.
86 See Arnold's 'Function of Criticism at the Present Time', *Lectures*, pp. 258–85.
87 'Baudelaire' (1930), *SE* 424.
88 Alice Chandler, *A Dream of Order: The Medieval Ideal in Nineteenth Century English Literature* (London: Routledge & Kegan Paul, 1971).
89 Professor Chandler also discusses the Lake Poets, Disraeli, Pugin, and the Pre-Raphaelites.
90 Ibid., p. 7.
91 Thomas Carlyle, *Past and Present* (London: Dent, 1960), p. 85.
92 Ibid., p. 93.
93 I am concerned here with the tradition rather than particular points of influence, but it is apparent that Eliot knew Ruskin's work well. He lectured on Ruskin in two of his extension courses (see Ronald Schuchard, 'T. S. Eliot as an Extension Lecturer, 1916–1919', *RES* New Series, XXV, 9 (1974), pp. 163–73, 292–304, particularly pp. 171, 173, and 292), and Ruskin's concern with *aesthesis* and *theoria* clearly lies behind Eliot's declaration that 'esthetic sensibility must be extended into spiritual perception, and spiritual perception must be extended into esthetic sensibility and disciplined taste before we are qualified to pass judgment upon decadence or diabolism or nihilism in art' (*Notes Towards the Definition of Culture* (New York: Harcourt, Brace, 1949), p. 29).
94 *Modern Painters*, ed. E. T. Cook and Alexander Wedderburn (London: George Allen, 1904), III, p. 333: Vol. V of this edition.
95 Joan Evans, *John Ruskin* (New York: Oxford, 1954), p. 165.
96 *The Crown of Wild Olive*, ed. E. T. Cook and Alexander Wedderburn (London: George Allen, 1905), p. 443: Vol. XVIII of this edition.
97 John D. Rosenberg, *The Darkening Glass: A Portrait of Ruskin's Genius* (New York: Columbia, 1961), pp. 85–6.
98 Ibid., pp. 86–7.
99 If any single view of history emerges from 'Gerontion' and *The Waste Land* it is surely a concept of history as nightmare.
100 Rosenberg, op. cit., p. 90. It is possible that Ruskin derived his method from Pugin's *Contrasts* (1836), which uses plates to contrast a town of 1440 with the same town in 1840, much to the latter's discredit.

101 What follows is a summary of ideas which Hulme did not live to put into a fully argued and polished form; he himself refers to the roughness of outline which characterizes most of the essays in *Speculations*, ed. Herbert Read (London: Routledge & Kegan Paul, 1936).
102 Ibid., p. 47.
103 Ibid.
104 Ibid., p. 53.
105 See 'Romanticism and Classicism', pp. 113–40, particularly pp. 126–8.
106 'The Serious Artist' (1913), *Literary Essays*, p. 54; the same passage is referred to in Pound's 1914 essay on Vorticism and the 1928 'How to Read', *Literary Essays*, pp. 22, 31.
107 Ezra Pound, *The Spirit of Romance* (New York: New Directions, 1952), pp. 25, 158.
108 Ezra Pound, 'Cavalcanti' (1934), *Literary Essays*, p. 150.
109 Richard Ellmann, *Yeats: The Man and the Masks* (London: Faber, 1961), p. 232. The gyres also represent other paired qualities such as beauty and truth, particular and universal, value and fact, etc.
110 W. B. Yeats, *A Vision* (New York: Macmillan, 1938), p. 292.
111 Ibid., p. 281.
112 Ibid., pp. 279–80.
113 'The Gyres', *Collected Poems of W. B. Yeats* (New York: Macmillan, 1956), p. 291; Yeats, *A Vision*, p. 135.
114 As in the case of Hulme, it is the eastern Middle Ages which are glorified; Yeats is more critical of the western Middle Ages. See Yeats, *A Vision*, pp. 287–90.
115 For Yeats's comments on Spengler, see ibid., pp. 18–19.
116 Ibid., pp. 22–3.
117 Ibid., p. 8.
118 *Letters of W. B. Yeats*, ed. Allan Wade (New York: Macmillan, 1955), p. 922.
119 A. G. Stock, *W. B. Yeats: His Poetry and Thought* (Cambridge: Cambridge University Press, 1964), p. 151. Cf. Eliot: 'A philosophical theory which has entered into poetry is established, for its truth or falsity in one sense ceases to matter, and its truth in another sense is proved.' ('The Metaphysical Poets' (1921), *SE* 288–9.)
120 C. K. Stead, *The New Poetic: Yeats to Eliot* (Harmondsworth: Penguin, 1967), p. 35.
121 Yeats, *Letters*, p. 922.
122 Stead, op. cit., p. 126.
123 Hence Stead's use of 'negatively' – presumably in Keats's sense.
124 Kermode, *Romantic Image* (London: Routledge & Kegan Paul, 1957; and New York: Vintage, 1957), p. 141.

3 Eliot as Rhetorician

1 *Anatomy of Criticism* (Princeton: Princeton University Press, 1957), p. 337.
2 Bernard Bergonzi, *T. S. Eliot* (New York: Macmillan, 1972), p. 26.
3 Literary argument does not, of course, deal in 'proof' in the usual sense: I use the term, as Holloway does, 'in the readily understood and familiar sense of straightforward argument' (*The Victorian Sage: Studies in Argument* (New York: Norton, 1965), p. 3).
4 Clark Lectures VIII:12, VI:2; cf. 'Contemporary English Prose', *Vanity Fair* XX, 5 (July 1923), pp. 51, 98.
5 Holloway, op. cit., pp. 7, 8.
6 Cited in Lyndall Gordon, *Eliot's Early Years* (New York: Oxford, 1977), p. 23.
7 Coleridge, *Aids to Reflection*, cited in Holloway, op. cit., p. 4.
8 Holloway, op. cit., pp. 8, 9.
9 Ibid., pp. 11, 18.
10 Pound reports that Eliot referred to the polite essay as 'that parlour game' ('Henry James', *Literary Essays*, p. 315).
11 Hugh Kenner, *The Invisible Poet: T. S. Eliot* (London: Methuen, 1960), p. 85. As Kenner reports, Eliot wrote five letters to the editor of *The Egoist* one month, simply to fill a column; each of the letters is a parody of a letter-writing 'type'.
12 Kenner, op. cit., pp. 85–6. Pound encouraged Eliot in his 'subversion': see Donald Gallup, 'T. S. Eliot and Ezra Pound: Collaborators in Letters', *Atlantic Monthly* CCXXV, 1 (January 1970), p. 60, and Kenner, op. cit., p. 83. A good discussion of Eliot's place in the tradition is John Gross, *The Rise and Fall of the Man of Letters* (London: Weidenfeld & Nicolson, 1969), pp. 233–9.
13 10 August 1929. The letter is in the first volume of the E. M. Forster Letter-Book in the collection of the King's College (Cambridge) Library. An intelligent anonymous review of *The Sacred Wood* also mentions 'a curious element of bluff' in Eliot's prose: see the *New Statesman* XVI, 45 (26 March 1921), p. 733.
14 The linking of literature, politics, and religion anticipates the polemical Preface to *For Lancelot Andrewes* (1928).
15 Holloway, op. cit., p. 51. Cf. an interesting remark by Eliot in conversation with Françoise de Castro, 23 August 1948: 'l'intelligence poussée dans toutes ses profondeurs conduit elle-même à la mystique.' ('Entretien avec T. S. Eliot', typescript by Mlle. de Castro, Item M4a in the Hayward Bequest, King's College, Cambridge.)
16 'Arnold and Pater', *SE* 432.
17 Cited in R. P. Blackmur, *The Lion and the Honeycomb* (New York: Harcourt Brace, 1955), p. 166.

18 'William Blake' (1920), *SE* 317.
19 'Seneca in Elizabethan Translation' (1927), *SE* 65.
20 'Religion and Literature' (1935), *SE* 388.
21 'In Memoriam' (1936), *SE* 328.
22 'Reflections on *Vers Libre*' (1917), *TCTC* 183.
23 'Literature, Science and Dogma', *Dial* LXXXII, 3 (March 1927), p. 243.
24 'Seneca in Elizabethan Translation' (1927), *SE* 96.
25 'Niccolò Machiavelli' (1927), *FLA* 51.
26 (1944); *OPAP* 165. See also pp. 198–9, and the opening sentence of 'John Dryden' (1921): 'If the prospect of delight be wanting (which alone justifies the perusal of poetry). ...' (*SE* 305)
27 'Verse Pleasant and Unpleasant', *Egoist* V, 3 (March 1918), p. 44.
28 'Shorter Notices', *Egoist* V, 6 (June–July 1918), p. 87.
29 'The Education of Taste', *Athenaeum* 4652 (27 June 1919), p. 521. The allusion is perhaps less obvious here than in the other cases, but it seems clear to me that Eliot is echoing Prospero's 'We are such stuff/ As dreams are made on, and our little life/Is rounded with a sleep'. He thus implies both the somniferous quality of the bibliographies and the ephemeral nature of the criticism they follow.
30 'Second Thoughts About Humanism' (1929), *SE* 487.
31 'Euripides and Professor Murray' (1920), *SE* 61.
32 'A Victorian Sculptor', *New Statesman* X, 256 (2 March 1918), p. 528.
33 'Shorter Notices', *Egoist* V, 6 (June–July 1918), p. 87.
34 'A Romantic Aristocrat' (1919), *SW* 28.
35 'Seneca in Elizabethan Translation' (1927), *SE* 70.
36 'Verse Pleasant and Unpleasant', *Egoist* V, 3 (March 1918), p. 43.
37 'Swinburne as Poet' (1920), *SE* 324.
38 E.g. *SW* 129, 157, 167.
39 'The Local Flavour' (1919), *SW* 36.
40 'The French Intelligence' (n.d.), *SW* 46. Eliot's only explicit criticism of Meredith can be found in 'Contemporary English Prose', *Vanity Fair* XX, 5 (July 1923), pp. 51, 98.
41 Cf. Eliot's references to G. K. Chesterton in 'In Memory of Henry James', *Egoist* V, 1 (January 1918), pp. 1–2; 'Verse Pleasant and Unpleasant', *Egoist* V, 3 (March 1918), p. 43; 'Professional, Or ...', *Egoist* V, 4 (April 1918), p. 61; 'Observations', *Egoist* V, 5 (May 1918), p. 69; 'Criticism in England', *Athenaeum* 4650 (13 June 1919), p. 457; 'A Preface to Modern Literature', *Vanity Fair* XXI, 3 (November 1923), p. 44.
42 'The Borderline of Prose', *New Statesman* (19 May 1917), pp. 157–8.
43 'Verse Pleasant and Unpleasant', *Egoist* V, 3 (March 1918), p. 44.
44 'Charleston, Hey! Hey!', *Nation and Athenaeum* XL, 17 (29 January 1927), p. 595.
45 'Introduction' (1920), *SW* xv.

46 'The Function of Criticism' (1923), *SE* 28; 'Commentary', *Criterion* XIII, 53 (July 1934), p. 624.
47 See *UPUC* 106, 111, 115, 116, 117.
48 'Francis Herbert Bradley' (1927), *SE* 451.
49 'An Extempore Exhumation', *Nation and Athenaeum* XLIII, 14 (7 July 1928), p. 470.
50 Review of J. M. Murry's *God*, *Criterion* IX, 35 (January 1930), p. 335.
51 'Mr Middleton Murry's Synthesis', *Criterion* VI, 4 (October 1927), p. 341.
52 'The Silurist', *Dial* LXXXIII, 3 (September 1927), p. 262.
53 'Francis Herbert Bradley' (1927), *SE* 444-5. Eliot claimed to share Bradley's incapacity for abstruse thought: see 'A Commentary', *Criterion* XI, 43 (January 1932), p. 274, and a letter cited by John D. Margolis, *T. S. Eliot's Intellectual Development, 1922-1939* (Chicago: University of Chicago Press, 1972), p. xv.
54 'To Criticize the Critic' (1961), *TCTC* 20.
55 'Professional, Or ...', *Egoist* V, 4 (April 1918), p. 61.
56 The phrase, originally the title of Eliot's poem, is from *Our Mutual Friend*, Chapter XVI.
57 'To Criticize the Critic' (1961), *TCTC* 14.
58 Bergonzi, op. cit., p. 69.
59 'The Perfect Critic' (1920), *SW* 14.
60 See 'On the Development of Taste in Poetry', *UPUC* 32-6.
61 'Swinburne as Critic' (1919), *SW* 20.
62 'Professional, Or ...', *Egoist* V, 4 (April 1918), p. 61.
63 'Introduction' (1920), *SW* xiii. The unnecessary question mark is Eliot's.
64 'A Note on the American Critic' (n.d.), *SW* 43.
65 No one can deny George Eliot's gifts as an ironist, and the criticism I have extrapolated from these remarks of T. S. Eliot may seem unfair to the novelist. But George Eliot's irony is rarely directed at her own ideas, and Eliot's criticism of an incomplete irony would presumably be that it is partial in both senses and therefore subjective.
66 Cf. – to give just one example – the statement in 'Hamlet' (1919) that *Coriolanus* is, 'with *Antony and Cleopatra*, Shakespeare's most assured artistic success' (*SE* 144).
67 'Seneca in Elizabethan Translation' (1927), *SE* 91.
68 'Swinburne as Poet' (1920), *SE* 326.
69 'William Blake' (1920), *SE* 321.
70 'Hamlet' (1919), *SE* 145.
71 'Ben Jonson' (1919), *SE* 155.
72 'Thomas Middleton' (1927), *SE* 166.
73 'Thomas Heywood' (1931), *SE* 181.
74 'John Marston' (1934), *SE* 232.
75 'A Note on Richard Crashaw' (1928), *FLA* 96.

76 Matthew Arnold, *Lectures*, p. 284.
77 'The Literary Influence of Academies', *Lectures*, pp. 232–57.
78 'The Function of Criticism' (1923), *SE* 28. The italics are Eliot's.
79 N.d.; *SW* 45–6.
80 *Lectures*, p. 345; 'William Blake' (1920), *SE* 321.
81 'Professional, Or ...', *Egoist* V, 4 (April 1918), p. 61. *Amos Barton* is, of course, one of the few well-written English novels. Eliot's standard of perfection in fiction is the work of Stendhal and Flaubert, who are mentioned with great frequency, often together, in the uncollected prose: see 'Beyle and Balzac', *Athenaeum* 4648 (30 May 1919), pp. 392–3, and, in the collected essays, *SW* xiii, 15, 34, 68, 77, 111, 139; *FLA* 78; *SE* 137, 178, 202, 297, 462, 502; *TCTC* 12. James is another exemplar, both of achievement and of single-minded dedication to his craft, but he is not mentioned as frequently as the French novelists. See 'In Memory of Henry James', *Egoist* V, 1 (January 1918), pp. 1–2.
82 'Philip Massinger' (1920), *SE* 218. Cf. Eliot's remark in 'The Possibility of a Poetic Drama' (1920) that 'the great ages did not perhaps *produce* much more talent than ours; but less talent was wasted' because of the existence of literary forms into which that talent could flow (*SW* 64).
83 'The Perfect Critic' (1920), *SW* 9.
84 'Whether Rostand Had Something about Him', *Athenaeum* 4656 (25 July 1919), p. 665.
85 'Preface' (1928), *SW* viii.
86 'John Bramhall' (1927), *SE* 355.
87 Despite the clarity of Eliot's definition, a remarkable number of commentators and critics still talk of the objective correlative as if it were a *symbol* of the character's emotion.
88 Holloway, op. cit., p. 224.
89 'Ben Jonson' (1919), *SE* 159; my italics.
90 See *SE* 123.
91 Raymond Williams, *Culture and Society, 1780–1950* (Harmondsworth: Penguin, 1961), p. 227.
92 Clark Lectures I: 11; 'Dante' (1929), *SE* 239; *Notes Towards the Definition of Culture* (1948), Chapter 1.
93 'Ben Jonson' (1919), *SE* 156.
94 See Chapter 1.
95 See, e.g., *SW* 7, 10, 15, 64–5, 67, 84, 110, 119.
96 Stead, p. 129.
97 For 'art-emotion', see *SW* 57, 87, 109; for usage that supports Stead's argument, *SW* 12–13, 101, 133, 168. Some of Eliot's statements, of course, do not fit Stead's conclusions. The famous remark that 'Poetry is not a turning loose of emotion, but an escape from emotion' ('Tradition and the Individual Talent' [1919], *SE* 21)

Notes to pp. 119–25

presumably ought to read 'Poetry is not a turning loose of feeling, but an escape from feeling into art-emotion', but Eliot had wit enough not to spoil an epigram. An interesting parallel to Eliot's distinction is that made by Stephen Dedalus between the 'static' emotion of tragedy and the 'kinetic' feelings excited by improper art. Joyce's concern with objectivity, also discussed by Stephen in Chapter V of *Portrait of the Artist as a Young Man*, suggests the possibility of Joyce's influence on Eliot's critical outlook.

98 R. P. Blackmur makes a similar distinction between 'feeling' and 'emotion': see op. cit., p. 172.
99 'Swinburne as Critic' (1919), *SW* 17.
100 'John Marston' (1934), *SE* 230–1. See also Eliot's capsule history of English prose in 'Contemporary English Prose', *Vanity Fair* XX, 5 (July 1923), pp. 51, 98.
101 'John Dryden' (1921), *SE* 314–15.
102 Clark Lectures VII:1.
103 *UPUC* 37–80. This tendency to put figures in diagrammatic relationship to one another is apparent elsewhere in Eliot's prose. In 'A Study of Marlowe', *TLS* 1309 (3 March 1927), p. 140, he writes: 'The value of Marlowe's verse is inseparable from the value of his thought; the value of Milton's verse has no relation to the value of his thought; we may say that the value of Shakespeare's verse transcends and includes the value of his thought.'
104 'Christopher Marlowe' (1919), *SE* 124.
105 *SE* 123. For the comparison of Marlowe and Jonson, see 'Ben Jonson' (1919), *SE* 147–60.
106 'Philip Massinger' (1920), *SE* 217.
107 *Dial* LXX, 6 (June 1921), pp. 687, 689.
108 See 'Contemporary English Prose', *Vanity Fair* XX, 5 (July 1923), p. 51.
109 'The Metaphysical Poets' (1921), *SE* 290.
110 'Tradition and the Individual Talent' (1919), *SE* 14.
111 'Baudelaire in Our Time' (1927), *FLA* 68–9.
112 'Euripides and Professor Murray' (1920), *SE* 62.
113 See Clark Lectures VIII:2.
114 'Ben Jonson' (1919), *SE* 155–6; 'John Dryden' (1921), *SE* 311.
115 'Andrew Marvell' (1921), *SE* 299; 'Milton I' (1936), *OPAP* 160; 'A Note on Richard Crashaw' (1928), *FLA* 93–97; 'In Memoriam' (1936), *SE* 331.
116 'Euripides and Professor Murray' (1920), *SE* 62; 'Baudelaire in Our Time' (1927), *FLA* 74.
117 'Lancelot Andrewes' (1926), *SE* 344–5.
118 See, e.g., *SE* 96, 136, 241, 244, 265, 270, 488.
119 M. C. Bradbrook, 'Eliot's Critical Method', in B. Rajan, ed., *T. S. Eliot: A Study of His Writings by Several Hands* (London: Dobson, 1947), p. 124.

120 (1947), *OPAP* 155.
121 'Andrew Marvell' (1921), *SE* 300; 'Dante' (1929), *SE* 268.
122 'Thomas Middleton' (1927), *SE* 164.
123 'In Memoriam' (1936), *SE* 333.
124 *UPUC* 90; 'What Dante Means to Me' (1950), *TCTC* 130–2.
125 'Euripides and Professor Murray' (1920), *SE* 61. For examples of the eloquent plainness which Eliot values in Dante, see his first two essays on the poet, *SW* 159–71 (1920) and *SE* 237–77 (1929).
126 'Philip Massinger' (1920), *SE* 209.
127 'Christopher Marlowe' (1919), *SE* 122.
128 'Dante' (1929), *SE* 241.
129 'Ben Jonson' (1919), *SE* 154.
130 'Thomas Middleton' (1927), *SE* 169.
131 'Tradition and the Individual Talent' (1919), *SE* 20; cf. 'Philip Massinger' (1920), *SE* 209.
132 E.g. *Inferno* XV, *SE* 18, 247; 'la sua voluntade e nostra pace', *SE* 136, 264, 270; parts of the Tourneur passage cited above, *SE* 20, 192, 209; of the Middleton passage, *SE* 169, 209; Chapman's 'fly where men feel/The cunning axle-tree ...', *SE* 74, *UPUC* 147; Othello's 'And say, besides, that in Aleppo once', *SE* 39, 130; Horatio's 'But look, the morn, in russet mantle clad', *SE* 88, 143.
133 Less than a page of 'Lancelot Andrewes' (1926) gives us 'A cold coming they had of it ...' ('Journey of the Magi', ll. 1–5), 'Christ is no wild-cat' (cf. 'Christ the tiger', 'Gerontion', l. 20) and 'the word within a word, unable to speak a word' ('Gerontion', l. 18; cf. *Ash-Wednesday* V, l. 5, 'the Word without a word'). A quotation in 'Dante' (1929) contains two references used in *Ash-Wednesday*, one used in *The Waste Land*, and the title of Eliot's 1920 volume *Ara Vos Prec*. The Middleton passage above suggests lines from 'Gerontion' ('I that was near your heart was removed therefrom/To lose beauty in terror ...', ll. 56–7) as does the Tourneur ('What will the spider do,/Suspend its operations, will the weevil/Delay?', ll. 66–8).
134 Vincent Buckley, *Poetry and Morality: Studies in the Criticism of Matthew Arnold, T. S. Eliot and F. R. Leavis* (London: Chatto & Windus, 1959), p. 52.
135 *Hamlet*, V, ii, ll. 347–50.
136 Cited in 'Seneca in Elizabethan Translation' (1927), *SE* 74, and in *UPUC* 147. The line is recalled twice in Eliot's poems: in Gerontion's 'whirled/Beyond the circuit of the shuddering Bear/In fractured atoms' (ll. 68–70), and the conjunction of axle-tree and stars in 'Burnt Norton' II.
137 It is too seldom noted that Arnold's definition of the activity of criticism – 'to try to know the best that is known and thought in the world' ('The Function of Criticism at the Present Time') – emphasizes the discursive element of literature and scants the

aesthetic. If one were to take Arnold at his word, the non-discursive arts such as painting and music would be excluded from the scrutiny of criticism altogether.
138 'Philip Massinger' (1920), *SE* 208.
139 'The *Pensées* of Pascal' (1931), *SE* 410.
140 'Charles Whibley' (1931), *SE* 499.
141 'John Marston' (1934), *SE* 225.
142 'Literature, Science and Dogma', *Dial* LXXXII, 3 (March 1927), p. 243.
143 'Charleston, Hey! Hey!', *Nation and Athenaeum* XL, 17 (29 January 1927), p. 595.
144 *UPUC* 147; 'Reflections on *Vers Libre*' (1917), *TCTC* 187.
145 *UPUC* 56. Cf. M. H. Abrams, *The Mirror and the Lamp: Romantic Theory and the Critical Tradition* (New York: Norton, 1958), especially 'Coleridge's Mechanical Fancy and Organic Imagination' (pp. 167–77) and 'Coleridge and the Aesthetics of Organism' (pp. 218–25).
146 'The Function of Criticism' (1923), *SE* 23. Eliot's use of the organic metaphor may reflect his reading of Burke as well as his knowledge of the Romantics.
147 'The Metaphysical Poets' (1921), *SE* 287.
148 *Biographia Literaria*, Chapter XIV; Eliot cites the relevant passage in 'Andrew Marvell' (1921), *SE* 298. Cf. Abrams on 'unity in multeity' in Coleridge, op. cit., pp. 220–21.
149 (1921); *SE* 300. The principle applies to individual words as well as to poetry. See 'A Commentary', *Criterion* V, 2 (May 1927) for Eliot's objections to the language of the revised Anglican prayer book.
150 'A Victorian Sculptor', *New Statesman* X, 256 (2 March 1918), p. 528.
151 ' "Rhetoric" and Poetic Drama' (1919), *SE* 42.
152 'Hamlet' (1919), *SE* 144.
153 'The Silurist', *Dial* LXXXIII, (3 September 1927), p. 259.
154 'Hamlet' (1919), *SE* 145.
155 'Contemporanea', *Egoist* V, 6 (June–July 1918), p. 84.
156 'Swinburne as Poet' (1920), *SE* 323; 'Tradition and the Individual Talent' (1919), *SE* 17–18. Cf. 'In Memory of Henry James', *Egoist* V, 1 (January 1918), p. 2: 'It is in the chemistry of these subtle substances, these curious precipitates and explosive gases, which are suddenly formed by the contact of mind with mind, that James is unequalled.'
157 'The Teacher's Mission' (1934), *Literary Essays*, p. 58; 'The Serious Artist' (1913), *Literary Essays*, p. 48.

Conclusion

1 Bornstein, pp. 1–26. The chief shortcoming of Bornstein's book is its

tendency to assimilate modernism completely into the Romantic tradition, its refusal to acknowledge what was genuinely new in modernist poetry and poetics.
2 Cited above.
3 'A French Romantic', *TLS* 980 (28 October 1920), p. 703.
4 Hulme, too, saw Keats as a 'classical' poet: see *Speculations*, ed. Herbert Read (London: George Routledge, 1936), p. 127.
5 Ibid.
6 See A. O. Lovejoy, *Essays in the History of Ideas* (New York: Capricorn, 1960), pp. 228–53.
7 See p. 93.
8 Basil Willey, *The Seventeenth Century Background* (Harmondsworth: Penguin, 1972), pp. 83–4.
9 'Ben Jonson' (1919), *SE* 159.
10 Ibid.
11 Bornstein, op. cit., p. 23. Bornstein speaks throughout as though no stricture on Romantic poetry were justified or justifiable; on two pages of his book (124–5) we find Eliot accused of 'frenzy', 'shrillness', 'absurdities', 'rant', 'nonsense', and 'precarious mental balance'. This name-calling defensiveness, which comes much closer to rant than anything in Eliot's prose, can only bring Bornstein's real arguments into disrepute.
12 Anthony Hecht, 'The Motions of the Mind', *TLS* 3923 (20 May 1977), p. 602.
13 Ibid.
14 E. D. Hirsch, Jr, *The Aims of Interpretation* (Chicago: University of Chicago Press, 1976), p. 147.
15 *CPP* 54; note to l. 412 of *The Waste Land*.
16 Hirsch mentions (p. 91) that Roland Barthes, engaged in controversy with Raymond Picard over Racine, 'was displeased when his intentions were distorted by M. Picard'.
17 Harold Bloom, *The Anxiety of Influence: A Theory of Poetry* (New York: Oxford, 1973); *A Map of Misreading* (New York: Oxford, 1975); *Kabbalah and Criticism* (New York: Seabury, 1975); *Poetry and Repression: Revisionism from Blake to Stevens* (New Haven: Yale University Press, 1976).
18 Denis Donoghue, 'Stevens at the Crossing', *New York Review of Books* XXIV, 14 (15 September 1977), p. 40.
19 Ibid.
20 Bloom, *Kabbalah and Criticism*, p. 122.
21 Ibid., p. 108.
22 Ibid., p. 125.
23 Ibid., pp. 125–6.
24 Hirsch, op. cit., p. 157.
25 'The Function of Criticism' (1923), *SE* 24.

26 'East Coker' V, *CPP* 128.
27 Ibid.
28 Ibid.
29 As Donoghue observes, much of Bloom's hostility to Eliot can be traced to the fact that Eliot does not fit Bloom's paradigm. 'Eliot is weak, presumably, because his relation to Dante was not a Freudian struggle of son against father; it was based upon Eliot's feeling that "there is no competition" ' (Donoghue, op. cit., p. 40).
30 'East Coker' V, *CPP* 129.
31 See José Ortega y Gasset, *The Revolt of the Masses* (New York: Norton, 1957), especially pp. 69–74, and Christopher Lasch, *The Culture of Narcissism* (New York: Norton, 1978).
32 See David Newton-de Molina, ed., *The Literary Criticism of T. S. Eliot: New Essays* (London: Athlone, 1977) and Balachandra Rajan, *The Overwhelming Question: A Study of the Poetry of T. S. Eliot* (Toronto: University of Toronto Press, 1976).
33 'Little Gidding' V, *CPP* 145.

Appendix A: Eliot, Pound and Modernist Criticism

1 See Frank Kermode, *Romantic Image* (New York: Vintage, 1957), pp. 119–61.
2 'Philip Massinger' (1920), *SE* 206.
3 See Valerie Eliot, ed., *The Waste Land: A Facsimile and Transcript of the Original Drafts Including the Annotations of Ezra Pound* (London: Faber, 1971), particularly Mrs Eliot's 'Introduction', pp. ix–xxix.
4 See, e.g., a letter to Ezra Pound, [?January] 1922, in *Selected Letters of Ezra Pound, 1907–1941*, ed. D. D. Paige (New York: New Directions, 1971), p. 170.
5 Yvor Winters, 'T. S. Eliot, or the Illusion of Reaction', in *In Defense of Reason* (Denver: Swallow, n.d.), p. 501.
6 Hugh Kenner, *The Pound Era* (Berkeley: University of California Press, 1971).
7 Pound to Harriet Monroe (30 September 1914), Paige, op. cit., p. 40.
8 I do not include Joyce simply because he appears to have been influenced by his contemporaries hardly at all.
9 'Andrew Marvell' (1921), *SE* 300.
10 (1918); *Literary Essays*, pp. 5, 12.
11 See Pound's review, 'T. S. Eliot' (1917), *Literary Essays*, p. 419.
12 Hulme 'Romanticism and Classicism', *Speculations*, ed. Herbert Read (London: Routledge & Kegan Paul, 1936), p. 127.
13 Pound himself attempts to correct the tendency to attribute too much to Hulme's influence in 'This Hulme Business' (1938), reprinted as an appendix to Hugh Kenner's *The Poetry of Ezra Pound*

(Norfolk, Connecticut: New Directions, 1951), pp. 307–9.
14 Ezra Pound, *Collected Shorter Poems* (London: Faber, 1968), p. 124.
15 These articles provide valuable support for Kermode's linking of Eliot with the Symbolist tradition and its preoccupation with the image of the dancer, but Kermode himself does not refer to them.
16 'The Hard and Soft in French Poetry' (1918), *Literary Essays*, pp. 288–9.
17 'The Function of Criticism' (1923), *SE* 24.
18 *Literary Essays*, p. 5.
19 'Philip Massinger' (1920), *SE* 206.
20 'The Hard and Soft in French Poetry' (1918), *Literary Essays*, p. 287.
21 'The Local Flavour' (1919), *SW* 35.
22 'The Teacher's Mission' (1934), *Literary Essays*, pp. 60–1. For Eliot's use of 'comparison and analysis' see 'Studies in Contemporary Criticism', *Egoist* V, 9 (October 1918), p. 113, and V, 10 (November/December 1918), p. 132, 'Criticism in England', *Athenaeum* 4650 (13 June 1919), p. 457, and *SW* 37, *SE* 32, 142, 206.
23 A good, sensible discussion of the affinities between Eliot and Pound is Herbert N. Schneidau, *Ezra Pound: The Image and the Real* (Baton Rouge: Louisiana State University Press, 1969), pp. 147–72 ('Tradition and Two Individual Talents: Pound and Eliot'). Lyndall Gordon is also helpful: *Eliot's Early Years* (New York: Oxford, 1977), pp. 66–9.
24 Pound, *Letters*, pp. 21, 23, 28; see also *Literary Essays*, pp. 80, 343; Eliot, 'To Criticize the Critic' (1961), *TCTC* 17. Pound's essay on Henry James appeared in 1917, as did Eliot's.
25 Pound, *Literary Essays*, pp. 33, 280–4; Eliot, Clark Lectures passim and many references in passing, e.g. 'Andrew Marvell' (1921), *SE* 292. Schneidau notes that Pound's interest in Laforgue 'went up sharply after he met Eliot' (op. cit. p. 158).
26 On Dante: Eliot, Clark Lectures, 'Dante' (1920), *SW* 159–71, 'Dante' (1929), *SE* 237–77; Pound, 'Hell' (1934), *Literary Essays*, pp. 201–13. On Flaubert and Stendhal, see Pound, *Literary Essays*, pp. 26, 31, 210, 216, 283, 305, 371, 399, 403, 418; Eliot, references in Chapter 1, fn. 58.
27 'Goethe as the Sage' (1955), *OPAP* 240–64; for Pound's opinion of Goethe, see 'The Renaissance' (1914), *Literary Essays*, p. 217.
28 'Hell' (1934), *Literary Essays*, p. 201. Cf. Eliot, 'Milton I' (1936), *OPAP* 156–64 and remarks in *SW* passim.
29 Eliot, *UPUC* 88; Pound, 'How to Read' (1928), *Literary Essays*, p. 33.
30 'The Perfect Critic' (1920), *SW* 9.
31 'How to Read' (1928), *Literary Essays*, pp. 21–2.
32 'The Serious Artist' (1913), *Literary Essays*, p. 48.
33 'Professional, Or …', *Egoist* V, 4 (April 1918), p. 61.
34 'A Retrospect' (1918), *Literary Essays*, p. 9.
35 'The Serious Artist' (1913), *Literary Essays*, p. 53.
36 1921; *SE* 295–301.

37 *Literary Essays*, pp. 361–70, 339–58, 295–338, 109–48.
38 Pound, 'Swinburne Versus his Biographers' (1918), *Literary Essays*, p. 293; Eliot, 'Swinburne as Poet' (1920), *SE* 324.
39 Pound, 'How to Read' (1928), *Literary Essays*, p. 36; Eliot, 'Euripides and Professor Murray' (1920), *SE* 61.

Appendix B: Eliot and Philosophical Aesthetics

1 'A Commentary', *Criterion* XI, 43 (January 1932), p. 274; 'To Criticize the Critic' (1961), *TCTC* 20–1.
2 John D. Margolis, *T. S. Eliot's Intellectual Development, 1922–1939* (Chicago: University of Chicago Press, 1972), p. xv; above, p. 97; 'Preface', *Knowledge and Experience in the Philosophy of F. H. Bradley* (London: Faber, 1964), p. 10.
3 The essay appeared in S. P. Rosenbaum, ed., *English Literature and British Philosophy* (Chicago: University of Chicago Press, 1971), pp. 251–77; Professor Bolgan's book was published by McGill-Queen's University Press (Montreal and London, 1973).
4 F. H. Bradley, *Appearance and Reality: A Metaphysical Essay*, 2nd edn. (Oxford: Clarendon, 1930), p. 335.
5 Richard Wollheim, 'Eliot and F. H. Bradley: An Account' in Graham Martin, ed., *Eliot in Perspective: A Symposium* (London: Macmillan, 1970), p. 189.
6 J. R. de J. Jackson, *Method and Imagination in Coleridge's Criticism* (Cambridge, Massachusetts: Harvard University Press, 1969), pp. 171, 172.
7 Elizabeth R. Eames and Alan M. Cohn have discovered ten 'new' reviews written by Eliot in 1917 and 1918, all of which deal with recent work in philosophy, psychology and religion. See Eames and Cohn, 'Some Early Reviews by T. S. Eliot (Addenda to Gallup)', *Papers of the Bibliographical Society of America*, 70, 3 (1976), pp. 420–4.
8 E.g. Eric Thompson, *T. S. Eliot: The Metaphysical Perspective* (Carbondale: Southern Illinois University Press, 1963) and Fei-Pai Lu, *T. S. Eliot: The Dialectical Structure of His Theory of Poetry* (Chicago: University of Chicago Press, 1966).
9 A. D. Nuttall, *A Common Sky: Philosophy and the Literary Imagination* (Berkeley: University of California Press, 1974).

Index

The index is arranged alphabetically by letter, not by word: thus Ford, John, is listed before *For Lancelot Andrewes*. Eliot's uncollected prose – except for the Clark Lectures – is not included. A number of the uncollected essays and reviews have long and cumbersome titles, and some of the shorter titles ('A Commentary' and 'London Letter', for example) refer to whole series of articles. Specific references to this material would therefore involve lists of dates and make the index too complicated for efficient use. References indicate pages on which the work referred to is cited or discussed.

Abrams, M. H., 173, 183
Adams, Henry, 86
Addison, Richard, 122, 167
After Strange Gods, 8, 161, 170
Allan, Mowbray, 158, 164
Anderson, Warren, 77
Andrewes, Lancelot, 124
'Andrew Marvell', 4, 48–9, 65, 69, 79, 124, 130, 131–4, 151, 156, 183
'Animula', 71–2
aperçu (as form of statement), 111–13
Aquinas, St Thomas, 19, 25
Ara Vos Prec, 182
Aristotle, 32, 51, 96, 160
'Arnold and Pater', 41, 99, 168, 174
Arnold, Matthew, 6, 7, 8, 41, 42, 76–81, 94, 96, 98, 99, 102, 103, 107, 113–15, 116, 117, 127–8, 136, 148, 182–3
Ash-Wednesday, 182
assumptions, Eliot's critical, 109
Auden, W. H., 100

Babbitt, Irving, 75, 173
Bantock, G. H., 163
Barthes, Roland, 146, 184
Barzun, Jacques, 171

Bate, W. Jackson, 64–5, 172
Bateson, F. W., 168
'Baudelaire', 6, 60, 81
Baudelaire, Charles, 42, 43, 51, 120, 122, 123, 124
'Baudelaire in Our Time', 123, 124
Beaumont and Fletcher, 117–18, 124
Beckett, Samuel, 55
Beddoes, Thomas Lovell, 67
Bell, Clive, 102, 103
Benda, Julien, 75, 114
'Ben Jonson', 11, 49, 52, 111, 116–17, 117–18, 124, 126, 140–1
Benziger, James, 173
Bergonzi, Bernard, 3, 15, 93, 108
Bergson, Henri, 114, 170
Berkeley, George, 23
Bernini, Gian Lorenzo, 34
Blackmur, R. P., 1, 177, 181
'Blake', *see* 'William Blake'
Blake, William, 62, 75, 100, 111, 138, 150
Bloom, Harold, 75, 141, 144–6, 185
Blunden, Edmund, 108
Bolgan, Anne, 158
Booth, Wayne, 170

189

Index

Bornstein, George, 6, 9, 10, 75, 135, 141–2, 173, 183–4, 184
Bradbrook, M. C., 3, 9, 125, 162
Bradley, F. H., 14, 18, 40, 41, 44, 52, 107, 108, 118, 144, 158–61, 172
Brémond, Abbé Henri, 170
Browning, Robert, 41, 151
Buckley, Vincent, 127
Burke, Edmund, 54, 183
Burne, Glenn, 44
Butler, Joseph, 158
'Byron', 174
Byron, Lord, 43, 75, 151

Carlyle, Thomas, 7, 41, 42, 82–3, 85, 89, 91
Castro, Françoise de, 177
Chace, William, 163, 174
Chalker, John, 162
Chandler, Alice, 82, 86
Chapman, John, 12, 65, 67, 127
'Charles Whibley', 128
Chaucer, Geoffrey, 63, 166–7
'Christopher Marlowe', 117, 122, 126
Clarendon, Earl of, see Hyde, Edward
Clark Lectures, 4–5, 15–16, 16, 17–19, 23–45, 53, 56–7, 59, 62, 81, 82, 91, 94, 113, 117, 121–2, 124, 129, 131, 135–7, 141, 163–4, 167
classicism, 60, 79, 81
Claudel, Paul, 105
Cobbett, William, 82
Coburn, Kathleen, 172
Cohn, Alan, 187
Coleridge, Samuel Taylor, 7, 57, 62, 68–70, 75, 95, 96, 119, 122, 129, 133, 137, 159, 160, 164, 172–3, 183
Collingwood, R. G., 51, 160
contrast (as rhetorical tactic), 124–5, 133
Cookson, William, 169
Copleston, Frederick, 19, 38
Corbière, Tristan, 15, 43, 154
Cowley, Abraham, 36–8, 91, 122
Crashaw, Richard, 33–6, 37, 112–13, 121–2, 124
criticism, contemporary, 143–9
'Cyril Tourneur', 49, 50

Dante, 17, 20, 21, 29–30, 33, 48, 49, 72, 91, 124, 125, 131, 135, 136, 154, 166, 167, 182
'Dante' (1920), 166, 182
'Dante' (1929), 1, 39, 117, 125, 126, 129–30, 182
definition (as form of statement), 115–17, 132, 134
Descartes, René, 19, 21–3, 24, 26, 36, 45, 55, 165, 165–6
'A Dialogue on Dramatic Poetry', 38
Dickens, Charles, 110
dissociation of sensibility, 3, 5, 9, 11–14, 20–3, 26, 29, 32, 34, 37–8, 44–7
distinction (as form of statement), 117–20
'Donne in our Time', 32
Donne, George, 42, 110, 179, 180
Donne, John, 12, 17, 21, 23, 24, 26–9, 30–3, 34, 36–7, 49, 58, 67, 75, 79, 91, 111, 121–2, 124, 131, 135, 166
Donoghue, Denis, 145, 185
Dryden, John, 16, 22, 24, 58, 63, 67, 120, 122, 124, 133
Duns Scotus, John, 19

Eames, Elizabeth, 187
eighteenth-century literature, 38–9
Eliot, George, 42, 110, 179, 180
Eliot, T. S., see titles of individual works
Eliot, Valerie, 150, 185
Ellmann, Richard, 88
Emerson, R. W., 9, 42, 139
entertained idea (as form of statement), 110–11, 132
Euripides, 103
'Euripides and Professor Murray', 103, 123–4, 126, 156, 174
Evans, Joan, 84

Fernandez, Ramon, 25
Fichte, J. G., 40, 94
Flaubert, Gustave, 43, 154, 167, 169, 180
Ford, John, 126
For Lancelot Andrewes, 9, 54, 56–7, 60, 177
forms of statement in Eliot's criticism, 108–21
Forster, E. M., 97, 158
'Four Elizabethan Dramatists', 38, 56
Four Quartets, 52–3, 57, 74, 80, 115, 147–8, 149, 166, 170, 173, 182
'Fragment of a Prologue', 57

Index

'Francis Herbert Bradley', 107, 108
Freed, Lewis, 158, 164, 168
'The French Intelligence', 104, 114
'The Frontiers of Criticism', 2
Frye, Northrop, 51, 93, 94, 109
'The Function of Criticism', 25–6, 74–5, 76–7, 81, 97–9, 114, 129, 147, 153, 173, 179

Gallup, Donald, 177
genealogy (as rhetorical tactic), 123–4
generalization (as form of statement), 113–15, 132–3
'Gerontion', 11, 43, 53, 74, 173, 175, 182
Gordon, Lyndall, 5, 53, 160, 163, 167, 177, 186
Gosse, Edmund, 106–7
Gourmont, Remy de, 10, 44–5, 47, 59, 75, 131, 154, 160, 168
Gregor, Ian, 76
Grierson, H. J. C., 12
Gross, John, 177

'Hamlet and His Problems' ('Hamlet'), 26, 48, 65, 80, 111, 116, 130–1, 180
Hayward, John, 164, 165
Hazlitt, William, 93, 119
Hecht, Anthony, 143
Hegel, G. W. F., 40, 94
Herbert, George, 34, 39
Herder, J. G. von, 9
Heywood, Thomas, 112
Hirsch, E. D., 143–4, 146, 172
historical survey (as rhetorical tactic), 121–3, 132
history and historiography, 11, 43–4, 62–92, 135, 139–41, 142
Hobbes, Thomas, 21, 38, 56
Holloway, John, 7, 41–2, 76, 94–6, 99, 116, 134, 167, 177
Homage to John Dryden, 15, 23–4, 57
Homer, 46
Hulme, T. E., 75, 86–7, 91, 136, 137, 139, 150, 152, 176, 184, 185–6
Hurd, Richard, 171
Hyde, Edward, 56
Hyman, Stanley Edgar, 162

impersonality, 25–6, 66, 67–8
'In Memoriam', 101, 124, 125

Jackson, J. R. de J., 159
James, Henry, 55, 100, 124, 154, 180, 183
James, William, 40
John, St, 24, 53
'John Bramhall', 116
John of the Cross, St, 23
'John Dryden', 120, 124, 178
'John Ford', 49, 50
'John Marston', 49, 74, 112, 120, 128
'Johnson as Critic and Poet', 102
Johnson, E. D. H., 77
Johnson, Lionel, 41
Johnson, Samuel, 7, 16, 23, 63, 67, 93, 96, 120, 133, 171
Jones, David, 168
Jonson, Ben, 12, 63, 68, 111, 117–18, 122, 124, 126, 132
'Journey of the Magi', 74, 182
Joyce, James, 43, 51, 85, 123, 169, 181, 185

Kant, Immanuel, 51, 94, 144, 160
Keats, John, 6, 59, 63–8, 75, 81, 136, 137, 138, 139, 148, 160, 173
Kenner, Hugh, 11, 96–7, 105, 151
Kermode, Frank, 6, 10, 14, 20, 65, 91, 135, 137, 150, 159, 171, 186
Kojecky, Roger, 68, 174

Laforgue, Jules, 42–3, 44, 51, 55, 122, 135, 154, 167
'Lancelot Andrewes', 5, 31–2, 124, 182
Landor, W. S., 67
Lanzon, S. A., 133
Lasch, Christopher, 148
Leacock, Stephen, 27
Leavis, F. R., 109, 147
Leishman, J. B., 166
Levine, Alice, 174
Lévy-Bruhl, Lucien, 71, 173
Lewis, C. S., 163
Lewis, Wyndham, 122, 123, 128, 131, 151, 152
literature, modern, 55–6, 142–3, 151–3
'The Literature of Politics', 170
'The Local Flavour', 2, 45, 104, 154
Locke, John, 24, 26, 82, 165
Lovejoy, A. O., 139

191

Index

'The Love Song of J. Alfred Prufrock', 53, 106
Lu, Fei-Pai, 187
Lucy, Seán, 174
Lukács, Georg, 51, 94
Luther, Martin, 24, 165–6
Lynch, William F., 170

Machiavelli, Niccolò, 102
Margolis, John, 163, 169, 170, 179
Marinetti, Filippo, 131, 152
Marino, Giambattista, 33, 37
Maritain, Jacques, 165
Marlowe, Christopher, 12, 24, 68, 117, 122, 126, 132, 181
Marston, John, 120
Martin, Graham, 162, 168, 174, 187
Martin, L. C., 33, 166
Marvell, Andrew, 12, 124, 131–4
Massinger, Philip, 122, 128
Matthiessen, F. O., 169, 174
Maurras, Charles, 75
Maxwell, D. E. S., 163, 173
'Mélange Adultère de Tout', 1
Menasce, Jean de, 164
Meredith, George, 104
metaphor (as rhetorical tactic), 128–31
'The Metaphysical Poets', 3, 5, 12, 13, 14, 15, 16–17, 40, 41, 72–3, 80, 116, 118, 122, 129, 176
metaphysical verse, 15–17, 32–3, 35–6, 43
Middleton, Thomas, 12, 112, 125, 126–7, 182
Milton, John, 12, 20–1, 49, 58, 67, 104, 120, 124, 133, 181
'Milton I', 49, 67, 124, 154
'Milton II', 57–8, 125
Monk, Samuel Holt, 165
Montaigne, Michel de, 128
More, Paul Elmer, 110, 158, 169
Morris, William, 48, 82, 124
Munby, A. N. L., 164
Murray, Gilbert, 123–4, 126
Murry, J. M., 98, 107, 179
myth, historical, 5–6, 13, 63–90; *see also* history

naïveté of vision, 45–7, 70–2, 78

Newman, J. H., 7, 25, 41, 42, 94–5, 96
Newton-de Molina, David, 162, 185
'Niccolò Machiavelli', 102
nominalism, 18–19, 22, 24, 25
'A Note on the American Critic', 110
'A Note on Richard Crashaw', 112–13, 124
Notes Towards the Definition of Culture, 76, 77, 117, 175
Nuttall, A. D., 161

objective correlative, 48
Ockham, William of, 19, 22, 24, 165
ontologism and ontology, *see* realism
Ortega y Gasset, José, 148

Pater, Walter, 41, 96, 168
'The *Pensées* of Pascal', 128
'The Perfect Critic', 3, 24, 109, 115, 131, 146, 155
personality, 49–51, 70, 80
Petersson, Robert, 166
'Philip Massinger', 12, 51, 63, 68, 115, 122, 126, 128, 150, 153, 168, 171, 181
philosophy and philosophical terms, 17–23, 25, 26, 40, 51, 69–70, 75, 158–61
Pieper, Josef, 165
politics, Eliot's, 54
'Portrait of a Lady', 53
'The Possibility of a Poetic Drama', 2, 66, 180
Pound, Ezra, 44, 60, 75, 86, 87, 90, 91, 131, 136, 137, 150–7, 165, 169, 176, 177
Praz, Mario, 18, 28, 166
pronunciamento (as form of statement), 110
Proust, Marcel, 60
psychologism, 17–18, 23, 25
Pugin, A. W. N., 175

quotation (as rhetorical tactic), 125–8, 133, 155–6

Rajan, B., 162, 181, 185
Ransom, J. C., 119
Read, Herbert, 25; *see also* Hulme
realism, philosophical, 18–21, 25
'Reflections on *Vers Libre*', 4, 101, 128–9

192

Index

religion, Eliot's, 53–4
'Religion and Literature', 101
Renaissance, Eliot's view of the, 38–9, 63–4
rhetoric, Eliot's, 93–134
'"Rhetoric" and Poetic Drama', 93, 101, 130
Richard of St Victor, 23, 165
Richards, I. A., 109, 167–8
Rimbaud, Arthur, 105
'A Romantic Aristocrat', 103
Romanticism, 4, 6, 7, 8, 10, 25, 40–1, 47, 51, 60–92, 135–9
Rosenbaum, S. P., 187
Rosenberg, John, 84–5, 85–6
Rousseau, Jean-Baptiste, 22–3
Rousseau, Jean-Jacques, 9, 25, 26, 165–6
Ruskin, John, 7, 41, 82, 83–6, 87, 89, 94, 96, 136, 137, 139

The Sacred Wood, 2, 5, 8, 15, 44, 52, 58, 76, 104, 106–7, 110, 115–16, 118
Schelling, F. W. J. von, 160, 172
Schiller, Friedrich von, 10, 45–7, 59, 66, 70, 78, 81, 136
Schleiermacher, Friedrich, 24, 155
Schneidau, Herbert, 186
Schopenhauer, Arthur, 40, 42, 94
Schuchard, Ronald, 175
Scott, Walter, 82
Scotus, Duns, *see* Duns Scotus
'Second Thoughts About Humanism', 102–3
Selected Essays, 5
Seneca, 101, 111
'Seneca in Elizabethan Translation', 38, 101, 103–4, 111
'Shakespeare and the Stoicism of Seneca', 166, 167
Shakespeare, William, 12, 26, 46, 47, 49, 61, 64, 66, 68, 84, 111, 124–5, 126, 127, 128, 130, 179, 181, 182
Shelley, Percy Bysshe, 63, 75, 124, 125, 140
Sidney, Philip, 122, 140, 160
Sitwell, Sacheverell, 102
Smith, Grover, 170, 172
Smith, James, 169
'The Social Function of Poetry', 70
solipsism, 19, 21, 24, 45, 52–3, 55–6, 64, 79–80, 143–8, 158
'A Song for Simeon', 74, 173
Spencer, Theodore, 166
Spengler, Oswald, 89
Spenser, Edmund, 65, 126
Stead, C. K., 6, 10, 60–1, 65, 71, 90, 118–19, 135, 153, 159
Stendhal, 43, 48, 110, 154, 167, 180
Stern, Karl, 165
Stevens, Wallace, 6, 56, 152
Stock, A. G., 89–90
style, Eliot's prose, 7–8, 93–134
suggested idea, *see* entertained idea
Super, R. H., 77
Swift, Jonathan, 50, 107, 164–5
Swinburne, A. C., 104, 109, 111, 119, 120, 131, 151, 156
'Swinburne as Critic', 3, 12, 66, 109, 119
'Swinburne as Poet', 2, 104, 111, 131, 156
symbolist historiography, 91–2
Symons, Arthur, 124

Tennyson, Alfred, Lord, 41, 43, 104, 110, 124, 125, 167
theological writing, 17–18, 21
Theresa of Avila, St, 23, 33–4
'Thomas Heywood', 112
'Thomas Middleton', 49, 112, 125, 126–7
Thompson, Eric, 187
Thompson, Francis, 41
'The Three Voices of Poetry', 169
Tillyard, E. M. W., 58
'To Criticize the Critic', 2, 9, 58–9, 108, 154, 158
tone in Eliot's criticism, 100–8
Tourneur, Cyril, 12, 50, 111, 127, 182
'Tradition and the Individual Talent', 6, 26, 47, 49, 56, 66, 68, 80, 81, 92, 115, 118, 122–3, 127, 131, 137, 172, 180–1
Trilling, Lionel, 81
Tuveson, Ernest, 165, 167

The Use of Poetry and the Use of Criticism, 27, 39, 45, 57, 63, 67–71, 73, 74, 75, 102, 103, 107, 113, 116, 122, 125, 128, 129, 154, 170, 174, 179

Index

Valéry, Paul, 57
Vaughan, Henry, 34, 39, 108
Victorian literature, 40–2, 76–86
Villon, François, 110

Wade, Allan, 176
Warton, Thomas, 171
Wasserman, Earl R., 171
The Waste Land, 13, 52, 53, 61–2, 74, 100, 108, 175, 182
Watson, George, 76
Webster, John, 12, 111
'What Dante Means to Me', 125, 166
'Whisper of Immortality', 13

Wilbur, Richard, 143
Wilde, Oscar, 41
Willey, Basil, 21–2, 72, 140
'William Blake', 75, 100, 111, 114
Williams, Raymond, 117, 174
Winters, Yvor, 147, 151
Wollheim, Richard, 159, 168
Woolf, Virginia, 55–6, 142
Wordsworth, William, 6, 62, 63, 64, 70–4, 75, 81, 103
Wyndham, George, 103

Yeats, W. B., 41, 62, 65, 86, 87–90, 91, 137, 139, 148, 150, 151, 153, 170, 176

For Product Safety Concerns and Information please contact our EU
representative GPSR@taylorandfrancis.com
Taylor & Francis Verlag GmbH, Kaufingerstraße 24, 80331 München, Germany